The Romance of the Three Kingdoms and Mao's Global Order of Tripolarity

The Romance of the Three Kingdoms and Mao's Global Order of Tripolarity

Lai Sing Lam

PETER LANG
Oxford • Bern • Berlin • Bruxelles • Frankfurt am Main • New York • Wien

Bibliographic information published by Die Deutsche Nationalbibliothek.
Die Deutsche Nationalbibliothek lists this publication in the Deutsche Nationalbibliografie; detailed bibliographic data is available on the Internet at http://dnb.d-nb.de.

A catalogue record for this book is available from the British Library.

Library of Congress Cataloging-in-Publication Data:

Lam, Lai Sing.
The romance of the three kingdoms and Mao's global order of tripolarity / Lai Sing Lam.
p. cm.
Includes bibliographical references and index.
ISBN 978-3-0343-0713-0 (alk. paper)
1. Mao, Zedong, 1893-1976. 2. Mao, Zedong, 1893-1976--Knowledge--Chinese literature. 3. Luo, Guanzhong, ca. 1330-ca. 1400. San guo zhi yan yi. 4. Tripolarity (International relations) 5. China--Foreign relations--Soviet Union. 6. Soviet Union--Foreign relations--China. 7. China--Foreign relations--United States. 8. United States--Foreign relations--China. I. Title.
DS778.M3L34 2011
327.51009'045--dc23
2011019655

ISBN 978-3-0343-0713-0

Hochfeldstrasse 32, CH-3012 Bern, Switzerland
info@peterlang.com, www.peterlang.com, www.peterlang.net

Printed in Germany

To the memory of my parents
Lam Wan Poh and Wong Keng Hei

Contents

Preface

Research on Mao's relations with the twin superpowers since the establishment of the People's Republic of China (PRC) in October 1949 has not been satisfactory. With the appearance of new documentation of his comments regarding the classical Chinese historical novel *Romance of the Three Kingdoms* and its influence on him in PRC publications in recent years, I was able to produce this original piece of work on Mao's foreign policies in relation to China's role among the superpowers.

This work argues that immediately following the establishment of the PRC, and inspired by the concept of the Chinese 'international' order of tripolarity as espoused in the above novel, Mao created a similar order by assigning China the role of a superpower in global power politics, though it was not yet a superpower. 'Sharing' the contemporary world with the twin superpowers, it was to contend with the powerful United States while *striving at all costs* to collude with Joseph Stalin's Soviet Union. Thus the post-war bipolar struggle between the Soviet and American blocs gave way to a more complicated pattern of international relationships in which the world was no longer split simply into two clearly opposed blocs.

During the last sixty years, I have been taking note of the development of the 'events' described in the historical novel. I find in my study of Mao that his perceptiveness was profound even regarding its minor details.

This work will certainly enlighten not only sinologists, political scientists and students, but also political leaders of both worlds regarding the relations of Mao's China with the twin superpowers.

My previous work *The International Environment and China's Twin models of Development* concerns Mao's defense-oriented economic development policy during the period 1950–76, dictated by the hostile international environment. Unavoidably, thus, part of the research material in each of Chapters Three to Five of this work is adapted from the previous work. These include the 'right opportunist' purge as well as the origins of the Liuist capitalist economic approach. They substantiate my arguments particularly regarding Mao's perception of the 'US-USSR collusion at the disadvantage of the PRC' in his global order of tripolarity.

The romanization in this work adopts the Pinyin system.

I am indebted to Mary Beltran for putting the finishing touches to part of the final version of the work.

Lam Lai Sing
Macau, China
January 2011

PROLOGUE

The Political Role of Classical Chinese Literature in Mao's Fight against the Twin Superpowers

When analysing the origins and development of Mao Zedong's fight for China's equality with the twin superpowers, it is difficult for us to do so effectively without considering the factor of classical Chinese literature, particularly the historical novel of the *Romance of the Three Kingdoms* (*San Guo*) (三国演义). These novels inspired Mao's thinking, shaped his character, and provided him with a viable alternative to contemporary power politics. Having drawn inspiration from their characters and events, Mao treated this literature as history. It was so profound a factor that he himself was consciously aware of this literature's pervasive influence on his view of reality.

Authors such as Luo Guanzhong (罗贯中) (1330–1400), Cao Xueqin (曹雪芹) (1715–1763), Feng Menglong (冯梦龙) (1574–1646), and Shi Naian (施耐庵) (? – ?) not only were brilliant historians, but also outstanding prose writers, as was Si-ma Qian (司马迁) (145 B.C.–86 B.C.), the Former Han dynasty's Grand Historian. These novels reflect the various political, social, economic conditions as well as human factors. The significance of these works lies in the intimate relationship between history and literature, for the life history of the characters and historical events are pre-dominant in the literature. For Mao, since these novels served as pure history, there was no demarcation line between history and literature. They are not only referred to by Chinese interpreters, but also by Western scholars as the finest pieces of Chinese literature in terms of realism of description, intricacy of the plot and excitement of character design, and above all, their colorful imagination. No wonder they have captured great masses of readers throughout the centuries. As a fan of these authors, Mao was therefore not exceptional. The realistic analysis of the warring situation in the historical novel of the *Romance of the Three Kingdoms* inspired him to analyse situations of his own time. The significance of this historical novel is that it also reflects these factors common to all ages.

This study entails a rather new approach to understanding Mao's fight against the twin superpowers with classical Chinese literature as his political weapons. This analysis of how the theme of the *Romance of the Three Kingdoms* inspired Mao and how he creatively applied it to the contemporary world is unprecedented. Mao's use of classical Chinese literature in different political contexts to fight US imperialism and Soviet 'revisionism' was original. In the following, I will first consider the novel *Romance of the Three Kingdoms*.

I argue that, inspired by this classical Chinese historical novel – which concerns contention initiated by a sovereign power, Shu, against another, Wei, by colluding with the third power, Wu, from a weak position in 220–80 – Mao initiated his own global order of tripolarity. This followed the establishment of the PRC in October 1949. It would fight for power with the United States through trying to collude with the Soviet Union.

In his fight for global power in relation to the powerful United States, China's primary enemy, in 1950 Mao adopted the united front strategy similar to that of the Shu state's premier, Zhuge Liang. He did so by striving *very hard* to get Stalin to sign the proposed Sino-Soviet Treaty and Agreements in Moscow that aimed at 'opposing the possible imperialist invasion'.

Referring to the theme of the historical novel as 'dialectic', Mao quoted it on a number of occasions, stating that the communist giants 'long united, must divide'. The Sino-Soviet alliance began to sour, however, when the 'US-USSR alliance at the disadvantage of China' became evident in 1954, as Mao saw it. Inspired by the same theme of the novel, he then dropped hints to the US about his wish to 'swim in the Mississippi River', implying that he would improve the Sino-US relationship at the expense of that with the Soviet Union. However, he was not taken seriously. In the late 1960s, the new Kissinger-Nixon Doctrine calling for gradual withdrawal of the US from Western Pacific region was initiated. Mao was then convinced that the United States and China 'long divided, must unite'. Thus he personally initiated the ping-pong diplomacy in 1971 leading to President Nixon's China visit and improving the Sino-US relationship.

Mao's 1974 concept of the 'Three Worlds', I argue, was based on the blueprint of Zhuge Liang's 'international order of tripolarity'. It referred to contending with the 'hegemonic' Soviet primary enemy through aiming to collude with the non-antagonistic secondary enemy of the First World, namely, the 'imperialist' United States.

The theoretical foundation of Mao's global order of tripolarity can be traced to (a) Cao Cao's *qi*, (b) Zhuge Liang's concept of the Chinese 'international' order of tripolar powers of Shu, Wei and Wu, and (c) the Battle of Chibi in the novel, which was won by small forces over big and by inferior over superior forces in a tripolar situation. Mao was impressed with Zhuge's conception of a Chinese 'international' order of tripolarity by colluding with the state of Wu, Shu's secondary enemy, to fight the powerful Wei, its primary enemy, from a weak position. Mao understood that the essence of the victory of the celebrated battle at Chibi was the firm cooperation of the allied forces so that astronomical power could be generated. However, he felt that, in the long run, lack of cooperation between the twin allies would render Zhuge's anti-Wei strategy ineffective. Moreover, he understood that Zhuge's basic strategy, which could not concentrate strong enough forces to defeat Shu's enemies one by one, was basically – geographically – faulty. Furthermore, he considered that Zhuge's staunch anti-Wei policy was overly rigid, due to the positions of the primary and secondary enemies being consistently fixed, thus eliminating the opportunity for the consideration of flexible reversion of their positions. Lack of cooperation between the Shu and Wu allied forces vis-à-vis the powerful Wei in the long run strengthened Mao conviction that Zhuge's consistent anti-Wei strategy would not work. In practice, Mao therefore made the positions of the primary and secondary enemies flexibly interchangeable, as he saw fit. Therefore, in the early 1970s, he successfully improved Sino-US relations at the expense of the Soviet Union by reversing the position of the US primary enemy into that of the secondary enemy, and vice versa, in a tripolar situation. The Shu leader Liu Bei would not have been defeated in the Battle of Yiling, had Zhuge advised him to try to collude with the Wei against Wu – reversing the positions of the primary and secondary enemies.

Treating the United States as the primary enemy and the Soviet Union as the *de facto* enemy in Mao's tripolar worldview following the establishment of the PRC in October 1949, Mao's foreign policy, inspired by Zhuge's 'international' order of tripolarity, entailed allying with the latter against the stronger former so that China might gain power from a weak position. However, in January 1954 he perceived this gradual 'US-USSR collusion to the disadvantage of the PRC'. The theme of the *Romance of the Three Kingdoms*, i.e., 'the world phenomenon under the heavens, long united, must divide, and vice versa', which Mao interpreted as 'the empires under the heavens, long united, must divide, and vice versa' was confirmed in Mao's prediction in January 1957 that 'a flare up of Sino-Soviet hostility would occur sooner or later'. Thus, his domestic policy of a national united front for China's defense against US imperialism and also to guard against the new 'US-USSR collusion' was devised. Based on the Yenan model as a prototype, Mao's mass line strategy, which was to serve as his collectivization drive, was aimed at 'uniting with all possible'. The drive was meant to ultimately lead to his defense-oriented communization goal.

Inspired by the theme of the *Romance of the Three Kingdoms*, he tried but in vain to collude with the United States against the Soviet Union in the late 1950s. He considered Peng Dehuai's 'collusion with the Russians to oppose the three red flags' as an act of high treason, and the 1959 dismissal of the 'right opportunist' Peng was part of a growing Sino-Soviet acrimony.

Taking a 'rightist-cum-revisionist' approach, which was considered as dangerously detrimental to Mao's mass line, Liu Shaoqi ignored the simple fact that the Soviet Union had become 'No. 1 accomplice of the US' primary enemy in Mao's tripolar worldview since 1954. Inspired by the theme of the *Romance of the Three Kingdoms*, Mao tried to befriend the United States at the expense of the Soviet Union during the period of 1959–69 without success. The US remained the primary enemy with the Soviet Union considered the 'No. 1 accomplice of the US'. Understandably, thus, Liu's US-inspired 'rightist-cum-revisionist' policies and his opposition to Mao's communization endeavors inevitably led to the latter's launching of the Cultural Revolution.

I argue that Mao's Cultural Revolution would have been delayed or his decision to launch the movement could even have been changed, if the United States had grasped the political meaning of his hints at wishing 'to swim in the Mississippi River' in the mid-1960s. However, it was not until the late 1960s that a golden opportunity for the improvement of Sino-US relations appeared and Mao initiated his 'ping-pong diplomacy' in 1971.

Mao's initiation of his 'ping-pong diplomacy' leading to President Nixon's China visit in 1972 was dramatic. China began to view the Soviet Union as its primary enemy and the United States as a non-antagonistic secondary enemy, leading to improved Sino-US relations. In 1974, inspired by the well-known theme of the historical novel as well as Zhuge Liang's tripolar concept, Mao envisioned his concept of the 'Three Worlds' to contend with China's primary enemy, the Soviet Union, while aiming to collude with the secondary enemy, the United States, plus the second and third world nations. Although Mao's global order of tripolarity did not help much in isolating the Soviet primary enemy, China's crucial strategy of establishing tripolar relationships was confirmed. As international environment was now conducive to his plan of opening up China to the outside world, Mao began to adopt a more relaxed economic policy starting in 1971. His four modernizations scheme was initiated to promote the acquisition of the US-led Western capital and modern technology along with its capitalist economic principles. This was not only to 'befriend' the US-led West at the expense of the Soviet Union, but also to improve the livelihood of the Chinese people.

Deng's 'good-neighbor' policy, which, starting in 1979, was designed to induce other countries worldwide to help modernize China, it subsequently included Russia, as a result of the collapse of the Soviet Union. Deng's policy helped maintain a peaceful and stable international environment. Ironically, the policy marked the end of Mao's global order of tripolarity. The collapse of the Soviet Union confirmed the end of Mao's global order.

In sum, inspired by the theme of the historical novel of the *Romance of the Three Kingdoms*, Zhuge Liang's 'international' tripolar order as well as the battle of Chibi, Mao sought to realize his own anti-imperialist and anti-'revisionist' aims through a global order of tripolarity during the period of 1950–76. In the following, I consider how, starting from depicting his animosity towards the pre-war fascist aggressors of Germany, Italy and Japan in May 1938, Mao made use of the stories and issues as described in classical Chinese novels to fight against US imperialism and Soviet 'revisionism', both externally and internally, in different political contexts during this period. He also 'fought' them with his own classical poetry. His approach was original with classical Chinese literature to serve his political objectives in relation to changing political climate.

First, in 1957, he attempted to consolidate the Sino-Soviet alliance and the Soviet camp with the statement that made reference to 'the East wind is prevailing over the West wind', a phrase first uttered by Lin Daiyu (林黛玉), the heroine of the classical novel of the *Dream of the Red Chamber* (红楼梦). Mao interpreted this phrase referring to how 'the forces of socialism are overwhelmingly superior to the forces of imperialism'.

Second, treating US imperialism as a ghost, Mao implanted the spirit of fearlessness into the mind of the Chinese people as well as in those of oppressed and bullied peoples around the world. He furthermore fought imperialism with the published book of the *Stories of Not Scared of Ghosts* (不怕鬼的故事). He made it very clear that 'We were not scared of ghosts, that was why (in 1958) we bombarded (the islands of) Quemoy and Matsu'.

Third, in his domestic anti-revisionist efforts in 1959, Mao exposed the 'treasonous right opportunists' with his description of his appreciation of Feng Menglong's (冯梦龙) historical novel of *Records of the Various Kingdoms of Eastern Zhou* (东周列国志). In addition, in a number of classical Chinese poems he composed in mid-1959, he referred to Peng Dehuai's 'treasonous act' of 'ganging up with the revisionist clique of Khrushchev' in criticism of his GLF and communization schemes.

Fourth, he made use of the Monkey King, Sun Wukong (孙悟空), from the novel of *Journey to the West* (西游记) to fight the 'revisionist clique of Khrushchev' in his classical Chinese poems. He described Khrushchev as the 'evil spirit' who 'rose from a heap of white bones' as described in the novel. He also challenged the Soviet leadership and claimed to be the leader of the international Communist movement.

Fifth, Mao 'fought' US imperialism and Soviet 'revisionism' through the utilization of his own classical *lu shi* and lyric poetry. In addition, in his lyric poem entitled 'Two Birds: A Dialogue', he used the hyperbolical legendary bird Kun Peng (鲲鹏) created by Zhuang Zi (庄子) (369 B.C.–286 B.C.) to depict the limitless 'harm' of the 'US-USSR collusion to rule the world'.

Sixth, he interpreted the surrender of Song Jiang (宋江) to the Song emperor in the novel *Shui Hu Zhuan* (水浒传) as 'good teaching material by negative example'. He 'criticized' Song Jiang who turns 'revisionist', Soviet 'revisionism' under Khrushchev and the new Soviet leadership as following Khrushchev's 'revisionism'. Internally, he accused both Liu Shaoqi and Lin Biao of practicing 'national capitulationism' towards the Soviets in the 1960s.

In the following, I will deal with Mao's contention with the US imperialist and Soviet 'revisionist' superpowers in terms of the above stories and issues featured in classical Chinese literature.

The Dream of the Red Chamber (红楼梦)

The celebrated classical Chinese novel of the *Dream of the Red Chamber*, written by Cao Xueqin (曹雪芹) (1715–63) of the Qing dynasty, was one of Mao's favorite classical novels. Politically, it helped him in his fight against US imperialism and Soviet 'revisionism' in the following ways.

First, in the early 1950s, the US grand design of the containment of communism and the domino theory was primarily directed against the PRC. The day after the Korean War had broken out, the United States dispatched the Seventh Fleet to 'neutralize the Formosa Straits'. At the same time President Truman announced increased aid to the French in Indochina and the strengthening of US forces in the Philippines. By dragging in the issues of Taiwan, Vietnam, and the Philippines, the US was determined to contain China. Reacting to the US's anti-communism with the success of his socialist revolution, China naturally needed to consolidate its alliance with the Soviet Union (and the third world nations) to form a united front against the United States. According to Mao, the Sino-Soviet Treaty and Agreements he signed with Stalin in April 1950 'serves us conveniently in our opposition towards the possible imperialist invasion'.[1]

Following the Soviet launching of the first inter-continental ballistic missile (ICBM) and space satellite, Mao suggested to the Moscow Conference of Communist Parties in November 1957 that the situation had reached a new turning point. Following the Soviet strategic achievement, he quoted the heroine of the above-mentioned classical Chinese novel, Lin Daiyu (林黛玉): 'the East wind is prevailing over the West wind'. In so doing, Mao referred also to his own attempts to consolidate the Sino-Soviet alliance and the Socialist camp in the face of US hostility.

> The international situation has now reached a new turning point. There are two winds in the world today, the East wind and the West wind ... It is characteristic of the current situation that the East wind is prevailing over the West wind. ... The forces of socialism are overwhelmingly superior to the forces of imperialism.[2]

The PRC's confidence was boosted by nuclear reactor materials 'received from Russia in 1956–7, and by the many Soviet physicists sent as advisers; there were also unconfirmed reports from Poland that the Soviet Union had agreed to supply China with atomic missiles'.[3] Thus Mao's description of this superiority during an address to some Chinese students in Moscow in mid-November 1957 reflected this sense of confidence:

> The world now has a total population of 2,700 million. The socialist countries account for nearly 1,000 million, the independent, formerly colonial countries account for more than 700 million, and the countries now struggling for independence, or for complete independence and the capitalist countries with tendencies towards neutralism, have 600 million. The population of the imperialist camp is only about 400 million, and what is more, is internally divided.[4]

That same month, in the Communist International and Workers Representatives Conferences held in Moscow, Mao repeated that they had reached a new turning point by quoting Lin Daiyu.[5] He tried to encourage confidence and consolidate it in the socialist camp. He (1977:321) quoted Lin repeatedly in his Speech at the Second Plenary Session of the Eighth Central Committee of the CCP in mid-November 1956.

Second, when analysing the origins of Mao's resolute spirit against the twin superpowers, we cannot fully understand without including Wang Xifeng (王熙凤), a female character in the novel of the *Dream of the Red Chamber*. Mao was drawn to Wang, admired her and tended to identify with her (1969:179, 189). He often advised others to emulate her, who claims: 'Even if it results in having my whole body cut in pieces, I dare to pull the emperor down from the horse' (1969:179). It became very common for him to quote lady Wang in his speeches, as he did in his Speech at the Second Plenary Session of the Eighth Central Committee of the CCP in mid-November 1956 and his speech at the CCP's National Conference on Propaganda Work in mid-March 1957.[6] Mao's favorite saying: 'dare to think, dare to say, and dare to act' is a virtual rephrasing of Wang's fiery statement.[7]

Mao's approach of making Lin Daiyu's statement relevant to real-life international relations of the second half of the 1950s was unprecedented. Also unusual was his original incorporation of references to Wang Xifeng's fiery character to reflect his stance as 'not scared of US imperialism and Soviet revisionism'. It is therefore in this context that in the following I will consider Mao's 'spirit of fearlessness' in the face of the US imperialist and Soviet 'revisionist' threats and pressures, beginning in the early 1950s.

Strange Tales of the Leisure Study (聊斋志异)

In many of his informal speeches to, and ordinary conversations with, different levels of society and even with foreign dignitaries, particularly in the late 1950s and early 1960s, Mao often unconsciously revealed his true self – a rational self of 'fearlessness'. His spirit of fearlessness, which was a critical element of his resolute contention with the imperialist and 'revisionist' superpowers, can be seen in many of his statements such as the following:

> Why fear! To fear does not get things done. We do not fear World War III though we do not like it started (1956).[8]

> Even when you (the US) have taken half of China, I still will not be scared. Had not Japan taken away more than half of China? Yet, later, have we not created a new China? (1957).[9]

> No matter what happens, don't be excited ... When the atomic bomb is dropped on us, we can't expect to be doing more than going to see Marx: To die is a natural thing ... In short, we are prepared to fight; when fighting a battle, don't be excited even if atomic bomb is used. Don't fear, the worst that can happen is the appearance of a chaotic world, or being killed. One has to die once – standing up or lying down. When not killed, we will fight on; even when half (of us) are killed, we will still have the other half left ... Don't be scared when facing imperialism. We will lose our strength when scared (1964).[10]

It was in this context that the *Strange Tales of the Leisure Study*, a collection of stories of ghosts, demons, fox spirits, and so on, compiled by Pu Songling (蒲松龄) (1640–1715) of the early Qing dynasty (1644–1911), became one of Mao's favorite classical Chinese novels to serve his political purposes. Based on folklore and popular legends with diverse occult themes ranging from romantic, fantastical to semi-historical and others such as the exploits of magicians or martial arts adepts, it is a collection of about five hundred tales of varying lengths from short anecdotes and jottings to fully fledged stories.[11] Written in classical Chinese style, the genre first appeared during the Jin (晋) dynasty (265–420), and continued to be popular throughout the centuries including the periods of the Tang (618–907), then the subsequent Song (960–1279), Yuan (1279–1368) and Ming (1368–1644) dynasties.

On 15 April 1959, speaking at the Sixteenth Supreme State Council Meeting regarding the 1958 Taiwan Straits Incident, Mao quoted the story 'the Mad Youth's Night Sitting' (狂生夜坐), a story from the celebrated collection of *Strange Tales of the Leisure Study* to demonstrate his own spirit of fearlessness. By virtue of contending fearlessly and therefore actively with the ghost, the Mad Youth, Mao argued, was determined to defeat the ghost as follows:

> We should not fear any threat. In one of the old stories called 'The Mad Youth's Night Sitting', it says that there is a mad youth who does his studies until quite late at night while a ghost tries to terrify him from the window by projecting his long tongue thinking that this student would be scared stiff. The mad youth, however, calmly picking up his brush, paints his own face just like Zhang Fei's (张飞) or like Yuan Shikai's (袁世凯) of our time. He then projects his own shorter tongue. Both of them (fearlessly) stare at each other. At last, the ghost retreats. The author of the *Strange Tales of the Leisure Study*, telling us not to be scared of ghosts, says, 'The more you are scared, the more certain it is ... you will not be alive. He certainly will devour you'. We were not scared of ghosts, that was why we bombarded Quemoy and Matsu.[12]

Overcome by horror, victims, as in most Chinese ghost stories, are usually in a passive position unable to initiate a fight. However, the Mad Youth's case is an exception. The protagonist battle with the ghost, motivated by his fearlessness, originates in rational thinking. It is in this context that we should understand Mao's contending spirit.

Mao understood that one of man's fundamental instincts is fear of the supernatural. With the understanding of this element in human nature, he deliberately drew the attention of his audience to the case of the Mad Youth's confronting a ghost. He believed that man's fear of the supernatural must be overcome through a scientific understanding of himself before he could deal with his enemy. In his work *Mao Tse-tung's Purposive Contention with the Superpowers*, I argue that Mao's understanding of the Mad Youth's confrontation with the ghost was that it sprang from realizing that the ghost could not do him any physical harm. This inspired Mao to contend with the most powerful nation in the world, namely, the United States, by initiating the Taiwan Straits Incident, given his understanding that the US dared not launch a nuclear confrontation with the PRC. Certainly Mao was convinced that 'in 1958 John Foster Dulles was dangerously isolated from both Allied support and American public opinion' (Snow, 1966:641). It showed that Mao 'understood himself as well as his enemy', that is, the US, before initiating the Incident. Therefore it would be inadequate to maintain that this resolute attitude sprang merely from Mao's spirit of fearlessness. Certainly his fearlessness was based on rational thinking.

First, from the viewpoint of rationality, 'to fear does not get things done', according to Mao, 'we will lose our strength when scared'. Second, Mao's sense of fearlessness indeed was built on the logic that from the military viewpoint 'to fear ... imperialism is to overestimate it – it is an improper attitude' (1969d:1162). Mao argued that 'imperialism all over the world ... (is) already rotten and has no future. We have reasons to despise it, and we are confident and certain that we shall defeat all the ... enemies of the Chinese people'. Thus, he went on, 'we must dare to think, dare to say, and dare to act'. Obviously, his rationale was that 'imperialism and all reactionaries, viewed in essence from a long-term perspective, must be seen for what they are – paper tigers. On this basis we must build our strategic thinking ....'[13] Thus his 'paper tiger' thesis is that imperialism was built on an unstable foundation due to its oppressive nature towards the majority of the people both internally and externally, and, as a result, imperialism would eventually crumble as it could not secure support from these great masses of the peoples (1969:99). 'On the other hand', he continued, 'there are living tigers, iron tigers, real tigers, which can eat people; they are not to be slighted. On this we should build our tactical thinking, instead of getting scared ....'[14]

In addition, the Chinese Leninist view of imperialism was rooted in, and therefore shaped by the modern Chinese historic experiences with the West (and Japan) since the mid-nineteenth century. Mao argued that 'the purpose of the imperialist powers invading China was to transform China into their own semi-colony or colony' (1967d:310) and that they 'had continued to use military, political, economic and cultural means of oppression against China' (1969d:1373). This had resulted in unequal treaties, extra-territorial rights, war indemnities, economic exploitation, concessions, the monopolization of China's banking and finance, occupation by foreign troops, massacres and the looting of Chinese cities resulting in not only bitter Chinese hatred, but acute fearfulness on the part of the Chinese people. Understandably, that Mao's implantation of fearlessness into the mind of the Chinese people was to rid them of fears and insecurity.

Having bombed the islands of Quemoy and Matsu, Mao claimed that the Taiwan Straits had become safe for navigation.[15] He declared that 'the imperialists were ghosts' and that 'not being scared of them could we defeat them'. His success inspired his decision to implant the spirit of fearlessness not only in the Chinese population, but also in the oppressed and bullied peoples around the world.

In April 1959, according to the Chinese, 'all over the world, imperialism, the reactionaries in various countries, and the revisionists organized a big anti-China chorus'.[16] In addition, they continued, 'the revisionists inside the country rose in response to international revisionism and launched a frenzied attack against the leadership of the Party'. In response, Mao commissioned He Qi-fang (何其芳), Editor-in-Chief of the Chinese Literature Section of the Chinese Academy of Science, to publish a book entitled *Stories of Not Scared of Ghosts* for his anti-'imperialist-revisionist' fight.

A month later, in a meeting with representatives and consuls of the Soviet Union and eleven other socialist countries, Mao confirmed the forthcoming publication of the *Stories of Not Scared of Ghosts*.[17] Relating the story of the Mad Youth to them, he continued, 'Our strategy is to inspire the Asian, African and American peoples not to be scared of ghosts'. This was because, according to him, 'there were lots of ghosts – imperialists – in the world: in the West as well as in Asia, Africa, and Latin America, who are the running dogs of imperialism and its reactionaries'. On the tenth of May that same year, talking to representatives of the German Democratic Party, he advised them not to be scared of ghosts: 'The more you are scared of ghosts, the more ghosts will appear', he continued, 'but if you are not scared of them, they will disappear'.[18] At the end of the year 1960, according to Mao, the Representative Conference of Eighty-first Communist and Workers Parties was convened in Moscow to announce the anti-imperialist, anti-reactionary and anti-revisionist stance of 'not to be scared of ghosts'.[19]

On 4 January 1961, having read He Qifang's draft of the *Stories of Not Scared of Ghosts*, Mao advised him, first, to strengthen the political nature of the manuscript, making it a tool for political and discursive struggles, and second, to emphasize his dictum that 'strategically we must utterly despise the enemy; tactically we must take it seriously', apart from featuring the character of each of the ghosts'.[20] These suggestions were raised to aim at 'defeating the ghosts', Mao argued. He also pinpointed the story of 'Magical Arts (妖术)' in the *Strange Tales* as a central one in that 'if the hero Yu (于) did not take the three magical puppets seriously – tactically – he would be killed'.[21] The story of the 'three magical puppets', Mao referred to, is as follows:

> A kungfu specialist by the name of Yu was in the capital for the palace examinations when much to his distress his personal servant fell ill. Yu decided to consult the expert fortune-teller, who frequented the marketplace, on his servant's behalf. However, the fortune-teller told Yu that he was in grave peril, but not his servant, and was fated to die in three days time. He suggested to Yu that he could intervene on Yu's behalf for ten taels of silver. However, Yu did not take his offer seriously, though his friends urged him to pay whatever the fortune-teller asked.
>
> On the third night, he sat calmly in his room with sword in hand waiting for whatever would happen. Suddenly he saw a tiny man with a spear on his back enter by the window and alight on the ground where he grew to ordinary size. Yu leaped to his feet and lunged out at the intruder and brought him down. He saw the figure of a man cut out of paper, severed at the waist.
>
> Another fearsome-looking monstrous creature bored its way in through a pane of the paper casement. The instant it touched the ground, Yu struck at it with force splitting it in two halves. He saw a clay figure lying on the ground broken into countless shattered shards.
>
> After a while, he heard what sounded like an ox snorting outside shaking the whole wall of the room. Yu rushed out into the night and saw a huge ghoul, high as the eaves of the house, its face pitch-black and its eyes glowing with a sinister yellow light. It held a bow in its hand and had a clutch of arrows attached to its waist. Yu was still reeling from the shock when this apparition flied a shower of arrows. Yu fended them off with his sword. Yu moved close up against the monster's ribs and dealt them a hefty thwack. He continued to strike blow after blow at it. Eventually he held high his lamp and saw a man-sized wooden puppet decorated in the most terrifying fashion. Blood was flowing from every place where his sword had struck.
>
> Yu realized that each one of the three monsters had been sent against him by the fortune-teller, who was determined to prove his clairvoyant powers, even if it meant killing him in order to do so. Next morning, Yu seized him with the magical art and hauled him before the Magistrate, who had him put to death.[22]

In addition, in his further discussion with He Qifang, Mao talked about the ghost story of 'Song Dingbo Capturing the Ghost' (宋定伯捉鬼),

in which the hero Song acquired the knowledge about the character and weaknesses of the ghost, in order to defeat it:

> In your book, the second case in point is 'Song Dingbo Capturing the Ghost': Carrying Song to cross the river, the ghost discoveries that his body is heavy. Thus Song lies to the ghost that he is a new ghost, (that is why he is heavy). Finding out the ghost's weaknesses by asking the right questions, Song could finally defeat it.[23]

Treating the ghost stories as fables, Mao used them as political tools against his international enemies as follows:

> 'If we are timid or our thought is not liberated', 'then we will be scared of the ghosts, who do not exist at all ... If we can rid our consciousness of superstition, then we will not be scared not only of ghosts, but also of imperialism, revisionism and reactionaries'.[24]

Mao advised He Qifang to add a few hundred words in the preface of the new book about the importance of this attitude for the defeat of the ghosts.[25]

On 16 January 1961, having read He's second draft, Mao wrote a preface on his behalf with the aim of 'counteracting the concerted attacks launched by the international revisionists and China's domestic revisionists'.[26] When the revisions were completed a week later, Mao designated He to send the amended second draft to Zhou Enlai, Deng Xiaoping, Zhou Yang and Guo Moruo, asking them to give their endorsement.[27] In addition, Mao instructed He to publish the preface in the journal of *Red Flag* and the *People's Daily* on the eve of the publication of the book, in addition to having the book translated into the major foreign languages. Under Mao's guidance, the *Stories of Not Scared of Ghosts* was finally published by the People's Literature Press in February 1961.

Judging from the preceding, Mao took his anti-imperialist propaganda work very seriously. After the book's publication, Mao frequently talked about it. For instance, at the beginning of January 1962, in a conversation with Chairman Kaoru Yasui (安井郁) of Japan's Anti-Nuclear Bomb Treaty Association, Mao said, 'The Japanese people are now full of guts, they are not scared of the US imperialist ghost any more'.[28]

In sum, Mao's original use of his psychological 'weapons' of the 'Stories of Not Scared of the Ghosts' to fight the twin superpowers indeed was an amazing feat of his political strategy.

The Records of Various Kingdoms of the Eastern Zhou Dynasty (东周列国志)

Mao often referred to various acts of treason committed in ancient China. For instance, the overthrow of Zhou Wang (纣王) of the Shang dynasty (sixteenth century B.C.–1066 B.C.), was due to the treacherous Shang minister Wei Zi's (微子) 'illicit relations with the foreign Zhou (周) dynasty'.[29] They were recorded in another of Mao's favorite texts, i.e., *The Records of Various Kingdoms of the Eastern Zhou Dynasty*, written by Feng Meng Long (冯梦龙) (1574–1646) of the Ming dynasty (1368–1644). On a number of occasions, Mao talked about the 'overthrow of a country with treason'.[30] Mao's conversations concerning this issue occurred around December 1959. This was after the Lushan Meeting, which featured the anti-'right opportunist' struggle against Peng who 'ganged up with Nikita Khrushchev' against his GLF and commune system.[31]

It is well known that during his 1959 spring tour to the Soviet Union, Peng Dehuai 'expressed misgivings' regarding Mao's GLF and commune scheme to Khrushchev who 'allegedly encouraged Peng to return to China to oppose Mao' and who was subsequently able to 'attack the Chinese communes in a speech in Poland'.[32] Mao's outrage at Peng's 'treason' was well understood. It is worth quoting my arguments from my work *The International Environment and China's Twin Models of Development* on Mao's views about high treason (Lam, 2007:63–5). Undoubtedly he regarded Peng's actions as 'most despicable', likening it to 'a family member who eats at home but crawls outwards' (吃里爬外). The international situation in the year 1959 was crucial to the confirmation of the Soviet Union as 'No. 1 accomplice of the primary enemy of the US' in Mao's worldview. The

Taiwan Straits Crisis confirmed that 'the US-USSR colluded to the disadvantage to the Chinese' in the face of the Sino-Soviet Friendship Treaty and Agreements (Snow, 1966:641), and that, after 1958, the PRC had to deal not only with the United States, but also with the Soviet Union, a new 'devil'. Mao considered Peng's 'collusion' with the Soviets, 'an attempt to push over Mt. Kunlun' as high treason (1969:94). Therefore Peng's fate was sealed as a result of the 1959 rectification campaign against 'right opportunism'. The case against Peng and his supporters resembled that of Gao Gang and Rao Soushi of 1954. In his 'speech at the second plenary session of the Eighth Central Committee of the CCP' on 15 November 1956, Mao denounced Gao's high treason as 'having illicit relations with foreign countries' (里通外国) (1977c:340). During the period of August–September 1967, three articles in a row in the *Beijing Review* were published to denounce Peng Dehuai's 'heinous crimes' of anti-Party activities particularly against both the GLF and the communization movements.[33]

In his domestic anti-revisionist struggles against the 'right opportunists' in mid-1959, Mao resorted to a couple of poems that expressed his thoughts as follows:

In a letter to the editors of the *Poetry Journey* (*Shi Kan*) in September 1959 concerning the publication of his two poems, 'Shaoshan Revisited' and 'Ascent of Lushan', Mao referred to the 'Right Opportunists' who 'ganged up with the anti-Chinese Soviet Revisionists against his GLF and communization schemes', as 'mayflies lightly plot to topple the giant tree', which 'is ridiculous!' At the end of his letter, in great temper, he referred to the 'Right Opportunists' as 'rotten eggs' (王八蛋).

In his *lu shi* styled poem entitled 'Shaoshan Revisited', written in June 1959, Mao was resolute regarding the workability of the Great Leap forward scheme:

> Bitter sacrifice strengthens bold resolve,
> Which dares to make sun and moon shine in new skies.
> Happy, I see wave upon wave of paddy and beans,
> And all around heroes home-bound in the evening mist.

Defending his GLF and communization projects in another *lu shi* styled poem entitled 'Ascent of Lushan', written a month later, he claimed that he could make the famous Prefect Tao Yuanming to 'till fields in the Land of Peach Blossoms'.

Using the above-mentioned poems as political 'weapons', Mao carried out his international anti-Soviet 'revisionist' and anti-'right opportunist' campaigns at home. They also aided his anti-Liuist 'capitalist-cum-revisionist' struggles as follows:

In the book mentioned above, I argued that Mao's acceleration of the process of his defense-oriented collectivization led to the onslaughts of the 'rightists' led by Liu Shaoqi on a number of occasions (Lam, 2007:38–41). The Liuist 'capitalists-cum-revisionists' were well known for opposing Mao's defense-oriented communization agenda. Their development policy was identified as US capitalist motivated as well as Soviet 'revisionist' in orientation. During the 'difficult period of 1959–61', a series of natural disasters exacerbated by the disastrous GLF led to the Liuist 'capitalist-cum-revisionist' policies being officially carried out. Measures were taken to increase material incentives, including allowing privately owned land and free markets, increased the number of small enterprises responsible for their own profits, and in some cases allowing peasants to leave communes to engage in private farming. This was the age of 'US-USSR collusion' against China, according to Mao.

In August 1962, I continued, bolstered by improved agricultural conditions, Mao began his counter-attack at the Central Committee work conferences in Beidaihe to curb the liberal features of the Liuist, pro-Soviet, 'revisionist' policy established during the difficult three years. In addition to curbing the emphasis on Liu's 'revisionist' material incentives, steps were taken to restrict 'small freedoms' including prohibiting the division of land among households, cutting back on large private plots, and tightening control over free markets and private speculative activities. In August 1965, the movement of study of Mao Zedong Thought, which emphasized 'self-reliance' and 'self-sacrifice' and the importance of collective interests, was directed at cadres and the masses alike. Furthermore, the movement of 'criticism and self-criticism' was carried out from mid-October 1965 to March 1966 to rid *xian* Party secretaries of their 'mandarin-like work styles' and 'negative behavior of looking for stability', which had risen from 'selfishness' and 'conservatism' thus disenabling them to 'unite with all who can be united'. It was in this period of Mao Zedong study and of emphasis in politics on 'taking command' that this Socialist Education Movement merged into the Cultural Revolution and led to revolt against 'the leading persons in authority taking the capitalist road'.

Journey to the West (西遊记)

The Monkey King Sun Wukong (孙悟空), the hero of the novel *Journey to the West*, written by Wu Chengen (吴承恩) (1500–82) of the Ming dynasty (1368–1644), was Mao's popular political means to depict his animosity towards the pre-war fascist aggressors, American imperialism and social imperialism. Mao used the character to play both positive as well as negative roles in his contention with his superpower enemies.

First, let us consider the positive role of the Monkey King as follows:

The Sino-Soviet split, which shattered the strict bipolarity of the Cold War world, turned the Soviet Union and the PRC into bitter rivals for leadership in the Communist and Third World. The Communist triumph in China was a disaster for the Soviet Union, for Mao inevitably refused to play the role of a subordinate. For instance, in his independent economic approach, upon the completion of his anti-capitalist cooperativization plan in 1957, he accelerated his communization endeavors. Politically, more important, he claimed that 'at the Twenty-second Congress of the CPSU in October 1961, the revisionist Khrushchev clique developed their revisionism into a complete system not only by rounding off their anti-revolutionary theories of "peaceful co-existence", "peaceful competition" and "peaceful transition", but also by declaring that the dictatorship of the proletariat is no longer necessary in the Soviet Union and advancing the absurd theories of the state of the whole people and the party of the entire people'. Mao criticized the Soviets in that, with the abolition of the dictatorship of the proletariat behind this camouflage, Soviet leadership under Khrushchev paved the way for the restoration of capitalism. As discussed above, the Taiwan Straits Crisis had confirmed the 'US-USSR collusion to the disadvantage to the Chinese'. Understandably, thus, in his *lu shi* poem entitled 'Reply to Guo Moruo', written in mid-November 1961, he likened the 'revisionist Khrushchev clique' to the 'devil' who 'rose from a heap of white bones' (1976c:41), which appears in the novel *Journey to the West*. In the same poem, playing the role of the revolutionary Monkey King, Mao challenged the Soviet leadership and claimed to be the leader of the international Communist movement. He aimed to be the single, superior authority as follows:

> The Golden Monkey wrathfully swung his massive cudgel
> And the jade-like firmament was cleared of dust.
> Today, a miasmal mist once more rising,
> We hail Sun Wu-kong, the wonder-worker.

In January 1964, Mao told American correspondent Louise Strong that in his anti-Soviet 'revisionist' struggle, which began in mid-July 1963, as a result of the Soviet attack on the PRC in the open, he did not have other personal weapons, apart from a few poems.[34] Inspired by the Monkey King's 'revolt against the heavens', he continued, he adopted 'the Chinese own revolutionary road' against the so-called 'Soviet authority without having to pay any attention to heavens' law' (天条).[35] The Monkey's 'revolt against the heavens' adopted from the chapters six and seven of the novel is as follows:

> Born of a stone egg on top of the Flower-Fruit Mountain of the Ao-lai Country at the East Purvavideha Continent, the Monkey King eradicated his name from the Register of Death and exercised his magic powers to disturb the heavens. The Jade Emperor threw down a decree of pacification and appointed him to look after the celestial stable, but he despised the lowliness of that position and left in rebellion. Devaraja Li and Prince Nata were sent to capture him, but they were unsuccessful, and another proclamation of amnesty was given to him. He then made himself the Great Sage, Equal to Heaven, a rank without compensation. After a while he was given the temporary job of looking after the Garden of Immortal Peaches, where

almost immediately he stole the peaches. He also went to the Jasper Pool and made off with the food and wine, devastating the Grand Festival. Half-drunk, he went secretly into the Tushita Palace, stole the elixir of Lao Tzu, and then left the Celestial Palace in revolt. Again the Jade Emperor sent a hundred thousand Heavenly soldiers, but he was not to be subdued. Thereafter the Efficacious Kuanyin from the Potalaka Mountain of the South Sea sent for the Immortal Master Erhlang and his brothers, who fought and pursued him. Even then he knew many tricks of transformation, and only after he was hit by Lao Tzu's diamond snare could Erhlang finally capture him. Taken before the Throne, he was condemned to be executed; but, though slashed by a scimitar and hewn by an ax, burned by fire and struck by thunder, he was not hurt at all. After Lao Tzu had received royal permission to get him refined by fire in the brazier to reduce him to ashes, and the brazier was not opened until the forty-ninth day. Immediately he jumped out of the Brazier of Eight Trigrams and beat back the celestial guardians. He penetrated into the Hall of Perfect Light and was approaching the Hall of Divine Mists when Wang Lingkuan, aide to the Immortal Master of Adjuvant Holiness, met and fought him bitterly. Thirty-six thunder generals were ordered to encircle him completely, but they could never get near him ....[36]

Second, the negative role of the Monkey King, the pre-war 'German, Italian and Japanese fascism' featured in Mao's paper 'On Protracted War' (1967d:147) written in May 1938 is as follows:

There is yet a third form of encirclement as between us and the enemy, namely, the interrelation between the front of aggression and the front of peace. The enemy encircles China, the Soviet Union, France and Czechoslovakia with his front of aggression, while we counter-encircle Germany, Japan and Italy with our front of peace. But our encirclement, like the hand of Buddha, will turn into the Mountain of Five Elements lying athwart the Universe, and the modern Sun Wu-kongs – the fascist aggressors – will finally be buried underneath it, never to rise again. Therefore, if on the international plane we can create an anti-Japanese front in the Pacific region, with China as one strategic unit, with the Soviet Union and other countries which may join it as other strategic units ... and thus form a gigantic net from which the fascist Sun Wu-kongs can find no escape, then that will be our enemy's day of doom.

Mao was inspired by the following episode in chapter seven of the novel, in which the Monkey is subdued by Buddha as follows.

Arriving in Heaven, Buddha and his disciples (Ananda and Kasyapa) heard a fearful din and found Monkey beset by the thirty-six deities. Buddha ordered the deities to lower arms and go back to their camp, and called Monkey to him. Monkey changed into his true form and shouted angrily, 'What bonze are you that you ask for me in the middle of a battle?' 'I am the Buddha of the Western Paradise. I have heard of the trouble you have been giving in Heaven ... How can you delude yourself into supposing that you can seize the Jade Emperor's throne? ... What capability have you got ... that would enable you to seize the blessed realms of Heaven?'

'Many,' said Monkey. 'Apart from my seventy-two transformations, I can somersault through the clouds a hundred and eight thousand leagues at a bound. Aren't I fit to be seated on the throne of Heaven?'

'I'll have a wager with you,' said Buddha. 'If you are really so clever, jump off the palm of my right hand. If you succeed, I'll tell the Jade Emperor to come and live with me in the Western Paradise, and you shall have his throne without more ado. But if you fail, you shall go back to earth and do penance there for many a kalpa before you come to me again with your talk'.

This Buddha, Monkey thought to himself, is a perfect fool. I can jump a hundred and eight thousand leagues, while his palm cannot be as much as eight inches across. How could I fail to jump clear of it? 'You're sure you are in a position to do this for me?' he asked.

'Of course I am', said Buddha.

He stretched out his right hand, which looked about the size of a lotus leaf. Monkey put his cudgel behind his ear, and leapt with all his might. 'That's all right,' he said to himself. 'I'm right off it now.' He was whizzing so fast that he was almost invisible, and Buddha, watching him with the eye of wisdom, saw a mere whirligig shoot along.

Monkey came at last to five pink pillars, sticking up into the air. 'This is the end of the World,' said Monkey to himself. 'All I have got to do is to go back to Buddha and claim my forfeit. The Throne is mine.'

'Wait a minute,' he said presently, 'I'd better just leave a record of some kind, in case I have trouble with Buddha.' He plucked a hair and blew on it with magic breath, crying 'Change!' It changed at once into a writing brush charged with heavy ink, and at the base of the central pillar he wrote, 'The Great Sage Equal of Heaven reached this place'. Then to mark his disrespect, he relieved nature at the bottom of the first pillar, and somersaulted back to where he had come from. Standing on Buddha's palm, he said, 'Well, I've gone and come back. You can go and tell the Jade Emperor to hand over the Palaces of Heaven.'

'You stinking ape,' said Buddha, 'you've been on the palm of my hand all the time.'

'You're quite mistaken,' said Monkey. 'I got to the end of the World, where I saw five flesh-coloured pillars sticking up into the sky. I wrote something on one of them. I'll take you there and show you, if you like.'

'No need for that,' said Buddha. 'Just look down.' Monkey peered down with his fiery, steely eyes, and there at the base of the middle finger of Buddha's hand he saw

> written the words 'The Great Sage Equal of Heaven reached this place', and from the fork between the thumb and first finger came a smell of monkey's urine. It took him some time to get over his astonishment. At last he said, 'Impossible, impossible! I wrote that on the pillar sticking up into the sky. How did it get on to Buddha's finger? He's practising some magic upon me. Let me go back and look.' Dear Monkey! He crouched, and was just making ready to spring again, when Buddha turned his head, and pushed Monkey out at the western gate of Heaven. As he did so, he changed his five fingers into the Five Elements, Metal, Wood, Water, Fire and Earth. They became a five-peaked mountain, named Wu Hsing Shan, which pressed upon him heavily enough to hold him tight. The thunder spirits, Ananda, and Kasyapa all pressed the palms of their hands together and shouted 'Bravo!'[37]

Making use of the elements of (a) the 'devil' who 'rose from a heap of white bones' to represent Khrushchev, (b) the revolutionary Monkey King to represent his fight against Heaven – the 'big brother' the USSR, and (c) the Monkey King to represent the pre-war fascist allies of Germany, Italy and Japan, all from the *Journey to the West*, to serve his political purposes, was unprecedented.

Classical Chinese Poetry

In the following, I will consider how Mao used his own poems as political 'weapons' to fight the twin superpowers in relation to relevant political situations.

As noted above, the Sino-Soviet alliance began to turn sour when the 'US-USSR alliance at the disadvantage of China' became evident in 1954, as Mao saw it. To reiterate, the Chinese claimed that in the Twenty-second Congress of the CPSU in October 1961 Khrushchev developed revisionism into a complete system by 'rounding off the anti-revolutionary theories of 'peaceful co-existence', 'peaceful competition' and 'peaceful transition'. They were obviously concerned about 'US-USSR collusion' against them. Understandably, in December 1962, in his anti-US imperialist and anti-Soviet 'revisionist' stance, Mao composed his *lu shi* poem 'Winter Clouds' using the respective symbol of 'tigers and leopards' to represent US imperialism while the 'wild bears' represented the 'revisionist' Soviet Union as follows: 'Only heroes can quell tigers and leopards and wild bears never daunt the brave' (1976c:45).

The Sino-Soviet dispute erupted in 1963. In his lyric composed in January 1963 to the tune *Man Jiang Hong* and entitled 'Reply to Comrade Guo Moruo', Mao (1976c:46) wrote: 'The west wind scatters leaves over Changan, and the arrows are flying, twanging'. These lines clearly hinted at incipient Sino-Soviet hostility at the time of Khrushchev's arrival in Beijing in August 1958. Mao composed the lyric in 1963, five years after the Taiwan Straits Crisis and when the Sino-Soviet dispute was starting to loom large. The 'sounding arrowhead' denoted Khrushchev, who arrived in Beijing in autumn 1958 to 'attempt to blockade China's coast', according to Mao, 'intending to establish a so-called united fleet with us in order to control our coast' (1969:432). In these lines, Mao meant that the 'arrows' was shot into the city of Changan (长安), the ancient capital, Khrushchev's destination in China was Beijing, the modern capital. The word 'arrows' was symbolic of the latent hostility between the PRC and the Soviet Union since 1956 and aggravated by Khrushchev's arrival in autumn 1958. In ancient China, a declaration of war was affixed to an arrow and shot into the enemy's territory. The arrival of Khrushchev can be interpreted in this light.[38]

To reiterate, the above poems were the 'personal weapons' Mao described to US correspondent Louise Strong in January 1964 as having been used in his anti-'revisionist' fight.

In addition, in autumn of 1965, by applying Zhuang Zi's (庄子) (369 B.C.–286 B.C.) hyperbolical-astronomical *qi*, Mao depicted the 'limitless harm' of the 'US-USSR collusion to rule the world'. In tracing Mao's *qi* he expressed to contend with the twin superpowers, we will begin with Zhuang Zi's interpretation of Lao Zi's (? – ?) Tao (the Way), which called for a hyperbolical approach.

In his celebrated paper 'Flying Freely' (逍遥游), expounding on the vastness of the cosmos and the immeasurable greatness of Tao, the Way, as conceptualized by Lao Zi, Zhuang Zi successfully brought home the hyperbolical image of the legendary bird Kun Peng (鲲鹏) as follows:

> In the Northern Dimness there is a fish and its name is Kun. The Kun is so huge that no one knows how many thousand li he measures. He transforms into a bird whose name is Peng. The back of the Peng measures, no one knows how many thousand li across and, when rises up and flies off, his wings are like clouds all over the sky ... This Peng sets off for the Southern Dimness, the waters are roiled for three thousand li. He beats the whirlwind and rises ninety thousand li ... (He) shoulders the blue sky ...[39]

However, it is important to realize that the hyperbolical action of the Peng generates astronomical power. In this context, the element of astronomical power was implied.

In his *Irregular Verses* to the tune *Nian Nu Jiao*, composed in autumn 1965 and entitled 'Two Birds: A Dialogue', Mao referred to the *qi* of Zhuang Zi to depict the 'limitless harm' of the 'US-USSR collusion to rule the world' as follows:

> The Kun Peng stretches its wings,
> soaring ninety thousand li;
> and rousing the raging cyclone called Ram Horn,
> carrying the blue sky on his back,
> he looks down.
> to survey Man's world with its towns and cities.
> Gunfire licks the heavens,
> shells pit the earth.
> ...
> 'Don't you know a triple pact was signed
> under the bright autumn moon two years ago?
> There'll be plenty to eat,
> potatoes piping hot,
> beef-filled goulash'.
> 'Stop farting,
> Look, the world is being turned upside down!'

By referring to the June 1963 Moscow Test Ban Treaty, signed by the US, USSR and UK, Mao depicted the limitless 'harm' of the 'US-USSR collusion to rule the world', which, turned 'the world upside down'.[40] Morton H. Halperin (1965:2) writes:

> Viewed from Peking, it was not so much the case that China had decided to confront the two superpowers as that the US and USSR had come together and were trying to establish a duopoly of power.

The application of Zhuang Zi's analogy of hyperbolical-astronomical *qi* to depict the 'limitless harm' of the 'twin superpowers' collusion to rule the world' was another original feat of Mao Zedong Thought.

Shui Hu Zhuan (水浒传)

The classical Chinese novel of *Shui Hu Zhuan* (水浒传) (i.e., *Water Margin*, or *All Men Are Brothers*), written by Shi Naian (施耐庵) (? – ?) of the North Song dynasty (960–1127), was Mao's political 'weapon' to fight Soviet 'revisionism' especially its feature of 'capitulationism'. Originally, this novel is about a peasant uprising that took place around the Liangshan Mountain (in the present-day Liangshan county of Shandong province) towards the end of the same dynasty. The movement is aborted with the onset of its new leadership.

Chao Gai (晁盖), founder of the Liangshan bandit army, Wu Yong (吴用) and others make their way to Liangshan in revolt after seizing a large amount of money, which was sent to the premier as a gift. They all pledge to unite and rise in revolt against the emperor. Chao, the genuine 'law and heaven defiant' (无法无天者) (to use Mao's term) (1969:185), is popularly known as the 'Heavenly King'. However, the Maoists argued that the author of the novel, Shi Naian, considered rising against the Song emperor and calling himself a king to be a case of lese-majesty. Thus, Shi decided, according to the Maoists in February 1976, 'to have him killed by a poisonous arrow in a battle with the armed forces of the landlords'.[41] The Maoists argued that this was meant to make way for Song Jiang (宋江), the defender of Confucianism, to succeed Chao Gai so that Song's policy of capitulationism could be put in practice. Song became a Liangshan bandit only in the fortieth of the seventy-chapter version of the novel. After Chao's demise in chapter 59, Song manages to win the confidence of the other insurgents and assumes leadership of the Liangshan army. Immediately he changes the Juyi Hall (聚义厅) (*juyi* meaning united fraternity), named by Chao Gai, into the Zhongyi Hall (忠义厅) (*zhongyi* meaning loyal to the emperor). Understandably, thus, the novel denounces Song Jiang as the No. 1 capitulationist.

Therefore Mao argued that the main targets of attack of the Liangshan peasant insurgents led by Song Jiang are the local corrupt officials, but not the emperor, and that the merit of the last ten chapters of the novel, in which Song Jiang is the bandit leader, lies precisely in the portrayal of capitulation. This is because Song Jiang surrenders to the Song emperor and carries out the royal order to put down the armed rebellion of Fang La (方腊). Therefore, to Mao, the beauty of Song Jiang's surrender was that it served as 'good teaching material by negative example' (反面教材). In 1974, he mentioned to Zhang Yufeng (张玉凤), his personal secretary, in Wuhan that Song Jiang was 'a capitulationist as well as a revisionist'.[42] He quoted Lu Xun (鲁迅) in stating that Song was an imperial 'slave' (奴才).

In late 1975, acting in accordance with Mao's instruction, the Chinese used the novel as teaching material by negative example to distinguish capitulationists and initiated critique of the novel. The Maoists claimed that to meet the needs of the court, Song Jiang 'pushed a capitulationist line and made acceptance of the offer of amnesty and enlistment the aim of the uprising'.[43] That same year, the Maoists pointed out: 'What the novel praises is just this specimen of revolt in order to accept the offer of amnesty and enlistment'.[44] Thus, they argued, Song's capitulationist theme dominates the narrative, while the anti-capitulationist theme of Chao Gai and others is less influential.

The 1975 political movement of criticism of Song Jiang's 'Confucian' attitude, and therefore his 'capitulationism' seemed aimed at criticizing Liu Shaoqi and Lin Biao 'who pushed a revisionist line towards the Soviet Union'.[45] More important, Mao emphasized the issue of Song Jiang's capitulationism as part of his anti-Soviet strategy. This political movement attacked Soviet 'capitulationism' towards the United States in the mid-1960s. Even as early as April 1965, in applying the novel's feature of 'capitulationism' to fight Soviet 'revisionism', the Chinese accused the new leadership of the CPSU of following Khrushchev's 'general line of foreign policy to uphold peaceful co-existence'.[46] They claimed that the Twentieth Congress of the CPSU 'was the first and the most significant sign of the emergence of Khrushchev revisionism'.

In sum, Mao's application of the character of Song Jiang in the novel of *Shui Hu Zhuan* to denounce, first, Khrushchev's 'revisionism', i.e., his use of Song Jiang's 'Confucian capitulationism' to criticize 'Soviet capitulationism' towards the United States, and second, the capitulationist attitude of Liu Shaoqi and Lin Biao, was unusual.

Conclusion

Inspired by the classical historical novel of the *Romance of the Three Kingdoms*, Mao initiated his own global order of tripolarity to contend with the United States and the Soviet Union, singly or in unison, following the establishment of the PRC. In order to fight US imperialism and Soviet 'revisionism', as well as the domestic pro-US and pro-Soviet 'revisionists', Mao made use of the stories and issues as described in romance and other classical Chinese novels for his political objectives. These included the 'ghost stories' in the anthology *Strange Tales of the Leisure Study*, the 'evil spirit' who 'rose from a heap of white bones' from the novel of *Journey to the West*, and the legendary bird Kun Peng in Zhuang Zi's article of 'Flying Freely', in addition to Song Jiang's 'surrender to the Song emperor' in the novel of *Shui Hu Zhuan*, the 'East wind is prevailing over the West wind' from the novel of the *Dream of the Red Chamber*, and the 'treasonous right opportunists' related with the treasonous personalities from the historical novel of the *Records of Various Kingdoms of Eastern Zhou*. Mao also 'fought' US imperialism and Soviet 'revisionism' with his own classical poems. With classical Chinese literature as his political weapons in relation to changing political climate, his approach was original.

Chronological Events of the Three Kingdoms Period

The 'international' order of tripolarity of the Three Kingdoms period gradually developed, starting at the end of the Eastern Han dynasty (25–220). Chronologically the important events of the Three Kingdoms period were as follows:

As the Han Empire began to disintegrate into chaos, and a mad scramble for power among various military warlords began.

In 196, Cao Cao (曹操) held the Han emperor Xiandi (献帝) to random with his base at Xuchang (许昌) making the feudal lords surrender to his command.

In 200, Cao defeated his major enemy Yuan Shao (袁绍) in the Battle of Guandu (官渡之战) with his meager force of 10 thousand men against Yuan's 100 thousand strong.

In 207, having an army of one million, Cao Cao established his firm despotic rule of the Wei (魏) in northeastern China.

In eastern China, ruler Sun Quan (孙权) of the Wu (吴) state was the third generation to hold a firm base there, with the geographical advantage of the Yangtze River as its natural protection.

Liu Bei (刘备), 'Royal Uncle' of the Han dynasty, was still in the political wilderness, as Cao Cao had strengthened his Wei regime at Xuchang after defeating Yuan Shao.

In 207, Zhuge Liang (诸葛亮) became Liu's premier.

In 208, with a small force of 30,000 men, the Sun-Liu alliance crushed Cao's mighty force of over half a million men at Chibi (赤壁).

In 209, Liu Bei took the strategic Jingzhou (荆州) districts thus his third of the tripolar powers was materialized.

In 215, with the regions of Yizhou (益州) secured, Liu established his capital in Chengdu (成都) in the Western Riverlands (西川). His regime was Shu (蜀).

In 219, Sun Quan killed Guan Yu (关羽), Liu's sworn brother, after his Commander Lu Meng (吕蒙) captured Guan and took over Jingzhou.

In 220, Cao Cao died, and his son Pi (丕) succeeded him.

In 221, Liu Bei invaded the Wu state, but was defeated in Yiling (彝陵) a year later.

In 223, following Liu Bei's death, Zhuge Liang made peace with Sun Quan against the Wei state.

In 228, Zhuge began his six expeditions out of the Qi Mountain (祁山) to fight the Wei state.

In 234, Zhuge Liang died.

In 249, Si-ma Yi (司马懿) was in firm control of Wei.

In 252, Sun Quan died, his son Liang (亮) succeeded him.

In 255, Si-ma Yi's son Zhao (昭) took over the Wei state.

In 256, Jiang Wei (姜维) of the Shu state invaded Wei but was defeated.

In 263, Si-ma Zhao of the Wei state invaded and wiped out the Shu state. The Shu emperor Liu Chan (刘禅) surrendered.

In 265, Si-ma Yi's grandson, Yan (炎), took over Wei and became Jin Wudi (晋武帝) of the Western Jin dynasty (西晋).

In 280, Si-ma Yan annihilated the Wu state, and the period of the Three Kingdoms ended.

The decisive events of the period of the Three Kingdoms were as follows:

First, after defeating Yuan Shao in the Battle of Guandu, Cao Cao established his rule in northeastern China.

Second, the Battle of Chibi resulted in the formation of the tripolar powers to scramble for the control of China.

Third, invading the Wu state, Liu Bei was defeated in the Battle of Yiling. Liu's demise enabled Zhuge Liang to carry out his consistent policy of making peace with Wu against the Wei state.

Fourth, Zhuge Liang died without achieving his aim of defeating Wei in his six expeditions.

Fifth, Si-ma Yi took control of Wei.

Sixth, Si-ma Yi's son Zhao wiped out the Shu state.

Seventh, Si-ma Yi's grandson Yan, who annihilated Wu, became emperor of the Western Jin dynasty thus ending the era of the Three Kingdoms.

CHAPTER ONE

Mao and the Theme of *The Romance of the Three Kingdoms*

In the early 1950s, John Dulles viewed the postwar world in dichotomous terms as had Harry Truman and, for that matter, Joseph Stalin. However, this thesis argues that, inspired by the historical novel *Romance of the Three Kingdoms* (三国演义), Mao Zedong initiated his own global order of tripolarity following the establishment of the People's Republic of China in October 1949. This was to contend with the United States through attempted collusion with Stalin's Soviet Union.

The historical novel concerns contention initiated by one sovereign power, Shu (蜀), against another, Wei (魏), by colluding with the third power, Wu (吴), from a weak position in the then China of 209–80. In order to crystallize the Chinese 'world order' of tripolarity, which Zhuge Liang (诸葛亮) (180–234), the Shu architect of contention, conceives of, his plan is to take the then West China as base for contention against the Wei and subsequently collude *at all costs* with East Wu, since West Shu will have to contend with the powerful North Wei from a weak position. This realistic analysis of the warring situation concerning the three kingdoms inspired Mao (1969:627) as he considered the international political situations of his own time.

Interviewed by Edgar Snow in 1936, Mao said he 'believed that he was much influenced by the historical novel read at an impressionable age'.[1] I argue that this 'influence' can be traced to the theme, characters, and events of the historical novel as follows:

(1) The *qi* of Cao Cao ((155–220), which inspired Mao to perceive the world in its totality,

(2) The following two components constitute the theme of the historical novel:
 (a) The concept of 'partition of the world under the heavens into three' (三分天下), that is, the Chinese 'international' order of tripolarity (209–80) initiated by Zhuge. Mao (1969:172) referred to this concept in his talks in the Chengdu Conference in March 1958. He noted then that he considered Zhuge to be 'competent'.[2]
 (b) 'The world phenomenon under the heavens is that long united, it must divide; and vice versa' (天下大势, 合久必分, 分久必合).[3] Mao often referred to this principle. It is important to note that Mao interpreted this ambiguous original statement as follows: 'The world phenomenon under the heavens is that empires, long united, must divide; and vice versa'. Therefore, in view of the irreparable breach between the Shu and Wu states in Zhuge Liang's Chinese 'international' order of tripolarity, Mao interpreted this statement in relation to Sino-Soviet relations in his global order of tripolarity as 'their animosity would occur sooner or later',[4] and to 'the Sino-US relations, which must make up with each other after a long period of hostility'.

(3) The battle at Chibi (赤壁), in which the victory was won by small forces over large and by inferior over superior forces in a tripolar situation. In his *Selected Works*, Mao (1967c:212–13, 252–3; 1967d:164, 192–3) referred to this battle on a number of occasions. Its outcome inspired him to *strive hard* to collude with Stalin's Soviet Union to fight the powerful United States in the early 1950s.

In chapter 21 of the novel, Cao Cao (曹操), the Wei ruler, refers to himself as a 'truly great hero' with the *qi* described as 'embracing the universe and swallowing the sun and the moon' (夫英雄者, 有包藏宇宙之机, 吞吐日月之志者也). Mao described Cao's *qi* as 'a great (writing) hand brush' (大手笔), and called him 'a true man' (真男子).[5] This *qi*, as noted above, inspired Mao to look at the whole world in its totality or from a 'bird's-eye' view. This meant that he perceived the whole of the world as basic to his policy formulation of China's relations with the superpowers.

Immediately after the establishment of the People's Republic, stimulated by Zhuge Liang's concept of 'international' order of tripolarity, he conceived of his own global order of tripolarity by virtue of assigning the PRC the role of a superpower in big power politics, though it was not yet a superpower. This was to 'partition the world under the heavens into three', which is Zhuge's celebrated phrase in chapter 38 that Mao (1969:172) often quoted.

It is well known that Mao was fond of Beijing opera and that in his leisure time he enjoyed singing particularly the 'Three Visits to the Thatched Hut' (三顾茅庐) concerning Royal Uncle Liu Bei's (刘备) request for Zhuge Liang's assistance to regain the former glories of the Han dynasty. The operatic piece begins with the following lines emphasizing Zhuge's concept of the tripolar world:

> I was honored with the Royal Uncle's three visits in order to urge me to assist him in regaining the former glories of the Han dynasty. I thus obliged to present my concept of the tripolar powers in which the Liu Han should collude with the Wu at all costs to fight the powerful Wei from a weak position ...
> (御驾三请, 保定乾坤, 算就了, 汉家业, 鼎足三分 ...).[6]

Certainly Mao's interest in this operatic piece gives us useful insights into his psychological depth. In his talks at the Hangzhou Conference in April 1957, he (1969:106) referred to Liu's request to Zhuge for assistance.

In April 1959, quoting Zhuge Liang's famous remark 'bending my back to strive on, until my end' (鞠躬尽瘁, 死而后已), Mao told his security guard Li Yinqiao (李银桥) that he would like to do the same to serve China.[7] He (1969:436) considered Zhuge as a man of the highest integrity and was impressed with his intellectual capability. He treated Zhuge's remark as his own motto. He quoted the phrase on a number of occasions, for instance:

(1) In May 1942, towards the end of his 'Talks at the Yenan Forum on Literature and Art', he (1969c:834) quoted the phrase to praise Lu Xun's (鲁迅) revolutionary spirit in serving the proletariat and the masses.

(2) In a written tribute to Zou Taofen (邹韬奋), a well-known contemporary Chinese journalist and political commentator, in his article 'In Commemoration of Mr Zou Taofen', published in the *Liberation Daily* (解放日报), 15 November 1944, he quoted Zhuge's phrase again.
(3) In his paper 'In Commemoration of Dr Sun Yat-sen' written in November 1956, Mao (1969e:312) quoted Zhuge's phrase again to pay tribute to Dr Sun Yat-sen. Zhuge Liang's phrase was coined in the last paragraph of the text of his 'Second Petition for a Campaign' (后出师表), an appeal to the young Shu emperor Liu Chan (刘禅) for the expedition against the Wei in the year 227.

In September 1961, expressing great reverence for Zhuge, Mao told Lord Montgomery in Wuhan that 'like Zhuge Liang', he was 'the Director General' (军师) of the Army.[8]

In his speech at a conference of cadres in Shanghai in July 1957, Mao (1977c:468) emphasized Zhuge's importance to the Shu leader Liu Bei as 'fish-in-water relationship' as follows:

> When Liu Bei got Zhuge Liang to help him, he said he felt 'just like a fish in water'. This is true. Their fish-water relationship is not only described in fiction but recorded in history. The masses are Zhuge Liangs, the leaders are Liu Beis.[9]

Certainly Mao considered Zhuge's 'international' order of tripolarity, that is, the 'partition of the heavens into three' to be logical. Therefore, he (1969:709) argued about the importance of the strategy of united front, when commenting on the following important battles described in the novel *Romance of the Three Kingdoms*:

> Cao Cao, using his powerful military forces to try to conquer Sun Quan, is defeated; Liu Bei who tries the same to Sun Quan also fails; and Si-ma Yi who also tries the same to Zhuge Liang also fails.

He implied that these decisive battles all end up in failure because the military designers do not adhere to the strategy of the united front of two states against the third in a tripolar situation. This was because they consider that with greater numbers they would win their respective battles without applying the strategy of 'united front'. In addition, the success of military operation does not depend on the greater numbers of men mobilized, but on how to mobilize them. Therefore, it is not surprising Mao (1969a:188; 1969b:458) stressed these principles again and again as he had been convinced of their validity, for instance, by the battle at Chibi in the novel and by many other battles fought throughout the centuries (by both China and the Western world).

This work argues that, inspired by Zhuge Liang's united front strategy of the famous battle at Chibi, in which victory was won by small forces over large and by inferior over superior forces, Mao aimed to collude with the Soviet Union in 1950 to fight the powerful United States from a weak position. Reacting to the start of an era of US anti-communism, China, according to Mao, needed to consolidate its alliance with the Soviet Union 'at all costs' (and the third world nations) to form a united front against the United States. During the months of January and February of 1950, he *strove hard* to get Stalin to sign the proposed Sino-Soviet Treaty and Agreements in Moscow. On a number of occasions during the period 1957–62, he (1969:85, 432) recalled that he and Stalin 'were at loggerheads during the above-mentioned two months over the ratification of the treaty and agreements', because, according to Mao, 'Stalin refused to sign it'. He even accepted, though 'unwillingly', the independence of Outer Mongolia as a condition for the signing of the treaty and agreements. He later argued that 'based on Sino-Soviet friendship and bound by law', the treaty and agreements were ratified to aim at 'opposing the possible imperialist (US) invasion'.[10] However, as it turned out, the 1950 Sino-Soviet treaty and agreements were signed in name only, and subsequently China had to fight the US-led UN in Korea without Soviet participation.

Therefore, the postwar bipolar struggle between the Soviet and American blocs gave way to a more complicated pattern of international relationships in which the world was no longer split into two clearly opposed blocs.

The following accounts for some of the main stream theses concerning the Sino-Soviet-American triangle since the beginning of the 1950s.

Dittmer (1987:29–46) considers the Sino-Soviet-American strategic triangle as an international game during the period from the end of the

Second World War to the mid-1980s. Robinson (1987:4) argues that 'the strategic triangle has been a central feature of the international system at earliest since 1950 and certainly since the early 1970s', and that 'the triangle has fundamentally configured international relations for a long time to come'. Hsiung (1987:230–52) proposes to examine Sino-US-Soviet relations in their triadic context, 'drawing upon some of the theoretical insights made available from studies of three-person games by sociologists and social psychologists'. Rummel (1987:253–78) considers the Sino-American-Soviet relationship as an exemplification of a general process of triadic conflict and accommodation, involving fundamentally a balancing of powers, and establishing a structure of expectations and core status quo based on the resulting balance. In his thesis, Tow (1994:122) argues that throughout the post-war era, the international strategic system was largely shaped by the 'US-Sino-Soviet strategic triangle'. According to him (1994:122), 'since the PRC's inception, its foreign policy has been most influenced by the balance-of-power, state-centric approach to international politics and security, with the aim of waging a "protracted struggle" against both superpowers'. The study of Camilleri (1980) is primarily concerned with the fluctuating triangular relationship between China, the Soviet Union and the United States. In her book *China's Global Strategy: Towards A Multipolar World*, Clegg (2009:39) writes that although the world situation was still dominated by the two superpowers during the post-Second World Cold War period, 'the shift in effect was the first step towards a qualitatively new stage of world history, that of multipolarity'. In his paper on the Sino-American relations, Shambaugh (1994:199) talks about the 'loose bipolar' character of the international system that prevailed during the decade of the 1960s, which 'remained constant', while the United States, China and Soviet Union added a new dimension to the international system with the creation of the so-called 'strategic triangle'. Ilpyong Kim (1987:1) writes that 'the trend toward détente and a multipolar world in the 1970 characterized by the Kissinger balance-of-power diplomacy was designed to restructure the bipolar international system to a multipolar system' and that 'the rise of China as a world power after the Cultural Revolution has created a new pattern of relations within the US-Soviet-Chinese triangle in world politics'. Levine (1987:72–85) deals with the Soviet views of US-Chinese relations from 1971 to the late 1980s on the question of Soviet-American relations insofar as both superpowers include a China factor in their political and strategic calculations. Chang (1987:90–108) writes about China's perceptions of the two superpowers and of American-Soviet relations from the eras of Mao and Deng. Without elaborating it, Robinson (1987:561) mentioned that 'the Maoist military component of revolutionary experience owed much to ... the heroics exhibited in such writings as the *Romance of the Three Kingdoms*'. However, I will go further to trace the origins of Mao's global order of the Sino-US-Soviet tripolarity to 1949 immediately following the establishment of the PRC and argue that his global order was inspired by the historical novel.

It is important to note that Mao considered Zhuge Liang's 'international' order of tripolarity to be too rigid, because Zhuge sticks to his anti-Wei strategy of colluding Shu with Wu throughout the novel. This strategy does not flexibly include a possible Shu-Wei united front against the state of Wu as an option when necessary. Understandably, therefore, following the establishment of the PRC in October 1949, Mao formulated his own global order of tripolarity basically including interchangeable primary and secondary enemies to suit the contemporary world of his time.

Mao's tripolar worldview of the contemporary world was gradually transformed in response of the politics and actions of the superpowers as he saw them. This had resulted in transitions from 'friend' to 'enemy', from 'secondary enemy' to 'primary enemy', and vice versa, and in the formulation of his scheme of collusion with the 'secondary enemies' against the 'primary enemy'. Mao's concept of the 'three worlds' was fundamentally formulated to aim at the 'primary enemy' of the first world. His struggle with the primary enemy, a superpower, or the superpowers combined, was carried out in the following ways:

(1) through colluding with (the imperialist) secondary enemy or enemies against the primary enemy;
(2) through inciting the third world nations or the second world nations to unite against the superpower enemy or enemies;
(3) through fanning revolutionary movements in the third world.

Beginning in 1954, Mao perceived that the twin superpowers 'actively colluded to the disadvantage of China'. However, the year 1964 witnessed the demise of Khrushchev and the United States began its involvement in Vietnam in 1965. Understandably he sought to realize his anti-'hegemonic' and anti-imperialist aims 'one by one' in his global order of tripolarity when possible particularly during the respective periods 1959–64 and 1965–9 as follows.

(1) While the Sino-Soviet dispute had hardened into bitter hostility in 1969, Mao dismissed the Soviet-backed 'right opportunists' at home in 1959. The Soviet secondary enemy was transformed into the primary enemy in Mao's global order of tripolarity during the period 1959–69.
(2) The US new involvement in Vietnam in 1965 gave Mao the opportunity to launch his Cultural Revolution to purge the 'capitalist-cum-revisionist' Liuists as part of the Sino-US acrimonious exchange. Further, in mid-1966 Zhou Enlai announced China's support of North Vietnam. President Nixon's new Guam policy was announced in October 1967; it played a role in the US primary enemy beginning to develop into the secondary enemy.

As early as January 1957, Mao (1977:344) argued that 'a flare up of the Sino-Soviet animosity will occur sooner or later' and implied that the Sino-US relations, long estranged, would in time improve. Therefore, on two separate occasions, inspired by the theme of the novel, he dropped hints to American correspondents Anna Louise Strong in February 1959 and Edgar Snow in October 1964 about his wish to 'swim in the Mississippi River'.[11] Mao's hints were meant to improve the Sino-US relationship at the expense of the Soviet Union.

In the early 1970s, in response to the new Kissinger-Nixon Doctrine, which called for gradual withdrawal of the US from Northeast and Southeast Asia, Mao saw a golden opportunity to normalize Sino-US relations in the face of the Soviet threat. Thus, encouraged by the theme of the historical novel, which he referred to on a number of occasions, and which he interpreted as 'the world phenomenon is that empires, long divided, must unite', Mao initiated the so-called 'ping-pong (table tennis) diplomacy'. After Nixon's China visit in 1972, this led to the decisive changes in China's relations with the superpowers in Mao's global order of tripolarity.

In February 1974, Mao created his new concept of the 'Three Worlds'. This was Zhuge Liang's 'international' order of tripolarity, enhanced by the theme of the novel *Romance of the Three Kingdoms*. Mao's new concept was fundamentally formulated to fight the primary enemy of the First World, i.e., the 'hegemonic' Soviet Union, through befriending the secondary enemy of this First World, namely, the 'imperialist' United States. His contention with the Soviet primary enemy was further carried out actively, both directly and indirectly, through inciting the Third World nations over which Mao always claimed China's leadership, or even trying to unite with the Second World nations against the Soviet Union.

In laying out its argument, this work will examine the following main sections:

(1) *The Romance of the Three Kingdoms* and the origins of Mao's global order of tripolarity,
(2) The period 1950–76 of Mao's global order of tripolarity,
(3) The period 1979–90: the collapse of Mao's global order of tripolarity.

While section 1 will include the transformation of the post-war bipolarity into Mao's global order of tripolarity, section 2 will focus on the following three main periods of tripolarity:

The first 1954–64 period witnessed the dissolution of the Sino-Soviet alliance, and the second period 1965–69 witnessed an era of Sino-US 'love signaling'. In addition, in between these two periods respectively, the following took place:

(a) Dismissal of the Soviet-backed 'right opportunists', and
(b) The Cultural Revolution which was to purge the 'capitalist-cum-revisionist' Liuists and Deng Xiaoping.

These two periods fall in the category of the United States as the primary enemy with the Soviet Union as 'No. 1 accomplice of the US'. The third period 1969–72 was dominated by Sino-US 'courtship'; in this period the Soviet Union was the primary enemy and the United States secondary enemy.

CHAPTER TWO

The Romance of the Three Kingdoms and the Origins of Mao's Global Order of Tripolarity

When analysing the origins and development of Mao Zedong's resolute spirit against the superpowers, we cannot operate effectively without considering the impact of the classical Chinese novel *Romance of the Three Kingdoms*. This historical novel inspired his thinking, shaped his character, and provided a viable alternative to power politics during his time. In order to plumb the significance of his remarkable contention with the superpowers, I argue that the novel had been so profound a single factor that exerted decisive influence on his view of reality. Its realistic analysis of the warring situation concerning the three kingdoms in the novel inspired him to analyse global political situations of his own time.[1] Mao drew inspiration from the novel's theme, characters such as Cao Cao (曹操) and Zhuge Liang (诸葛亮), and narrative events such as the 'international relations' of the three kingdoms of Wei, Shu and Wu of the then China during the period 209–80, and its famous battle at Chibi.

Interviewed by Edgar Snow in 1936, Mao emphasized:

> What I enjoyed were the romances of Old China ... (For instance), I read *San Kuo* (*Romance of the Three Kingdoms*), while still very young ... I used to read them in school, covering them with a Classic when the teacher walked past. So did most of my schoolmates. We learned many of the stories almost by heart, and discussed and re-discussed them many times. We knew more of them than the old men of the village, who also loved them and used to exchange stories with us ... I believe that perhaps I was much influenced by them read at an impressionable age.[2]

The novel reflects the various political, economic, military and social conditions of the three kingdoms. Mao (1969:529) considered it a source of the history of the period. Through its succinct clarity of style and refined literary treatment, the historical novel of the *Romance of the Three Kingdoms*, written by Luo Guanzhong (罗贯中) (1330–1400) of the Yuan – Ming dynasties, was based on the book *Records of the Three Kingdoms* (三国誌) compiled by Chen Shou (陈寿) (233–97) of the Western Jin (西晋) period, in addition to the following texts:

(1) *Annotated Records of the Three Kingdoms* (三国志注) by Pei Song Zhi (裴松之) (372–451) of the South Dynasties' Song era,
(2) *Later Han Book* (後汉书) by Fan Ye (范晔) (398–445) of the same Song era and
(3) *Oral Records of the Three Kingdoms* (三国誌平话) of the Yuan dynasty

Luo Guanzhong not only was a brilliant historian, but also an outstanding prose writer, as was Si-ma Qian (司马迁) (145 B.C.–86 B.C.), the Former Han dynasty's Grand Historian. With the use of the colloquial style of prose writing, the *Romance of the Three Kingdoms* is excitingly dramatized. Its masterly prose writing, its lucid narration, its vivid descriptions and, above all, its colorful imagination, had captured great masses of readers throughout the centuries.

This historical novel focuses on the political, military and diplomatic struggles among the three kingdoms. It consists of 120 chapters. Chapters 1 to 33 are about the uprising of the Yellow Turbans, the chaotic struggles of the warlords and Cao Cao's unification of northeast China. Chapters 34 to 50 focus on the events that preceded the battle of Chibi and the battle itself. Chapters 51 to 115 are about the post-battle tripolar powers, the establishment and strengthening of the Shu state, its struggles against the states of Wei and Wu, and those among the three powers. The last 5 chapters concern the relations of the three kingdoms, which lead to the establishment of the Jin (晋) dynasty. The historical novel's eventful framework and activities of the actors are largely based on the history of the period of the three states. In the novel, Luo Guanzhong also made up his own stories, in combination with folk stories and legends. It is a story of the heroic leaders and warriors of the time in their struggles for control of China. Its fictitious episodes are interesting and exciting, for instance, Zhuge Liang's borrowing of Cao

Cao's arrows with a ruse, Zhuge's supplicating of the divine wind, Guan Yu attending the henchmen hidden banquet with only a saber and the exciting episode 'Playing a Tune on a Stringed Instrument, Zhuge Repulses Si-ma Yi (司马懿)'. The novel is a captivating epic. The characteristic descriptions of the various battles and their strategies are dramatic. Based on actual events in third century China, it has always been considered a novel of 'seven-parts fact and three-parts fiction'. Characters such as Cao Cao, Liu Bei (刘备), Zhang Fei (张飞), Zhao Yun (赵云), Guan Yu (关羽), Zhuge Liang and so on have become well loved and even divine for the last two cases in the hearts of the Chinese, young and old, man and woman, throughout the centuries. Mao once stated that 'one cannot be considered as a Chinese, if he has not read the *Romance of the Three Kingdoms* [together with the *Shui Hu Zhuan* (*Heroes of the Marshes*) (水浒传) and the *Dream of the Red Chamber* (红楼梦)].[3]

The Romance of the Three Kingdoms and Mao

In May 1938, in his talks at the Anti-Japanese Military Academy in Yenan, he referred to an occasion during the Jinggangshan period when he asked about the historical novel and other classical novels, which might be found in the house of a liquidated landlord.[4] This demonstrated that even during wartime, he remained eager to re-read the novel.

What makes the novel fascinating is its wide appeal to many types of readers. Chinese and Western scholars claim that ordinary Chinese have read it because of the heroic and fraternal leaders and warriors, whereas rulers have been attracted to its descriptions of battle strategies. Both these two conditions applied to Mao. I will discuss later how Mao was attracted to the strategies of the three major battles at Chibi, Guandu and Yiling. In the following, I will first show how Mao responded to the heroic acts of warrior Guan Yu.

In his poem entitled 'To Peng Dehuai', written in September 1935 after Peng's successful breakthrough in the battle in Lazikou (腊子口) of Northern Shensi province, he painted a true warrior image of Commander Peng who was, like Guan Yu, 'reigning in his steed with his lance-like saber across his chest' (谁敢横刀立马,惟我彭大将军). This very image of the heroic Guan Yu is portrayed in Chapter 27 of the novel entitled 'Commander Guan with a Beautiful Beard Rides on a Solitary Journey of a Thousand Li Slaying Six Generals and Breaching Five Passes' (in Cao Cao's territory).

On a number of occasions, Mao referred to Guan Yu's lance-like saber (青龙偃月刀), for instance:

(1) In November 1957, during his second visit to the Soviet Union, Mao discussed with Guo Moruo (郭沫若) Hu Qiaomu (胡乔木) and others about the 'killing effect between Guan Yu's lance-like saber and the atomic bomb'.[5]
(2) In the Eighth Central Committee's Second Plenary Session (May 1958), he told the audience about his attempt to convince India's Prime Minister Nehru that modern weapons were not as effective as Guan Yu's lance-like saber.[6]

Undoubtedly Mao equally enjoyed reading the celebrated Chapter 66 entitled 'Guan Yu Attends the Henchmen Hidden Banquet with Only a Saber'. Briefly, it relates the following:

Liu Bei who has become the ruler of the Shu state refuses to 'return' the Jingzhou districts to the Wu state, even though he has promised to do so after conquering the Western Riverlands (西川). Instead, he has appointed Guan Yu to defend the districts. Thus, the Wu leadership cooks up the plan of inviting Guan to a meeting where they would try diplomacy if he accepts, but let the hidden henchmen kill him if he resists. They also decide that if Guan refuses to accept the invitation, they would send troops to recover Jingzhou.

Guan Yu accepts the invitation and turns up with only a small army.

Warmed by the wine, Lu Su (鲁肃), a Wu official, asks about the retrieval of the districts. Considering it as a state business, Guan refuses to talk about it ... Guan's expression turns ugly. In his right hand, he holds the lance-like saber that he snatched from his adopted son Zhou Cang (周仓), his left is wrapped around Lu Su. Feigning that he is drunk, he demands they drop the subject of Jingzhou. Lu feels his frightened soul part from his body as Guan drags him to the river bank. Lu Meng (吕蒙) and Gan Ning (甘宁), set to strike, hold off, seeing Guan armed and Lu's life in danger. Reaching his boat with his army, Guan releases his hostage.

Mao considered the rendezvous in Chongqing with Chiang Kaishek in August 1945 as '(Guan Yu) attending the meeting with only a saber' (单刀赴会) to 'reveal Chiang's treacherous plot'.[7]

In the following, I will consider one of Zhuge Liang's heroic acts and remarkable performances described in the novel: 'Zhuge Liang repulses Si-ma Yi of the Wei state, playing a tune on his stringed instrument' (Chapter 95). This episode has been well known as the 'Empty City Strategy' (空城计) throughout the centuries. It was one of the 'stories' Mao told Edgar Snow in Yenan in 1936 that he 'enjoyed' equally as other Chinese, young and old.

While Si-ma Yi (司马懿) of the Wei state is leading squadrons of one hundred and fifty thousand towards the Shu's western guard tower, Zhuge Liang finds that he has no commanders of importance available. Half of the five thousand men in his command have been dispatched to move food supplies leaving the other half in the city. All of the officials turn pale at the news of Si-ma Yi's approach. Mounting the city wall, he saw dust clouds in the distance as the Wei's field army advance for attack.

Zhuge Liang orders everyone to keep quiet and all flags and banners put out of sight. Then he instructs that the four gates of the guard tower be opened wide; at each a squad of twenty soldiers disguised as commoners, were to sweep the streets. They are told to not make a move when the Wei troops arrive. He himself puts on his crane-feather cloak and sits in front of a stringed instrument, playing a tune as incense burns. Meanwhile, Si-ma Yi has reached the wall of the western guard tower with his troops, seeing Zhuge smiling, while playing his instrument. To his left, a boy holds a sword, to his right, another holds a feathered whisk. By the city gate, sweepers ply their brooms, as if no one else is about.

Puzzled, Si-ma turns his army around and retreats. He considers that Zhuge has always been a man of extreme caution and firmly believes that he has opened the city gates because he has set an ambush. Thus he orders the Wei troops to withdraw.

Inspired by Zhuge Liang's 'Empty City Strategy', Mao created his own version of the strategy to ward off KMT's 'Bandit Suppression' Commander-in-chief Fu Zuoyi (傅作义) and his squadrons of 100 thousand, only with a page of radio script. The following eyewitness account taken from the book *Beside Mao Zedong for 15 Years* (在毛泽东身边15年), written by Li Yinqiao (李银桥), Mao's bodyguard,[8] is even more spectacular than Zhuge's fictitious strategy:

In August 1948, determined to regain the liberated city of Shijiazhuang (石家庄), Fu Zuoyi advanced upon the CCP and PLA Headquarters in Xibaipo (西柏坡) with cavalry squadrons of 100 thousand men from Beiping (today's Beijing) and Baoding. Xibaipo was at the time far from the PLA main force. And Zhou Enlai had to make arrangements for the Central's organizational units to disperse, having dispatched Wang Dongxing (汪东兴) to escort Mao as he left the Party headquarters.

With his attention focused on formulating his strategy of operations for the forthcoming Liaoxi-Shenyang Campaign, Mao did not take the advance of Fu's army seriously. However, when the situation became desperate, he decided to 'show Fu some true colors' as he put it. Drafting a radio script, with a sense of humor, he began: 'We are well prepared. There is no point for you to come'. Making use of Zhuge's 'Empty City Strategy', he continued:

> Now (your city) Beiping is not well protected. Do you intend to keep it intact or not? You only have stationed the (weak) 208th Division there. It is virtually empty. It is also empty in Tongzhou (通州) ... In short, Chiang Kai-shek's whole northern front line as well as your (Fu Zuoyi's) fighting system will be finished in a few months' time. Yet, you are still dreaming of recapturing Shijiazhuang. Would it be ridiculous![9]

Having drafted the script, he instructed the New China News Agency to broadcast it immediately.

Panicking, Fu ordered his troops to retreat hastily back to Beiping. Likewise, he ordered the troops, which stationed in Baoding to retreat to the capital.

Having scared off Fu and the multitude of 100 thousand in his command with the short radio script and without firing a bullet, Mao sang the Beijing opera '(Zhuge Liang's) Empty City Strategy':

> While enjoying the mountain views on the guard tower, I heard utter chaos outside the city with flags in a flutter. I found that Si-ma Yi was leading squadrons of 150 thousand towards the western guard tower ...

Having sung the famous opera, Mao continued with another operatic piece '(Liu Bei's) Three Visits to (Zhuge Liang's thatched hut in) Wo Long Gang (卧龙岗)' (三顾茅庐), which starts with the line 'I am Zhuge Liang originally from Wo Long Gang ....'[10]

In the following, I will argue how Mao identified with Zhuge, who 'thrice riles Zhou Yu' (Chapters 51 to 57). This episode, which has been well-known throughout the centuries, was another of the 'stories' Mao told Edgar Snow in Yenan in 1936 that he 'enjoyed'.

After the decisive battle at Chibi, both the Shu and Wu states intend to capture the Nanjun (南郡) from the Wei. While Zhou Yu is battling with Cao Ren (曹仁), Cao Cao's commander-in-chief, Zhuge Liang dispatches Zhao Zilong to take over several southern districts and sends Zhang Fei and Guan Yu to capture Jingzhou and Xiangyang (襄阳) respectively. As a result, Zhou Yu passes out from exasperation and finally ruptures an old wound that he had received in a battle against Cao Ren.

The news of Governor Liu Qi's (刘琦) death triggers the Wu to reclaim Jingzhou from the Shu state. However, Zhuge successfully pacifies the Wu minister Lu Su by writing a document to guarantee that the Shu can borrow the districts as its temporary base and that Jingzhou would be restored to the Wu state after the Shu has taken the Western Riverlands. Zhou Yu realizes that Lu Su has been fooled.

The sudden news of the passing of Liu's wife is now a golden opportunity for Zhou Yu to put forward his plan to marry Liu into the Wu family.

Holding Liu prisoner instead of going through with the marriage, this plan is meant to 'retrieve' the districts of Jingzhou in exchange for his release.

Matrimonial arrangements are made for Liu Bei to cross the Yangtze River. While denouncing Zhou Yu for plotting out the treacherous act, when the State Matriarch realizes that Liu Bei is the imperial uncle of the Han dynasty, a virtuous and eminent man of the era, she decides to meet him. Impressed by Liu's extraordinary bearing and appearance, she happily accepts the proposed marriage. Thus Zhou Yu's ruse becomes reality.

Under Zhuge Liang's plan, Liu flees the Wu state with his new wife. Zhou pursues the couple with his fleet, but is ambushed and defeated. Zhuge directs his troops to jeer from shore: 'Commander-in-chief Zhou's brilliant scheme of conquest not only has cost the Lady, but also the troops to boot'. Rage wells up in Zhou, his old wound bursts and he collapses.

Zhou Yu works out another plan. He proposes to the Shus that as the Suns and Lius are now in one family, the Wu would raise an army to take the Riverlands and turn them over to the Shu state as a dowry in exchange for the Jingzhou districts. As a pretext, Zhou means to catch the Shus unaware and capture Jingzhou. Zhuge Liang pretends to agree with Zhou's scheme.

With land and naval forces, Zhou's squadrons of fifty thousand men marched toward Jingzhou; he is confident that Zhuge is trapped. However, Shu Commander Zhao Zilong emerges from Jingzhou's guard tower to reveal Zhou's ugly scheme of 'trying to borrow a passage in order to capture Jingzhou'. Realizing that he has failed again, Zhou cries out and falls from his horse.

Soon after, a letter that just arrived advises him not to be so foolish as to try taking the Riverlands. Groaning several times, he drops dead.

With Commander Zhao and five hundred warriors, Zhuge attends Zhou's funeral. Kneeling on the ground, Zhuge reads his eulogy:

> Woefully fallen in your prime! Heaven leaves man to grieve. Heartbroken, I spill this wine. May your spirit savor my libation ... While a heart beats here, this sorrow cannot end. Heaven darkens over. Your lord mourns. Your friends pour out their hearts ...

Zhuge is prostrate with grief. Deeply moved, the Wu commanders think that Zhuge is a man of great depth, while Zhou was narrow.

In the following, I will consider that, inspired by Zhuge Liang's 'thrice riling Zhou Yu', Mao (1967f:265–6) staged his own 'thrice riling Chiang Kai-shek' to highlight Chiang's defeat in the Liaoxi-Shengyang campaign during the period between mid-September and early November 1948:

The Liaoxi-Shengyang campaign was a massive campaign fought by the Northeast People's Liberation Army in the western part of Liaoning Province and in the Shengyang-Changchun area. Jinzhou, on the Peiping-Liaoning Railway, was the strategic link between northeastern and northern China. The KMT forces defending the Jinzhou (锦州) sector consisted of 8 divisions, with more than 100,000 men under Fan Hanjie, Deputy Commander-in-Chief of the KMT's Northeast 'Bandit Suppression' Headquarters. The capture of Jinzhou was the key to the success of Mao's Liaoxi-Shengyang campaign. Chiang Kai-shek hurriedly flew to the Northeast to take personal charge of the operations. According to Mao, the complete collapse of the KMT troops in the Northeast was already a foregone conclusion in the month of October 1948. But in mid-October, Chiang still 'dreaming of recapturing Jinzhou', gave orders to the army under Liao Yaoxiang to continue its advance towards Jinzhou. The three crucial stages of Mao's campaign were as follows:

First, after taking Jinzhou, the PLA immediately swung back to the northeast and closed in on Liao's army from the north and south of Heishan and Dahushan.

Second, in late October, the PLA succeeded in surrounding the enemy in the Heishan-Dahushan-Xinmin sector and wiped them out, capturing army commander Liao Yaoxiang, corps commanders Li Tao, Bai Fengwu and Zheng Tingji, and more than 100,000 men.

Third, the PLA followed up the above victory and liberated Shengyang and Yingkou in early November, wiping out over 149,000 KMT troops. The whole of the Northeast was thus liberated.

Mao described the above three successful stages of the campaign, in which a total of more than 470,000 KMT troops were wiped out, as 'thrice riling Chiang Kai-shek' (三气蒋介石).[11]

Origins of Mao's Concept of Global Order of Tripolarity

This thesis focuses on the global order of tripolarity which Mao initiated immediately following the establishment of the PRC. Inspired by the struggles among the tripolar powers of Shu, Wei and Wu, he sought to realize his anti-imperialist and anti-hegemonic aims. As noted above, Mao told Edgar Snow in 1936 that he 'believed that he was much influenced' by the historical novel 'read at an impressionable age'. I argue that this 'influence', which laid the theoretical foundation of Mao's global order of the tripolar powers, can be traced to the following major sources:

(1) The *qi* of Cao Cao (155–220), which inspired Mao to perceive the world in its totality,
(2) The following two components which constituted the theme of the historical novel:
    (a) The concept of 'partition of the world under the heavens into three' (三分天下), that is, the Chinese 'international' order of tripolarity (209–80) initiated by Zhuge Liang (180–234).
    (b) 'The world phenomenon under the heavens is that long united, it must divide; and vice versa' (天下大势, 合久必分, 分久必合). Mao often referred to this principle. It is important to note that this original statement is ambiguous, and he interpreted it as follows: 'The world phenomenon under the heavens is that empires, long united, must divide; and vice versa'. Mindful that the colluding states of Shu and Wu against the powerful Wei often breach their agreements, Mao applied this principle to the Sino-Soviet relations in his global order of tripolarity, which added 'their animosity would occur sooner or later'. He also flexibly included 'Sino-US relations must make up with each other after a long period of hostility'.
(3) The battle at Chibi in which the victory was won by outnumbered and inferior over superior forces. The outcome of this battle inspired Mao to *strive extremely hard* to collude with Stalin's Soviet Union to

fight the powerful US, immediately following the establishment of the PRC.

Firstly, I will trace Mao's theoretical strategy of acquiring 'astronomical power' from Cao Cao's *qi* and how he used it to carry out his anti-imperialist and anti-hegemonic fights. Mao's foreign policy of treating the United States and the Soviet Union as the primary enemy started in 1950 and 1969 respectively.

Secondly, by implementing his policy on an unprecedented scale in contention with the superpowers, Mao's theoretical grounding was strengthened, inspired by Zhuge Liang's 'international' order of tripolarity.

Thirdly, inspired by Zhuge Liang's concept of the Chinese 'international' order of tripolarity and stimulated by the theme of the novel *Romance of the Three Kingdoms* as he interpreted it, Mao's tripolar worldview of the contemporary world of his time was featured with the transformation of 'friend' to 'enemy', from 'secondary enemy' to 'primary enemy', and vice versa. Thus, following the establishment of the PRC, his scheme of colluding with the 'secondary enemies' plus the third world nations against the 'primary enemy' was formulated.

Finally, the battles at Chibi, Guandu and Yiling, in each victory was won by outnumbered and by inferior over superior forces, inspired Mao to contend with the superpowers (either singly or united) even when in a weak position.

In the following, we will first consider Cao's *qi*, which served as an inspiration to Mao.

Cao Cao's *Qi*

Towards the end of the Eastern Han period (25–220), the Han Empire began to disintegrate into chaos, after the uprising of the Yellow Turbans in the year 184. A scramble for power among various military warlords started.

In 196, Cao Cao established his despotic rule over the Wei in Xuchang (许昌) and made the feudal lords surrender to his command through holding the Han emperor Xiandi (献帝) for ransom. In 200, he wiped out the last major warlord Yuan Shao (袁绍). In 207, having defeated the Wu Huan (乌桓), he unified north eastern China.

Cao's victory in his campaign against the Wu Huan inspired his aggrandized ambition to conquer the 'world'. This psychological insight can be seen in his poem 'Gazing the Great Sea' (观沧海) in which he hyperbolically identified his own spirit with the vastness of the universe:

> Eastwards to Jieshi I gaze over the waters
> Why is the sea so calm,
> While the mountain island rears up awfully?
> There are trees all round and the grass abundant.
> While the autumn wind is sighing,
> Huge billows are swirling.
> The sun and the moon seem to be contained in it;
> The Milky Way appears to have originated from it.[12]
> Most lucky am I to be in such a position
> To sing about my (hyperbolical) mind.

This is the very *qi* associated with Chinese styled heroism that he reveals to Liu Bei, the 'Royal Uncle', in Chapter 21 of the historical novel as follows: 'A truly great hero has an immense consciousness of embracing the universe and swallowing the sun and the moon'. What he means is that a truly great hero cherishes lofty plans in his bosom and assumes he has the means to achieve them; he has all-embracing schemes of the world, which is at his mercy.

Completely disregarding the major warlords of his time such as Yuan Shu (袁术), Yuan Shao (袁绍), Liu Biao (刘表), Liu Zhang (刘璋) and Sun Ce (孙策), Cao Cao considers himself a true hero.[13]

Calling Cao Cao 'a true man' (真男子), Mao considered Cao's *qi* as 'a great hand brush' (大手笔).[14] This vision of *qi* inspired Mao to look at the whole world in its totality, from a 'bird's-eye view'. It also strengthened his 'methodology of thinking' by 'making the universe my greater self … who is concerned with the affairs of the whole world and ten thousand future generations'.[15] His methodology was to acquire astronomical power through the strategy of uniting with the secondary enemy (and the oppressed peoples around the world) against the primary enemy in a tripolar situation. His hyperbolical task was to 'annihilate US imperialism' or Soviet 'revisionism', starting from 1950 and 1969 respectively.

It was in this context that in his poem 'Kunlun' written in 1935 Mao 'cleaves' Mt. Kunlun as a metaphor for imperialism in three:

> Could I but draw my sword o'ertopping heaven
> I'd cleave you in three:
> One piece for Europe
> One for America
> One to keep I the East.
> Peace would reign over the world,
> The same warmth and cold throughout the globe.

According to Mao, Mt. Kunlun of imperialism, which 'lies like dead weight on the people', must be 'up-rooted'. With the 'immense consciousness' of his ability to contend with the superpowers and ultimately defeat them by tapping astronomical power for this hyperbolical task, Mao was clearly inspired by Cao Cao's *qi*.

Understandably, therefore, Mao 'reversed the verdict' on Cao Cao who is treated in the *Romance of the Three Kingdoms* as a 'traitor' and 'usurper of the legitimate ruling Han dynasty'[16]. In the novel, Cao is posed in contrast Liu Bei, the 'Royal Uncle', who is the direct off-spring of the Han royal family and is treated as the novel's moral actor. And, in the eyes of the author of the novel, the kingdom of Shu is the legitimate regime. However, according to Mao's research, in reality Cao Cao was a very capable political leader.

On 20 November 1958, Mao convened a meeting in Wuhan to discuss the novel *Romance of the Three Kingdoms* and the historical text on which it was based. In the meeting, he focused on Cao Cao. According to him, the historical text presents Cao as 'an extraordinary man' (非常人) in a chaotic age. However, Mao declared that he 'respected' and treated Cao as a 'hero'.[17]

Mao's *qi* is well expressed in his poem 'Snow' to the tune of *Qin Yuan Chun*. It was written in February 1936, about four months after he had composed the above poem 'Kunlun':

But alas! Qin Shihuang and Han Wudi
Were lacking in literary grace,
And Tang Taizong and Song Taizu
Had little poetry in their souls;
And Genghis Khan,
Proud Son of Heaven for a day,
Knew only shooting eagles, bow outstretched.
All are past and gone!
For truly great heroes
Look to this age alone.

I argue that written within such a short span of time, the above two poems are related particularly regarding 'cleaving the mountain of imperialism' and the 'heroic deeds'. Just like Cao Cao who completely disregards his contemporaries, Mao disparaged the famous ancient emperors of China to which he referred in his poem 'Snow'. In this poem, Mao claims that his *qi* to be expressed in his future deeds will be far greater than that of these ancient emperors. Pointedly, in the last two lines of the poem, Mao hinted that he would be the 'truly great hero' who, representing the PRC – the moral actor like the minor Shu state of the Three Kingdoms period – aimed to 'wipe out' imperialism with *qi* for the exploited and bullied peoples around the world.

Zhuge Liang's Concept of the Chinese 'International' Order of Tripolarity

We discussed above how Mao identified with Zhuge Liang. In his 'Seminar Records' (讲堂录), the teenage Mao had already praised Zhuge for being 'capable'.[18] In a paper entitled 'Beat Back the Attacks of the Bourgeois

Rightists' in his *Selected Works V*, written in July 1957, Mao (1977c:468) referred to Zhuge's important role in the historical novel as follows:

> When Liu Bei got Zhuge Liang to help him, he said he felt 'just like a fish in water'. This is all true. Their fish-water relationship is not only described in fiction, but recorded in history. The masses are Zhuge Liangs, the leaders are Liu Beis.

Zhuge Liang was the creator of the 'international' order of the then China of 209–80.

As Mao 'believed' that he had been influenced by the novel *Romance of the Three Kingdoms*, this thesis suggests that not only did Mao perceive the relevant positions of the three powers in the pattern as Zhuge Liang set out, but also that he was inspired by the resolute spirit of Premier Zhuge of the principal warring power, the Shu state. Confirmatory evidence can be seen in Mao's well-known scheme to construct his own 'world order of tripolarity' (三分天下),[19] immediately after the establishment of the PRC. He often referred to the term.

In Mao's favorite pastime singing of the 'Three Visits to the Thatched Hut' regarding the Royal Uncle Liu Bei's request for Zhuge's assistance to regain the former glories of the Han dynasty, Zhuge's concept of the tripolar world of the then China was emphasized.[20]

In Chapter 38, prior to the materialization of the Shu state, Zhuge Liang charts the tripolar course for Liu Bei to consider as follows:

From the outset, he analyses the 'international' situation in then China at the end of the Eastern Han dynasty (25–220). By first introducing the powerful Cao Cao who has an army of one million and holds captive the Han emperor to make the feudal lords surrender to his command, Zhuge initially thinks there is no way Liu Bei can defeat him. However, he considers, Sun Quan, who holds the power of his family's third generation in the then south-eastern China, has a firm grip there. The territory is not easily accessible, with the Yangtze River as its natural protection, and the people are loyal to him. Thus, according to Zhuge, the Wu state may serve as a supporting ally but should not be a strategic objective.

In the central plain, the Jingzhou districts command the Han and Mian Rivers to the north, while they draw wealth from Nanhai in the south. Eastwards, they communicate with Wu's southern regions; and westwards, they offer access to the Western Riverlands, today's Sichuan province. He therefore urges Liu to take the Jingzhou districts first. Then, the next target in Zhuge's strategy should be the Yizhou districts (益州) to the west of Jingzhou. Strategically located, they are inaccessible, with fertile lands extending thousands of li. Accordingly, Zhuge argues, the first emperor of the Han consummated his imperial achievements by establishing a base there. The existing regional protector, Liu Zhang (刘璋), he continues, is weak and feeble, even though the people are well off and the region is thriving. The people there are yearning for enlightened rule.

Zhuge Liang advises Liu Bei to sit astride the Jing (荆) and Yi (益) regions, guard their strategic centers, come to terms with the minority tribes on the west, appease the people of the Yi (彝) and the Viets (越) to the south, make a diplomatic alliance with Sun Quan and initiate a region program in his own territory.

Finally, according to Zhuge, Liu should wait for the opportunity to drive north to Cao Cao's Luoyang (洛阳) from the Western Riverlands. This plan is to fulfill Liu's aim of reviving the Han dynasty.

In short, Zhuge Liang proposes that Liu Bei should take Jingzhou first and make it his home base. Liu should then move to the Western Riverlands and build his third of the tripolar powers there. Eventually his objective should be to aim to take the northern and central plains. Meanwhile, according to his recommendation, Liu should collude at all costs with the Wu state, since the Shu was ultimately to contend with the powerful Wei from a weak position. This means that in the contention of the Shu state with the Wei, the kingdom of Wu would be reduced to a position level with the Shu state whose primary enemy is the Wei.

Liu Bei carries out Zhuge Liang's recommendation.

In the twelfth month of 208, with a meager force of 30,000 men, the Shu-Wu colluding forces crushed Cao Cao's mighty force of over three-quarters of a million by setting fire to his linking fleet at Chibi. A year later, Liu Bei took the strategic Jingzhou of Wei, as advised by Zhuge Liang. Thus his third of the tripolar powers was materialized. In 215, with the regions of Yizhou in the west of Jingzhou secured, Liu established his capital in Chengdu (成都).

The decisive battle at Chibi, in which the colluding Shu-Wu states against the Wei state resulted in the Chinese 'international' relations of the Three Kingdoms period of 209–80, changed the course of Chinese history.[21]

Stimulated by Zhuge who sets out the pattern of the three kingdoms to materialize Liu Bei's role in the tripolar powers, Mao created his own global order of tripolarity immediately after the establishment of the PRC which I will focus on in the next chapter.

The Theme of *The Romance of the Three Kingdoms*

Mao was familiar with the theme of the historical novel *Romance of the Three Kingdoms* which is emphasized at the beginning of its first chapter as well as towards the end of its last chapter as follows:[22] 'The world phenomenon under the heavens is that long divided, it must unite; and vice versa. Thus it has ever been. (天下大势, 久合必分, 久分必合)'

As discussed above, he interpreted this statement as 'The world phenomenon under the heavens is that empires, long divided, must unite; and vice versa'. Therefore, according to him, the dissolution of the alliance of the colluding Shu and Wu states confirms its validity. Liu Bei launches an attack on the Wu, who have taken over the strategic Jingzhou after killing Liu's sworn brother, Guan Yu. On a number of important occasions, from 1954 to 1969, during which the US was treated as the primary enemy and the USSR as 'No. 1 accomplice of the US', Mao referred to the novel's theme in reference to the contemporary world of his time.

In September 1964, Mao (1969:578) confirmed that the communist giants 'long united, must divide'. According to him, 'this statement is dialectic'.[23] In mid-January 1954, the Sino-Soviet alliance began to weaken when Pospelov, Secretary of the Soviet Communist Party's Central Committee under Khrushchev, responded positively to US President Eisenhower's proposed 'peaceful transformations' which, as Mao saw it, were aimed at 'the disadvantage of the PRC'. In 1959, the Sino-Soviet relations turned sour and the Soviets aborted the Sino-Soviet agreements and withdrew all their economic advisers and aid.

Inspired by the same theme, on two separate occasions, he dropped hints to American correspondents Louise Strong in February 1959 and to Edgar Snow in October 1964 about his wish to 'swim in the Mississippi River'.[24] Mao's hints were meant to improve the Sino-US relationship at the expense of China's relationship with the Soviet Union. At the beginning of the 1970s, inspired by the theme of the historical novel, Mao was convinced that both the United States and China 'long divided, must unite'. A golden opportunity arose, and he personally initiated the ping-pong diplomacy in 1971 that led to an improved Sino-US relationship.

The Battle of Chibi and Other Major Battles Described in *The Romance of the Three Kingdoms*

A total of eight chapters of the 120-chapter *Romance of the Three Kingdoms*, i.e., Chapters 43 to 50, accounts for events related with the battle at Chibi. The narrative unfolds as follows:

(1) Zhuge convinces the Wu politicians and military strategists of the importance of the Shu-Wu collusion to fight the powerful state of Cao Cao,
(2) Pang Tong has a shrewd plan for linking the Wei's vessels,
(3) Zhuge supplicates the divine 'southeast wind' to enhance the fire set to Cao Cao's linking fleet,
(4) Commander Guan Yu fraternally sets free the escaping Cao Cao following the latter's defeat in the battle, and

(5) Dramatic conflicts ensue between the colluding Zhuge Liang and Zhou Yu, the Wu Commander-in-chief, while they both deal with their common enemy Cao.

It is well known that Mao enjoyed reading the exciting episode of the Battle of Chibi.[25] This celebrated battle described in the *Romance of the Three Kingdoms* was based on history recorded in Chen Shou's *Records of the Three Kingdoms* and Pei Song Zhi's *Annotated Records of the Three Kingdoms.*

Inspired by the Battle of Chibi, Mao's theoretical foundation of his global order of tripolarity he initiated in 1950 was to aim at colluding with Stalin's Soviet Union to fight the powerful United States from a weak position. This theoretical foundation was strengthened by his understanding of the following theses:

(1) The basic military principle concerning 'the strategic defensive and strategic offensive' and
(2) The thesis that 'incorrect subjective direction can change superiority and initiative into inferiority and passivity, and correct subjective direction can effect a reverse change'.

According to Mao (1959a:212–13), these principles are well illustrated in the *Romance of the Three Kingdoms* concerning the famous battle and many others throughout the centuries carried out by both China and the Western world. Mao argued (1967d:165) that in these instances, victory was won by small over much larger and by inferior over superior forces.

On two occasions in his *Selected Works*, Mao referred to the Battle of Chibi described in the historical novel of the *Romance of the Three Kingdoms* regarding the victory won outnumbered and by inferior over superior forces. In his thesis 'Problems of Strategy in China's Revolutionary War', written in December 1936 (Volume I), and in another thesis 'On Protracted War', written in May 1938 (Volume II), Mao (1967c:212) talked about the battle of the Wu-Shu alliance against the more powerful Wei, the battle of Guandu between Cao Cao and Yuan Shao, and the battle of

Yiling between the states of Wu and Shu. In each example, the warring sides were unequal and the weaker side ultimately defeated the stronger.

In the above-mentioned first thesis, Mao commented on the battle at Chibi with regard to the policy of a 'strategic defense' taken by the weaker side in response to that of the 'strategic offense' taken by the stronger side. His comments (1967c:213) were as follows:

> Both sides were unequal, and the weaker side, yielding some ground at first, gained mastery by striking only after the enemy had struck and so defeated the stronger side.

In the above second thesis, Mao (1967d:164) argues:

> The thesis that incorrect subjective direction can change superiority and initiative into inferiority and passivity ... when we look at the record of defeats suffered by big and powerful armies and of victories won by small and weak armies.

In the above-mentioned theses, Mao clearly pointed out how the decisive Battle of Chibi was won by small and weak over big and strong armies as follows:

> Chibi is situated on the south bank of the Yangtze River in Hubei province. In 208, Cao Cao led an army of over three quarters of a million men, which he proclaimed to be one million strong, to launch an attack on Sun Quan. Sun, in alliance with Liu Bei, mustered a force of 30,000. With the knowledge that Cao's army was plagued by epidemics and was unaccustomed to action afloat, the Sun-Liu allied forces set fire to Cao's linking fleet and crushed Cao's forces completely.[26]

It was plain enough for Mao to conclude that the battle at Chibi was won by the colluding parties because they were able to concentrate their combined forces with firm cooperation to defeat their powerful enemy Cao. For instance, Zhuge 'supplicates the divine southeast wind' to enhance the fire set by Zhou's team to Cao's linking fleet.

On another occasion, referring to the same battle, Mao (1969:709) commented that 'Cao Cao tried to use his powerful military forces to try to conquer Sun Quan, but was defeated'. He condemned Cao for 'slighting his enemies tactically' simply because he had the greater numbers. Cao

Cao's psychological make-up is revealed in Chapter 49 of the *Romance of the Three Kingdoms*. Charged with emotion on the eve of the battle, he says of his allied enemies:

> You do not reckon for much with your puny force, Liu Bei and Zhuge Liang. How foolish of you to attempt to shake Taishan (Mt. Tai).[27]

First, Cao Cao's troops were in greater numbers, this was why he 'slighted his enemies tactically'. Second, unconcerned that he was facing the most important battle of his life, he boasted:

> I broke up the Yellow Turbans, captured Lu Bu, destroyed Yuan Shao and subdued his brother, Shu, whose armies are now mine. In the north, I reached to Liaodong and I stretched out over the whole north. I never failed ...[28]

In the above-mentioned theses in the two volumes of his *Selected Works*, Mao (1967c:252–3; 1967d:192–3) also clearly pointed out how the other two decisive battles were won by small and weak over big and strong armies. They were the battle at Guandu between Cao Cao and Yuan Shao and that of Yiling between the states of Wu and Shu. Let us first discuss Mao's comments concerning the battle at Guandu as follows:

> In the year of 200, Cao Cao scored a victory at the Battle of Guandu against the powerful forces of Yuan Shao. This battle occurred in the northeast of the present Zhongmou county, Honan province. Yuan had an army of 100,000, while Cao Cao had only a meager force and was short of supplies. Due to a lack of vigilance on the part of Yuan's troops who belittled their enemy, Cao Cao made use of his light-footed soldiers to spring an attack on them and set fire to their supplies. Yuan's army was thrown into confusion and was eventually wiped out.

The following are Mao's comments concerning the Battle of Yiling:

> Yiling is situated at the east of the present Yiling, Hubei province. In 222, Liu Bei, ruler of Shu, invaded Wu. Liu's troops scored successive victories at beginning of the war and penetrated five or six hundred li into the territory of Wu as far as Yiling. Lu Xun, who was defending Yiling, avoided battle for over seven months until Liu Bei was at his wits end and his troops were exhausted and demoralized in high summer. Lu crushed his troops by taking advantage of a favorable wind to set fire

to his camps propped up by timber structures in a wet ravine and closely linked up under the forest trees.[29]

In Chapter 58, 'Lu Xun Biography' (陆逊传) of the Wu Section (吴书) of his *Annotated Records of the Three Kingdoms* (三国志集解) concerning Lu Xun's defeat of Liu Bei by setting fire to the latter's timber camps, Lu Bi (卢弼) quotes Qing scholar Qian Zhen Huang's (钱振鍠) question that if Liu used mud and stone to build his camps, how could Lu defeat Liu? Based on his experience of his decades long revolutionary struggles, Mao responded to Qian's question as follows:

> Even without using the forest timber to build military camps, food supplies were difficult to reach Yiling for Liu Bei to fight a protracted war. Thus Liu's effective way should be to use the 'mobile warfare'. That is, first, attacking Wu's weaker defense in the Li River (澧江) region at the south of Yiling to divide its forces, second, concentrating on Shu's forces to defeat Wu's forces one by one.[30]

Liu Bei was defeated primarily because far away from his home base of the Western Riverlands, his adviser, Zhuge Liang, was not with him. The Battle of Yiling confirms the validity of the theme of the historical novel that 'the empires under the heavens, long united, must divide'.

Mao and the Battle of Chibi Described in both the *Records of the Three Kingdoms* and *Romance of the Three Kingdoms*

Having read both the *Records of the Three Kingdoms* and *Romance of the Three Kingdoms* a number of times, Mao cautioned the Chinese readers that the former was more factual than the latter.[31] On 20 November 1958, a day before the Central Government's Work Meeting in Wuhan, according to Tao Lujia (陶鲁笳), Mao convened a special seminar on the *Records of the Three Kingdoms*, in which he drew a comparison between the historical text and the historical novel.[32] In the following, I will deal with the different versions of the Battle of Chibi featured in these two texts.

Records of the Three Kingdoms, the official historical record for the period of the Three Kingdoms, as noted above, was compiled by Chen Shou in the third century, based on the histories of the rival states of Wei, Shu and Wu. Considering the brevity of this text, Pei Song Zhi annotated a new version, which became another celebrated source regarding the history of the three kingdoms. Throughout the centuries, Chinese military experts sought to learn the strategies of the military struggles featured in both the *Records of the Three Kingdoms* and *Annotated Records of the Three Kingdoms*. The Battle of Chibi recorded in these two historical texts is well reflected in details in the *Romance of the Three Kingdoms* as discussed above. (We can also find the other two major battles at Guandu and Yiling featured in details in these three sources, which show valuable insights into the principles of winning victory despite being outnumbered and battling superior forces. Mao was very attracted to the descriptions of the battles featured in the three books).

In Chapter 5 entitled 'Zhuge Liang's Biography' of the 15-chapter 'Shu Volume' of the *Records of the Three Kingdoms*, Chen Shou focused on Shu Premier Zhuge Liang who charts the tripolar course for Liu Bei. It describes in a short paragraph his emphasis on the importance of, first, taking the strategic districts of Jingzhou, second, occupying Yizhou and subsequently the Western Riverlands as the Shu's base. This is meant to substantiate the tripolar order in its contention with the powerful Wei state through colluding with the Wu state. In a short paragraph in Chapter 9 of the 'Wu Volume', it emphasizes the concluding talks of Sun Quan and Zhou Yu to resist Cao Cao's invading forces at Chibi. In the subsequent paragraph, it describes how Zhou Yu schemes to set fire to Cao's linking fleet.

In order to gain further insights into the Battle of Chibi, Mao read *Zizhi Tongjian* (资治通鉴) literally the *Guiding Mirror to Aid in Government*, which features the battle from a different angle.

Mao and the Battle of Chibi Described in *Zizhi Tongjian*

It is well known that Mao was crazy about the text *Zizhi Tongjian*, a pioneering reference work in Chinese historiography compiled by Si-ma Guang (司马光) (1019–86) and his assistants of the Song dynasty (960–1279).[33] Considering that it is well written, he read the historical text 17 times.[34] Apart from advising his personal staff to read it, he recommended it be read by leadership of various levels.[35] The battle described in the text as in those mentioned above gave Mao valuable insights into the principles of successful military operations and winning victory despite being outnumbered or facing superior forces. Not only did he read the book critically, he also studied the historical lessons described in it.[36] During the Long March, reportedly he often read on his horse.[37] On one occasion, he did the same again, this time reading the episode of the Battle of Chibi featured in the *Guiding Mirror to Aid in Government*. He was so absorbed in the story of this amazing victory of the Sun-Liu alliance of merely 30 thousand men against Cao Cao's army more than half a million strong, without realizing he had already been at his destination for half an hour.[38]

In this classical historical text, Si-ma Guang devoted 21 chapters to the account of the Three Kingdoms section, that is, Chapters 60 to 81. In Chapter 65 of the Han Annals (汉纪) section, three related topics were included. These were Zhuge Liang's life history, the Sun-Liu collusion and the Battle of Chibi. They were to motivate Zhuge's policy of realizing the 'international' tripolar order of then China through a Sun-Liu alliance to fight Cao Cao's mighty naval forces at Chibi towards the end of the year 208.[39] These topics were based on Chen Shou's *Records of the Three Kingdoms*.

In the first topic, a short paragraph of slightly less than a page was devoted to Zhuge Liang's rationale for the Shu-Wu collusion against the Wei state in the year 207. The first paragraph of slightly less than four pages was focused on the second topic, concerning the vital debate leading to Sun Quan's decision on the Wu-Shu collusion to fight Cao Cao in 208. The second paragraph of the same topic was about the analysis of the forthcoming battle at Chibi by officials of the Wu state who were confident in winning the conflict with their meager force of 30 thousand soldiers. In the third topic, a short paragraph of a page was about the battle itself that led to Cao Cao's defeat.

To reiterate, Mao enjoyed reading the three different versions and an annotated account of the Battle of Chibi; from these he gained remarkable insights that motivated his conception of the tripolar international relations of his own time.

Zhuge Liang's 'Limitations'

Although Mao agreed with Zhuge's logic on the Chinese 'international' order of tripolarity through colluding with the state of Wu against the powerful Wei from a weak position, he felt that Zhuge's strategy had 'limitations'. In November 1957, in a speech at the Moscow Meeting of Representatives of the Communist and Workers' Parties, Mao highlighted (1977c:514) Zhuge Liang's 'limitations' as follows: 'A Chinese proverb says that three cobblers with their wits combined equal to Zhuge Liang the mastermind. Zhuge Liang by himself can never be perfect, he has his limitations'. Zhuge Liang's limitations can be summed up in the following three categories.

The geographical factor

Mao criticized Zhuge's strategy as having loopholes geographically.[40] According to Mao, right from the beginning, Zhuge's policy disastrously divided the Shu's military forces in the regions of the Western Riverlands and the strategic Jingzhou districts.[41]

After taking Jingzhou, Liu Bei designated Guan Yu to defend it, while aiming to take over the Western Riverlands, as advised by Zhuge Liang.[42] After securing the Western Riverlands and the Central Han areas, Zhuge needs to station some of the Shu troops there. This, according to Mao, badly divided the Shu's meager military forces.[43] In 215, the Wu state began to fight for the strategic Jingzhou districts defended by Guan Yu, Liu's sworn brother. Sun Quan killed Guan and took over Jingzhou after his commander-in-chief Lu Meng captured Guan. In 221, Liu Bei launched an attack on Wu to avenge Guan's death, contrary to Zhuge Liang's consistent grand strategy of colluding with the Wu against the powerful Wei. This further divided and weakened Shu's military forces. The decisive battle occurred in Yiling to the west of the present Ichang, Hubei province. A year later Liu was defeated there by the Wu's Commander Lu Xun.

In the thesis 'Xiang Ji' (項籍) of his work *The Authoritative Book* (权书), Su Xun (苏洵) of the Song dynasty (960–1279) referred to the relationship between the geographical characteristics of the Sichuan province and its historical-political features.[44] He argued that 'as a base for defense, the province is not ideal' and that 'as a base for controlling the whole of China, it was impossible'.[45] Mao's response to Su's statement was that in the end, the Shu state was not able to unify China, because Zhuge Liang's strategy designed for Liu Bei to adopt, as first revealed in the celebrated 'Long Zhong Dialogue' (隆中对) of taking the Western Riverlands as home base after securing Jingzhou for the realization of a tripolar China, was basically, – geographically – faulty.[46] Mao concluded that Zhuge's policy could not concentrate 'astronomical power' to defeat the primary enemy Wei, because, early on, the Wu would lay claim to the strategic Jingzhou districts, which were far away and difficult to access from Shu's home base of the Western Riverlands.

An imperfect Shu-Wu collusion rendering Zhuge's anti-Wei strategy ineffective

The colluding Shu and Wu states against the Wei state often breached their agreements. For instance, on one occasion, Zhuge advises the Wu to attack the Wei together with the Shu.[47] Lu Xun, the Wu's grand strategist, argues against the plan and presents an alternative, which is eventually accepted by Sun Quan, the Wu ruler:

> Lu Xun said: 'This shows that Zhuge fears Si-ma Yi's scheme. Since we have agreed to collude against Wei, it is detrimental to us to refuse. However, we should pretend to be in full military alert in our response to the Shu's request (but actually wait and see ...) and while Zhuge attacks Wei in full swing, we should take the opportunity to take Central China ourselves.'[48]

This shows the lack of cooperation between the two allies vital to defeat of the powerful Wei, their deadly enemy. Mao (1969:709) recognized such non-cooperation as detrimental to both allies and as rendering Zhuge's anti-Wei strategy ineffective. It could not concentrate great forces to defeat the primary enemy. This lack of cooperation is further featured in chapter 46 of the historical novel entitled 'Zhuge Liang borrows Cao Cao's arrows with a ruse'. This is another example of Shu-Wu conflict even before the important Battle of Chibi as follows:

After being outsmarted by Zhuge Liang on a number of occasions, the jealous Zhou Yu, the Wu Commander-in-chief, is determined that Zhuge, the colluding party against Cao, must die.

He assigns the latter to undertake the production of one hundred thousand arrows to use against Cao Cao. Under martial law, Zhuge pledges to complete the job in three days. Zhou considers that to fix Zhuge's punishment, all he needs to do is to have his artisans to delay their delivery of whatever Zhuge needs.

In a deal, however, Zhuge gets Lu Su, Zhou's subordinate, to lend him twenty ships arrive lined up, carrying a thousand bundles of straw wrapped in black cloth on both sides of each ship. This puzzles both Zhou and Lu.

On the third night, fog spreads across the sky and the river mists are thick. At the fourth watch, Zhuge sends for Lu Su to go with him to fetch the arrows. By the fifth watch, Zhuge orders the vessels to sail into the deep fog nearing Cao's riverside. Cao's crews are alarmed and began to beat their drums. Cao Cao, thinking this sudden arrival of enemy forces must mean an ambush, orders the archers and crossbowmen to fire upon the unseen enemy toward the river at random. Their shots come down like rain.

When the sun appears dispersing the fog, Zhuge orders the vessels to sail backward, with the straw bundles are bristled with arrow shots. He also orders the crews to loudly thank Prime Minister Cao for which Cao Cao is at a loss for words, having been played the fool.

Lu Su puzzles over what has happened. Zhuge Liang considers that a military commander should be well versed in the changes in weather and explains that, three days earlier, he had predicted the occurrence of fog.

In sum, the Shu-Wu conflicts partly resulting from Zhuge's continuous acts of 'outsmarting' the jealous Zhou, weaken Zhuge's anti-Wei strategy and make the Shu-Wu collusion against the strong Wei state more difficult.

Zhuge Liang's rigid anti-Wei strategy

As noted above, in 215, the Wu scrambles for the strategic Jingzhou and kills Guan Yu, which led to the Shu-Wu battle at Yiling. Liu Bei's death following his defeat makes possible Zhuge Liang's consistent policy of making peace with Wu vis-à-vis Wei. Consequently, though there was no major conflict between the Shu and Wu states, Zhuge maintained a consistent anti-Wei strategy through collusion with the Wu until his death; the end of the Three Kingdoms period witnesses the state of Shu being wiped out by the Si-ma Wei. Although he agreed with Zhuge Liang's logic on the Chinese 'international' order of tripolarity, Mao implied that, from the beginning, in the tripolar situation, without flexibly including a possible Shu-Wei united front against the state of Wu as an option when necessary, Zhuge Liang's staunch anti-Wei strategy was overly rigid.

Mao's Solutions to Zhuge Liang's 'Limitations'

With his argument that the theme of the *Romance of the Three Kingdoms* 'is dialectic', Mao classified his own enemies as the primary and secondary ones and made their positions flexibly interchangeable. This was Mao's solution to Zhuge's rigid anti-Wei strategy. In addition, Mao's classification of these positions could resolve the Shu's geographical problem, with the Shu-Wei combined forces to attack Wu's new Jingzhou districts and subsequently cross the Yangtze River to aim at Wu's territories at the 'Eastern Yangtze' (江东). Further, needless to say, this new conceptionalization nullified the problem of imperfect Shu-Wu collusion.

Understandably, therefore, in reality, in the early 1970s, with this model, a golden opportunity arose and Mao was able to scheme at improving the Sino-US relations at the expense of the Soviet Union in a tripolar situation. The United States, which was Mao's primary enemy during the period 1945–70, became his nonantagonistic secondary enemy starting from 1972. The Soviet Union, his secondary enemy during the period 1945–53 and 'No. 1 accomplice of the US' during the period 1954–69, became his primary enemy starting from 1972. I will deal with Mao's new strategy of a global order of tripolarity in chapters three, four, five and six.

Conclusion

The theoretical foundation of Mao's global order of tripolarity can be traced to the following:

(1) Cao Cao's *qi*,
(2) Zhuge Liang's concept of the Chinese 'international' order of the tripolar powers of Shu, Wei and Wu,
(3) The theme of the *Romance of the Three Kingdoms* – 'the world under the heavens long divided, must unite, and vice versa' – which Mao claimed was 'dialectic' and interpreted it as: 'The world phenomenon under the heavens is that empires, long united, must divide; and vice versa'. He applied this statement to the Sino-Soviet relations in his reference 'their animosity would occur sooner or later'. He also noted that the Sino-US relations must be established after a long period of hostility.

(4) The victory of the celebrated battle at Chibi was won by outnumbered and inferior over superior forces in a tripolar situation. Mao believed that victory would be the result of the firm cooperation of the Shu-Wu allied forces such that astronomical power was generated. The outcome of the battle at Chibi, described in the historical novel as well as the classical historical texts to which I referred, was decisive in the development of the tripolar events in the era of the Three Kingdoms.

As discussed above, Zhuge's basic policy for the Shu state, which could not on its own concentrate great forces to defeat the powerful Wei, was geographically faulty. Although Mao agreed with Zhuge's logic of a Chinese 'international' order of tripolarity in relation to colluding with the state of Wu to acquire astronomical power to aim at defeating the powerful Wei from a weak position, he considered that, in the long run, lack of cooperation between the twin allies rendered Zhuge's anti-Wei strategy ineffective. Furthermore, he considered that Zhuge's staunch anti-Wei policy was rigid. Zhuge's policy did not include the vital exchange of the positions of the primary and secondary enemies. The Shu leader Liu Bei would not have been defeated in the battle at Yiling, had Zhuge advised him to try to collude with the Wei state against Wu – by reversing the positions of Wei and Wu. Mao's exchange of the positions of the primary and secondary enemies resolves Shu's geographical problem, with the end result of Shu-Wei combined forces against the Wu. It also nullifies the problem of an imperfect Shu-Wu collusion. Thus, in reality, Mao classified his enemies as primary and secondary ones in the contemporary world of his time and made their positions flexibly interchangeable as he saw fit. Understandably, therefore, in the early 1970s, he successfully improved the Sino-US relations at the expense of the Soviet Union in a tripolar situation. This reversed the position of the US primary enemy into that of the non-antagonistic secondary enemy, thus making the 'No. 1 accomplice of the US', i.e., the Soviet Union, the antagonistic primary enemy. In the next chapter, I will consider how, inspired by Zhuge Liang's scheme of colluding with Wu to fight Cao Cao's powerful Wei state, Mao sought to realize his anti-imperialist aim in China's attempt to collude with Stalin's Soviet Union. In chapters five and six, our focus will be on how, inspired by Zhuge's Chinese 'international' order of tripolarity and stimulated by the theme of the historical novel, he aimed to befriend the United States at the expense of the 'hegemonic' Soviet Union.

CHAPTER THREE

Mao's Tripolar Methodology: From Theory to Praxis

As noted above, Mao told Edgar Snow that he 'believed he was much influenced by the historical novel read at an impressionable age'. This influence, as discussed above, was related to a theme consisting of two major components as follows:

(1) 'Partition of the world under the heavens into three', a concept originally created by Zhuge Liang, the Shu state's architect of war, to collude with the Wu state to fight the powerful Wei state from a weak position, and
(2) 'Empires, long divided, must unite and vice versa' as Mao reinterpreted the novel's original theme.

Mao referred to both parts of the theme on a number of occasions. In January 1957, as noted above, he argued that 'a flare up of the Sino-Soviet animosity will occur sooner or later' and implied that the Sino-US relations, long divided, should be established. Thus, as noted in chapter one, on two separate occasions, inspired by the theme of the novel, he dropped hints to American correspondents Anna Louise Strong in February 1959 and Edgar Snow in October 1964 about his wish to 'swim in the Mississippi River'. Mao's hints were meant to improve the Sino-US relationship at the expense of the Soviet Union. In the early 1970s, inspired by the same theme, Mao was convinced that both the United States and China must make up with each other after a long period of hostility. A golden opportunity arose, and he personally initiated the ping-pong diplomacy in 1971 leading to an improved Sino-US relationship.

As noted in the preceding chapter, the death of the Shu state leader Liu Bei following his defeat in the battle at Yiling allows Zhuge Liang's consistent policy of making peace with Wu vis-à-vis Wei to continue. Consequently, right up to his death, though there remains no major conflict between the Shu and Wu states, Zhuge's consistent anti-Wei strategy of colluding with the Wu state at the end of the Three Kingdoms period witnesses the state of Shu being wiped out by the Si-ma Wei. As argued above, Mao did not fully agree with Zhuge's rigid 'international' order of tripolarity. He implied that, without flexibly including the alternative of a Shu-Wei united front against the state of Wu as an option when necessary in the tripolar situation of the period, Zhuge Liang's staunch anti-Wei strategy was too rigid.

Considering the novel's theme to be 'dialectic', Mao corrected what he viewed as its fundamental principle's limitation through making the positions of the primary enemy and secondary enemy in a tripolar situation flexibly interchangeable.

Mao's tripolar worldview of the contemporary world following the Second World War had been gradually transformed in response to the politics and actions of the superpowers as he saw them. This had resulted in the transformation of 'friend' into 'enemy', of 'secondary enemy' into 'primary enemy', and vice versa. Therefore, he initiated his scheme of collusion with China's 'secondary enemy' against its 'primary enemy'. Thus, Mao's concept of the 'three worlds' was basically formulated to be able to contend with the 'primary enemy' of the first world. His struggle with the primary enemy, a superpower, or the superpowers combined, was carried out in the following ways:

(1) through colluding with (the imperialist) secondary enemy or enemies against the primary enemy,
(2) through inciting the third world nations and the second world nations to unite against the superpower enemy or enemies,
(3) through fanning revolutionary movements in the third world.

In short, Mao's scheme was to 'concentrate astronomical power' by colluding with the secondary enemy to effectively defeat the primary enemy. Mao sought to realize his anti-imperialist and anti-'hegemonic' aims in the respective periods 1950–69 and 1969–76.

In January 1954, he perceived the gradual 'US-USSR collusion to the disadvantage of the PRC'. Further, the Sino-Soviet alliance broke down in open hostility, which was likened to the Shu-Wu split, in 1959. Thus, Mao's domestic policy of a national united front was devised; his mass line strategy, which was to serve his collectivization drive, was aimed at 'uniting with all possible' to deal with the 'US-USSR collusion'. Furthermore, Mao's drive, based on the Yenan model as a prototype, was meant to ultimately realize his defense-oriented communization goal for a united population to fight the imperialist and 'hegemonic' superpowers during the respective periods 1950–64 and 1965–76 'one by one'. I argue that the dismissal of the Soviet-backed 'rightist opportunist' Peng Dehuai in 1959 and the purge of the 'capitalist-cum-revisionist' Liu Shaoqi in the period 1965–9 demonstrated the respective acrimonious Sino-Soviet and Sino-US relations.

With the conception of the flexibly interchangeable positions of the primary and secondary enemy, Mao skillfully made possible the Sino-US united front at the expense of the Soviet Union during the period starting in the early 1970s. The United States, which was Mao's primary enemy during the period 1950–69, became his non-antagonistic secondary enemy starting in 1972. The Soviet Union, his secondary enemy during the period 1950–3 and 'No. 1 accomplice of the US' during the period 1954–69, became his primary enemy starting in 1972. The following is a list of periods of Mao's global order of tripolarity:

1950–1954: The United States is the primary enemy, while the Soviet Union is the secondary enemy

1954–1958: The United States is the primary enemy, and this is the period of 'the US-USSR collusion against the PRC'

1958–1969: The United States is the primary enemy, and the Soviet Union shifts from 'No. 1 Accomplice of the US' to become the primary enemy

1969–1972: The Soviet Union is the primary enemy, while the US becomes the secondary enemy

1972–1976: As above

In the following, I will first focus on the bipolar world order that immediately followed the Second World War.

CHAPTER FOUR

From Post-War Bipolarity to Mao's Global Order of Tripolarity

In Chapter Two, I argued that the theoretical foundation of Mao's global order of tripolarity can be traced to the *qi* of Cao Cao, Zhuge Liang's concept of a Chinese 'international' order of the tripolar powers of Shu, Wei and Wu, the theme of the historical novel as well as the battle at Chibi, in which victory was won by small forces over large and by inferior over superior forces in a tripolar situation. Stimulated by Cao Cao's *qi*, Mao looked at the whole world from its totality or from a 'bird's-eye' view. This meant that he perceived the whole of the world as fundamental to his policy formulation of China's relations with the superpowers. Immediately after the establishment of the People's Republic, he began to make China one of the tripolar powers, though it was far from being a superpower at the time.

As noted above, in Mao's favorite pastime singing of the 'Three Visits to the Thatched Hut' regarding Royal Uncle Liu Bei's request for Zhuge Liang's assistance to regain the former glories of the Han dynasty, Zhuge's concept of the tripolar world of the then China was emphasized. I also dealt with the major battle of Chibi and others such as those at Guandu and Yiling described in the novel *Romance of the Three Kingdoms*, and the classical historical texts *Records of the Three Kingdoms* and *Zizhi Tongjian*.

In this chapter, I will consider that, in 1950, inspired by the strategy of the battle at Chibi in terms of the weak Shu-Wu forces combined to fight the powerful Wei in a tripolar situation, Mao strove to collude with the Soviet Union, China's secondary enemy, to fight the powerful United States, its primary enemy, from a weak position in attempt to 'partition' the contemporary world with the superpowers 'into three'.

From the Post-War Bipolarity of 1945–1950 to Mao's Global Order of Tripolarity

The end of the Second World War witnessed two new ideologically opposing camps in the realm of international relations, i.e., the East and the West, with the former headed by the socialist USSR and the latter by the imperialist US. In attempt to 'partition' the contemporary world 'into three' with the superpowers (三分天下), Mao was inspired by the central theme of the historical novel, his conviction of the need to collude with Soviet Union under Stalin to fight the powerful United States from a weak position was strengthened by it. As Mao saw it, this was the start of an era of bipolar world order, in the light of the global preoccupation with animosity between the two camps.

In its anti-communist stance, the United States, as Mao saw it in August 1946, was making worldwide large-scale military arrangements and setting up its military bases worldwide to contain the Soviet Union. Mao (1967f:99) also argued that 'attacking the USSR would be out of the question until the US had subjugated the rest of the world'. He (1969d:1089–90) stressed that after the Second World War, 'it was not the Soviet Union that was the first to suffer US aggression, but those countries where these military bases were located'. Although Mao had yet to carry out his 'new democratic revolution' against the Kuomintang (KMT), his worldview gradually took shape in this light (1969d:1089–90). In his worldview, the First and Secondary Intermediary Zones had not yet materialized during the period 1945–9, and the Chinese Communists were still in the wilderness. His post-war worldview was that the US anti-communist stance was a 'smoke-screen' for its attempt to 'subjugate the intermediary world' (1969:239, 256). In actuality, he believed, US policy had several targets, the three main targets being Europe, Asia, and the Americas. China, according to Mao (1969d:1380–1), was the center of gravity in Asia. Therefore, by seizing China, the United States would possess all of Asia.

According to American correspondent Anna Louise Strong, the US White Paper released by the State Department in August 1949 disclosed that US aid to help Chiang Kai-shek start the civil war against the PRC was equivalent to 'more than 50 per cent of the monetary expenditures' of the Chiang Kai-shek government and was of 'proportionately greater magnitude in relation to the budget of that government than the United States had provided to any nation of the Western Europe since the end of the war' (1967f:101). Just a month before the establishment of the PRC, Mao (1969d:448–9) wrote that 'the US aid to China during and since the close of the Second World War, totaling over 5,914 million US dollars, given to help Chiang Kaishek slaughter several million Chinese ... had one purpose, namely, that it consistently maintained those fundamental principles of the US foreign policy toward China, which included the doctrine of the Open Door and opposition to any foreign domination of China'. According to Strong, one of the main purposes of the US government aid was to gain control of China's wealth, which they hoped to exploit and grow rich on for another 50 years.[1]

John Garver argues: 'the leaders of the People's Republic of China had the option in late 1949 and early 1950 of developing a working relationship with the United States and Mao's choice not to pursue that option lost Taiwan for the PRC' (2003:128–9). However, back in January 1945, according to Harrison Salisbury (1992:85), Mao 'had sent a personal message to President Franklin Roosevelt saying that he and Zhou Enlai were ready to come to Washington and negotiate an arrangement' for Sino-US cooperation. Salisbury's research (1992:85) shows that Mao had 'never gotten a reply'. Therefore, Garver's claim (2003:129) that the US policy in late 1949 and early 1950 aimed 'to wash its hands of the Kuomintang to condone an anticipated PLA takeover of Taiwan' is far from convincing. Moreover, Mao concluded in his report to the Central Committee of the CCP in late December 1947, 'The Present Situation and Our Tasks' that the United States had inevitably become the PRC's primary enemy: 'Irreconcilable domestic and international contradictions menace US imperialism everyday. This situation drove the US imperialists to draw up a plan for enslaving the world' (1967f:172). Further, in his articles 'Cast Away Illusions, Prepare For Struggle', 'Farewell, Leighton Stuart', 'Why It Is Necessary to Discuss the White Paper', 'Friendship Or Aggressors' and 'The Bankruptcy of Idealist Conception of History', all written in August 1949, around the time when 'the US washed its hands of the KMT' as Garver claims, as well as in the US State Department's White Paper and Dean Acheson's Letter of Transmittal, Mao (1967f:425–9) concluded that 'the imperialist nature (of supporting Chiang Kai-shek and anti-communism) of the US policy towards China had been sealed'. According to Mao (1967f:425–9), 'The White Paper is a counter-revolutionary document, which openly demonstrates US imperialist aggression and intervention in China'. 'It is a war', he (1967f:426) continued, 'in which the United States supplies the money and guns and Chiang Kai-shek supplies the men to fight for the United States and slaughter the Chinese people. ... The war to turn China into a US colony ...'.

In the fall of 1969, Burns (1969g:797) wrote that China played 'such a part in current superpower relationships that we are obliged to see them as now tripartite'. However, as I argued above, the PRC had been playing the role of a superpower in global power politics, immediately after the success of its new democratic revolution, even though it was not yet a superpower.

As noted above, Mao told Edgar Snow in 1936 that he 'believed he was much influenced by the novel *Romance of the Three Kingdoms* read at an impressionable age'. Stimulated by Zhuge Liang's 'international' concept of tripolarity, which spurred Liu Bei's third of the tripolar powers, Mao strove to *artificially* transform the world order of bipolarity into one of tripolarity by colluding with Stalin's Soviet Union. While it took Zhuge quite an effort to convince the Wu leadership to collude with the Shu to fight the powerful Wei from a weak position (Chapter 43), Mao considered it equally strategic for the Sino-Soviet collusion to fight US imperialism in the name of the 'consolidated communist brotherhood' as Zhuge's proposed Shu-Wu collusion against the Wei, a 'usurper of the legitimate ruling Han dynasty' as he put it. This was because the end of the Second World War witnessed a crucial transformation to ideologically opposed camps in the realm of international relations. Thus, immediately after the PRC was established, he visited Moscow to strive *at all costs* to get Stalin to ratify the proposed Sino-Soviet Treaty and Agreements. However, according to Mao (1969:432), during the period January–February 1950, 'Stalin and I were at loggerheads over the ratification of the treaty and agreements. He refused to sign it'. This was because Mao also sought to replace the pact of alliance and friendship, which Stalin had signed with Chiang Kai-shek. It had been agreed upon in a protocol of the February 1945 Yalta Meeting between Stalin, Churchill and Roosevelt concerning Russian privileges on Chinese territory such as the ice-free naval bases in Lushun and Dalian. In the end, he even tacitly accepted the independence of Outer Mongolia as a condition for the Sino-Soviet Treaty and Agreements which were signed in mid-February 1950.[2] Mao argued that 'based on Sino-Soviet friendship and bound by law', the treaty and agreements were ratified to aim at 'opposing the possible imperialist invasion'.[3] His worldview was now shaped by the new world situation, which motivated his attempt to form a united front with the Soviet Union against the United States primary enemy.

Mao's plan to establish a new global order hastened Stalin's plot to encourage his protégé, Kim Il-sung of North Korea to start the Korean War. This was, according to Harrison Salisbury, to embroil China in a war with the United States to destroy the new PRC (1969:107–15). Snow (1966:654) contends that the 'well-planned, well-supplied offensive (by North Korea) could have been undertaken' with prior consultation with and approval by Stalin. All of this was obvious. The Russians firmly believed that China's victory in its civil war was a real menace to them. With Mao's striving to secure the Sino-Soviet military treaty in mid-February 1950, Stalin sensed his central ambition to make China a power of the same standing as the superpowers. Salisbury's well-documented account shows that in the second half of February 1950, having secretly instigated his protégé, Kim Il-sung, to attack South Korea, Stalin promised Mao that the Soviet Union would send its air force to aid the Chinese troops in the war. Kim returned to North Korea in early March 1950 and the fighting erupted along Korea's thirty-eighth parallel on 25 June that year. However, Stalin 'triple-crossed the Chinese', as Salisbury put it (1969:112–13), by breaking his promise while the Chinese forces were already pouring toward the Yalu border. Salisbury's research (1969:113–14) shows that with this very scheme, 'Stalin lured the Chinese down a path of no return'. The celebrated Wang Gungwu pointed out that it was still not clear why the Soviets walked out of the United Nations Security Council over the issue (on 27 June 1950[4]). However, I would argue that under the pretext of protesting against United Nations' continued seating of Nationalist China thus depriving the PRC's representation in it, the Russians purposely boycotted its SC giving up their right of veto so as to let its resolution of providing troops for the 'police action' in Korea being passed. While the Chinese fought the sixteen member states of the US-led United Nations in the Korean War, the Soviets were sitting on the fence. Stalin's plot certainly gained the upper hand for the Soviet Union in the new tripartite US-USSR-PRC power structure. However, even without Stalin's 'promise', Mao would still defend North Korea, acknowledging the need to 'stop' the eventual war spillover into Manchuria.[5] He described this as 'damage to the lip would make the teeth vulnerable to the cold' (唇亡齿寒). Thus, he believed that he had no choice but to go to war, contrary to Lin Biao's argument on the American superior and nuclear weaponry and difficulty in winning the guerrilla war in foreign land.[6] According to Mao, 'if the whole of Korea was taken away by the Americans, the whole Far East would be exposed to considerable danger' (1999:97). Undoubtedly Mao realized that Stalin's deadly plot was hardly surprising. This was the price the maverick Mao had to pay for his initiative of establishing his new world order prematurely.

The Sino-Soviet Relations in Mao's Worldview of 1945–1950

Reacting to the start of an era of US anti-communism after the Second World War, Mao needed to consolidate its alliance with the Soviet Union 'at all costs' (and the third world nations) to form a united front against the United States. Mao believed that in enhancing China's efforts to counter US imperialism, it was necessary to gang up with the Soviet Union at this crucial stage. Thus, in 1946, he *artificially* made the USSR the 'angel' in his worldview or the 'defender of world peace' as he put it. However, by scheming and manipulation, the Soviet Union under Stalin had virtually annexed Outer Mongolia from China only a year earlier, and the US-USSR predominance at the Yalta Conference permitted Russian entry into Xinjiang province. All this had occurred against the Chinese will. Furthermore, Mao

(1969:164) revealed in 1969 that Stalin had tried to make Xinjiang and Manchuria provinces Moscow's 'colonies'. In addition, he would have to complete his socialist revolution before he could defend his country from any imperialist intrusion. At this stage US imperialism was too strong all around the globe in its confrontation with the socialist camp.

In my latest work *The International Environment and China's Twin Models of Development*, I trace Mao's interest in Outer Mongolia back to the time of the Edgar Snow interview in 1936[7] and other occasions as well.

In July 1936, Mao told Snow that following the victory of the Chinese revolution, Outer Mongolia was to 'automatically become a part of a socialist federation of China'.[8] The Soviet Union recognized Chinese suzerainty over Outer Mongolia as a result of the Mutual Defense Pact signed in 1936.[9] Snow (1966:396) writes that during the Bolshevik revolution the Russians helped create the Mongolian People's Republic (MPR) after overthrowing the Lama priesthood. According to Snow, though the Soviet government continued to 'recognize the PRC's nominal sovereignty over *all* (emphasis existing) Mongolia, the Soviets made an armed alliance with Outer Mongolia and stationed troops there' (1966:396). In 1945, Snow writes (1961:49–50), by signing the Sino-Soviet military alliance against Japan with the KMT government, Stalin obtained Chiang Kai-shek's full recognition of Outer Mongolian independence. That alliance, according to Snow, died a natural death once Mao achieved victory, but Outer Mongolia retained its independence and was still a military ally of Moscow (1961:50). In February 1949, Mao asked the Soviet leaders for their opinion about the amalgamation of the MPR with China.[10] Stalin replied that he did not believe the MPR would give up its independence in exchange for autonomy as part of China even if all Mongolian areas including Inner Mongolia were to be united.[11] As mentioned above, under the terms of the Chinese alliance with the Soviet Union in 1950, Mao had tacitly accepted the independence of Outer Mongolia though 'unwillingly' with the crucial consideration of 'socialist unity'. In 1954, during Khrushchev's visit to Beijing, the Chinese had offered a new amalgamation 'deal', but the Soviet delegation refused to discuss it.[12] In 1956, the Chinese declared that Outer Mongolia should be returned to China, and in the publication of Beijing's World Atlas, the MPR was made part of China.[13]

Salisbury (1992:13) traced the origins of the dispute between Mao and Stalin back to 1927 when the latter supported Chiang Kai-shek even after 'he turned on the Communists in the massacre that year at Shanghai'. According to Mao, China's revolution was 'successfully carried out against Stalin's objection' (1969:164). From the beginning of 1937 to August 1938, through Wang Ming, Stalin tried to stop Mao's attempt to carry out the revolution.[14] During the anti-Japanese Communist-KMT united front period of the 1930s, Salisbury (1992:14) argues, Stalin sent Chiang planes, arms and military advisers but only a planeload of propaganda leaflets to the Communists. Salisbury further writes that in 1946 'when Chiang began preparing an all-out drive against the Communists, Stalin urged Mao to enter into a coalition with Chiang and take a secondary role'. Thus, Mao realized that 'to get Stalin's financial assistance is just like trying to get a piece of meat from a tiger's mouth'.[15] Moreover, as is well known, Stalin tried hard to prevent Mao's victorious armies from completely destroying Chiang in the late 1940s. Thus, at the end of 1948, seeing Lin Biao's army sweeping down south from Manchuria, Stalin quickly sent an envoy to Xibaipo to dissuade Mao from crossing the Yangtze River.

Stalin's attempt to create two Chinas was obvious. The paranoid Stalin could have considered that a liberated China would be a grave threat to the Soviet Union.

It has been alleged that Stalin conspired with Gao Gang (高岗) to set up an 'independent kingdom' in Manchuria. This was plausible. In the days of the Comintern, Stalin appointed and sometimes even executed leaders of other parties. He also used the Cominform to expel Marshal Tito of Yugoslavia from the movement as a result of the conflict between them in 1948. Gao committed suicide in 1954 rather than face charges of treason, with the discovery of his secret alliance with Stalin. According to Mao, 'Stalin bribed Gao Gang with a car and Gao sent Stalin a birthday telegram on 15 August every year' (1969:163). Mao (1969:163) described the Gao-Rao (Shushi 饶漱石) anti-Party betrayal as a 'shocking earthquake of grade eight'. In his paper 'To Recall the Gao-Rao Event' published in 2005, Yang Shangkun confirms that 'Gao-Rao anti-Party betrayal was backed by Soviet great power chauvinism'.[16] In his memoirs, Khrushchev claims that 'Because of Stalin's betrayal of Gao Gang, we lost a true friend who supplied us with valuable information about the true attitude of the Chinese leadership toward the Soviet Union'.[17] It seemed that Mao (1969:163) bitterly tolerated the Russian animosity and betrayal for the sake of 'socialist unity' in the face of the threat of US imperialism.

A World of Tripolarity: The Korean War of 1950–1953 and the US Containment of China

We considered above that Stalin instigated President Kim Il-sung to start the Korean War in early 1950, with the intention of seeing the new PRC to be destroyed by the powerful United States. In mid-October 1950, direct Sino-US military confrontation began as the US-led United Nations forces crossed the thirty-eighth parallel in Korea. In its attempt to 'share' the contemporary world with the superpowers, this military confrontation confirmed China's role as a tripolar actor. Rolling back the Americans in a counter-offensive that took McArthur's headquarters by surprise, the PRC forces pushed the US-led UN troops to near-disaster.[18] The American Tenth Army Corps, faced with isolation and destruction, particularly in the vicinity of the Changjin Reservoir, withdrew in bitter fighting to Hungnam on the east coast and was evacuated by sea to Pushan in the south.[19] This indeed gave the new PRC a sense of strength, generating more confidence for its subsequent contention with the 'invincible' US superpower. Forcing the US-led UN to negotiate a truce starting in June 1951, Mao (1977c:117) said, 'the Chinese people are now organized, they are not to be trifled with'. Bitter fighting continued for two more years as each side sought to improve its tactical position. The armistice was signed in July 1953. US Commander Clark admitted that 'I was the first commander in American history to sign a ceasefire agreement'.[20] In his paper entitled 'Imperialism and All Reactionaries Are Paper Tigers', Mao wrote that 'The apparent 'power' and 'strength' of imperialism was, historically speaking, merely a transient phenomenon factor playing only a temporary role'. According to

Strong, the moment when the United States brought the United Unions into the Korean War marked the high point in America's world prestige. From that act, it began to decline'.[21] Stalin's plot to embroil the new PRC in the Korean War was backfired leading to the materialization of Mao's Zhuge-inspired global order of tripolarity.

At the beginning of the Korean War, the US dispatched the Seventh Fleet to 'neutralize the Formosa (Taiwan) Straits', and President Truman announced increased aid to the French in Indochina. At the same time the United States strengthened its military forces in the Philippines. With all this, the United States was determined to contain China. With the crystallization of the China policy of containment and the domino theory of the United States, there were, as Welfield (1974:6) put it, 'the unprecedented and sustained build-up of US nuclear, naval, and air power in Asia and the Pacific from the Aleutians, through Japan, Korea, Taiwan, and Southeast Asia to Australia; the formation of an extensive network of interlocking military alliances such as the Southeast Asia Treaty Organization; the efforts to isolate the PRC militarily, diplomatically, economically; persistent large-scale military intervention in North and Southeast Asia'. Therefore, the United States' China policy of containment was central to its worldwide containment of communism. Thus, according to Mao, in an attempt to neutralize Communist Chinese influence in Asia's intermediary zone, the United States sought economic, and therefore military, domination (1969:239). This was contrary to Akira Iriye's simplistic argument (1992:292) that 'the US must now resist any further alteration of the status quo by force after the Korean War'. Quoting MacArthur, he further wrote that 'The loss of Taiwan might well force our western frontiers back to the coasts of California, Oregon and Washington', and that 'similar considerations motivated a departure in policy toward Indochina'.

Long before the monumental US aid to South Vietnam was proposed, President Eisenhower's speech concerning US policy at a Governors' Conference on 4 August 1953, which had lent credence to Mao's argument was that 'if we lost Indochina, several things happen right away. (For example,) the tin and tungsten that we so greatly value from that area would cease coming'. 'So', he continued, 'when the US votes $400,000,000 to help the war, we are voting for the cheapest way that we can to prevent the occurrence of something that would be of a most terrible significance to the US, our security, our power and ability to get certain things we need from the riches of Indo-China territory, and from Southeast Asia'.[22] Therefore, Mao's position was a reaction against the US imperialist global, particularly Southeast Asian, scheme as he saw it. Understandably, he initiated 'collusion' with the Soviets 'at all costs', and in principle, with the 'oppressed peoples' of the world to form a united front with 'all who can be united' against US imperialism, China's primary enemy.[23]

A World of Tripolarity: The USSR in the Crucial 1954 – From Secondary Enemy to 'No. 1 Accomplice of the US'

In late 1949, the Republic of China under Chiang Kai-shek met final defeat on the mainland, despite more than a decade of US assistance. Of Chiang's vast Nationalist China, only Taiwan and offshore islands remained. Mainland China became Communist as the People's Republic of China. Incredulous Americans seeking an explanation for the disaster blamed the Truman administration, attacking Communist sympathizers in the US State Department for the loss of China, rather than the mismanagement and weakness of Chiang's forces.[24] Resentment against the Truman administration increased when the Communist government of North Korea launched an invasion of South Korea in June 1950.[25] The entry of Chinese troops into the conflict and the subsequent failure of McArthur to unify all of Korea resulted in an American retreat as discussed above.

The PRC's role as a tripolar world power was now confirmed.

It was in this background that, giving the Council of Foreign Relations 'an overall view' of the foreign policies of the new Eisenhower Administration, Secretary of State John Dulles announced in mid-January 1954, six months after the truce, the United States' 'great strategic change'. This important change, initiated in 1953 during the Korean War to further aim at isolating the PRC, resulted in President Eisenhower's so-called 'peaceful transformations', tacitly taking the PRC as a global tripolar power.[26] Referring to this new US policy, Mao cautioned his colleagues, pointing to the US aim of 'colluding with the Soviet Union against China'.[27] Less than a fortnight later, Pospelov, Secretary of the Soviet Communist Party's Central Committee, responded that 'Russia would do everything to ease international tension and solve all disputed problems by peaceful means'.[28] Quoting Lenin's theory of the Soviet struggle for easing international tensions, he emphasized that 'the Soviet Union could exist together peacefully with capitalist countries'.[29] On 27 January, Dulles made it clear to Soviet Foreign Minister Molotov that the latter should prevent 'the Chinese Communist aggressors' from joining the Berlin Conference, which was to be convened a few days later, 'for the purpose of dealing with the peace of the world'.[30] As Mao perceived it, this development not only was a watershed in the Sino-Soviet relations, but threw light on the gradual 'US-USSR collusion to the disadvantage of the Peoples' Republic of China'.[31]

The Chinese were outraged at Nikita Khrushchev's secret de-Stalinization movement at the Twentieth CPSU Congress in February 1956, which put further pressure on Mao. To him, the movement could dangerously exert a destabilizing influence on Mao Zedong Thought and his leadership. Thus, in his speech 'On the Correct Handling of Contradictions among the People' at the Enlarged Eleventh Session of the Supreme State Conference towards the end of February 1957, Mao stated that 'revisionism or right opportunism is a bourgeois trend of thought which is even more dangerous than dogmatism'. The PRC denounced Soviet 'revisionism' as cowardly acquiescence to Western, especially US domination. In his concluding remarks on the 'Provincial and Urban Committee Secretarial Meeting' in January 1957, Mao (1969:578) quoted the theme of the historical novel *Romance of the Three Kingdoms* as spelled out at the beginning of its first chapter as well as towards the end of its last chapter: 'The world phenomenon under the heavens is that long united, must divide; and vice versa. Thus it has ever been'. As discussed above, Mao (1969:83) interpreted this as follows: 'The world phenomenon under the heavens is that empires long united, must divide; and vice versa'. He thus considered that 'a flare-up of the Sino-Soviet animosity would occur sooner or later'.

In mid-1957, the Soviet Union launched the first intercontinental ballistic missile and space satellite. In an attempt to find out the real position of the Sino-Soviet 'friendship' in the face of the 'US-USSR collusion to the disadvantage of China', Mao stated in the Conference of Communist Parties on 18 November 1957: 'The international situation has now reached a new turning point' that 'the forces of socialism are overwhelmingly superior to those of imperialism'.[32] On this basis, Mao suggested to consolidate 'the Sino-Soviet alliance and the Socialist camp in the face of the US hostility'.[33] The Russians and their European comrades flatly refused to accept his assessment of the international situation. Mao's position was now quite clear.

In April 1955, the Bandung Conference was hosted to celebrate neutrality and an end to 'the old age of the white man' and to castigate the imperialist West. In the Conference, China attempted to marshal the animosity already nursed by the Third World against US imperialism into an Afro-Asian alliance under the slogan of anti-old or new colonialism.[34] At the 1957 Cairo Conference, the Chinese, in the name of the liberation movements of the 'Moscow Declaration', encouraged the Afro-Asian alliance to expand its united front on anti-colonialism and anti-imperialism.[35] After the Conference, the Chinese strongly fanned anti-imperialist revolutionary flames in many Afro-Asian nations in an attempt to wean aligned nations from the West, for instance, by supporting the Indonesian communist movement, the Iraqi rebel government, and the demand by the Laotian Communists for the formation of a coalition government.[36] Support for all these movements was geared to the Chinese policy of anti-US imperialism. At the end of the Bandung Conference, China was able to establish diplomatic relationships with thirty Afro-Asian nations.[37] Its diplomatic achievements in making these nations neutral prevented them from joining any anti-communist alliance. However, its anti-US activities were not effective in facing the superpower.

With the emergence of the Soviet 'revisionists', Mao's aim of colluding with the USSR superpower against the powerful US in the new tripolar world did not work out. Thus, he had no choice but to resort to the defense-oriented collectivization scheme by organizing and consolidating the whole Chinese population (1967d:186), because 'the richest source of power to wage war lies in the masses of the people'.

From Agricultural Producers' Cooperatives to Defense-Oriented Collectivization Scheme

In the preface of his new book *Mao's Great Famine: The History of China's Most Devastating Catastrophe 1958–1962*, Dikötter (2010: ix) begins: 'Between 1958 and 1962, China descended into hell. Mao Zedong threw his country into a frenzy with the Great Leap Forward, an attempt to catch up with and overtake Britain in less than fifteen years ... to catapult his country past its competitors'. Dikötter dismisses Mao's ideas and policies and regards the failure of the GLF as resulting from Mao's personal competitiveness with Khrushchev and his obsession with a Chinese model of socialist modernity. This is simplistic.

In mid-June 1953 Mao (1977c:93) estimated that the transition period of the Party from the founding of the PRC to the basic completion of socialist transformation would take 'ten to fifteen years, or a little longer'. However, in the opening speech at the National Conference of the CCP in March 1955, Mao cautioned his colleagues that apart from being surrounded by US imperialist forces, the country's position was worsened by the new appearance of the 'US-USSR collusion to the disadvantage of the PRC'; and he (1977c:156) urged that they 'must be prepared against all possible emergencies'. 'If the imperialists should unleash a war in the future', he continued, 'very likely they would launch a surprise attack, as in World War II'. Therefore, he (1977c:156) urged again, 'we must be prepared, mentally and materially, to avoid being caught unaware by such a sudden turn'. Understandably, thus, from the summer of 1955, Mao changed the above-mentioned time-table and accelerated the process of transformation. As a result, the second half of 1955 saw an upsurge of the cooperatization effort of the agricultural producers. At the end of that year, the number of cooperatives reached 1.9 million from 650 thousand previously. This meant that only about 63 percent of China's peasant households were in co-op farms. About 3.9 per cent of the nation's peasant households were in the more advanced socialist type of co-op farms – collective farms.[38] A year later, in his speech 'On the Ten Major Relationships' at an enlarged meeting of the Political Bureau of the Central Committee of the CCP, Mao (1977c:289) emphasized that 'being bullied and encircled by our enemies, we must strengthen our national defense; and we must first of all strengthen our work in economic construction'. By June 1957, 96.8 per cent of all farm households were in collective farms or co-op farms.[39] With Mao's international perception of the United States as China's primary enemy and the gradual 'US-USSR collusion to the disadvantage of the PRC', he considered that his defense-oriented strategy for China's political economy needed to be accelerated.

Devising the national united front strategy was vital, as great masses of peasants were available as defense against the aggressors. In the Beidaihe Enlarged Political Bureau Meeting on 'the Resolution of the Question of the People's Communes in the Peasantry', 17–30 August 1958, Mao introduced the principle of a defense-oriented commune system, which was characterized by the unified mobilization of the whole population. This was based on the People's Republic's various wartime experiences.[40] Characteristic of Mao's military-based communism was the concept of an 'equalized livelihood' for the population in which soldiers and the people were to be treated equally and the military officials and the soldiers were also to be treated the same. Using this system, the Communists were able to defeat Japanese imperialism and the KMT. On many occasions, Mao stressed the absolute prohibition of the 'leftist communist wind' of 'robbing the peasants' or illegally ordering them about. It was in this context that his mass line strategy was formulated to develop the collectivization scheme. His defense-oriented economic development strategy, based on the Yenan model, was to ultimately lead to his communization goal. In the following, the development of the agricultural producers' cooperatives (APC) will be discussed.

The Development of Agricultural Producers' Cooperatives

Mao's collectivization scheme, which had begun in 1953, was the basis for building a defense-oriented economy. Characteristic of the Chinese peasantry were small-scale individual economies. These would not only fail to unify and cement all the individual scattered units, but also breed capitalism. This, in turn, would lead to exploitation, thus rendering his mass line strategy difficult to improve the people's livelihood, repel US imperialism, and guard against the looming Soviet enemy. Thus, according to Mao, 'by-passing' capitalism was needed. In promoting 'by-passing' of capitalism in his collectivization scheme, Mao (1977c:214) argued that agricultural cooperatives were aimed at 'consolidating the CCP's alliance with the peasants on the basis of proletarian socialism and not of bourgeois democracy'. This was meant to 'isolate the bourgeoisie once and for all and facilitate the final elimination of capitalism' (1977c:214). To Mao, proletarian socialism could unite and consolidate the masses, but bourgeois democracy could not, 'like a pot of loose sand', as he put it. In 'wiping out capitalism', which breeds individualism, and uniting the masses against the United States, his primary enemy, cooperativization, the basic principle of collectivization, was his answer. This was especially the case in view of the then Chinese conditions where frequent national disasters rendered the land incapable of producing sufficient food for the vast population and where land management was primitive. Although land reform had improved their livelihood, Mao continued, the Chinese people remained beset with difficulties. The wealthy were in the minority, and the majority – more than 70 per cent of the whole population – was poor.[41] Thus, Mao's rationale was to cement all people together by 'cooperativizing'. In mid-December 1951, according to Mao, there were three hundred or more agricultural producers' cooperatives, and two years later, the number grew to more than 14,000, a 46-fold increase (1999:420). In June 1955, the number reached 650,000 (1999:420).

Mao's policy of 'uprooting the mountain of feudal landlordism', a continuous process inspired by the agrarian revolution in Hunan in 1927, ended in October 1952. However, the 1950–2 land reform was also aimed at promoting the rich peasant economy essential for post-war national economic construction. In Mao's land reform movement, tapping the people's power achieved by his strategy of 'uniting with all possible' temporarily included the rich peasants. It should be noted that Mao's land reform program during the periods 1946–9 and 1950–2 was the precondition for his gigantic task of 'wiping out capitalism'. However, this program, initiated to temporarily protect the rich peasants, indicated the essence of China's post-war national economic reconstruction. On the surface, socialist cooperativization seemed to be an economic solution. However, more importantly, in terms of national defense, this strategy was basic, because the whole population 'must be mobilized to be prepared against all possible emergencies'.

In sum, with the primary aim of restricting capitalist development and minimizing individual land ownership in the short term and eventually abolishing it, Mao's uprooting of feudal landlordism in terms of land reform – an integral part of transforming agriculture to pave the way to collectivization – was a precondition for his task of 'wiping out capitalism' and a basic strategy for 'uniting all who can unite' against US imperialism and the looming socialist enemy.

'By-Passing Capitalism' and the Collectivization Scheme

As a precondition for his task of 'wiping out imperialism' and a basic strategy for 'uniting all who can unite' against US imperialism and the looming socialist enemy, Mao's collectivization scheme was implemented. It was divided into three phases, namely, (a) the phasing out of the rich peasant economy, (b) the implementation of mutual aid teams (MATs) which are the foundation for his cooperatives, and (c) the commune system. The first two phases paved the way for Mao's defense-related commune system which will be discussed in the next chapter. In the following, Mao's policy of the rich peasant economy will be examined.[42]

Following the defeat of feudal landlordism, the phasing out of the rich peasant economy was seen as crucial for Mao's collectivization drive since he was primarily concerned with preventing capitalist development. Phasing out the rich peasant economy was essential to realizing Mao's egalitarian goal for national defense through his cooperativization scheme, which called for the support of the whole population and the formation of one class. Winning over the well-to-do middle and middle peasants to isolate the rich peasants and landlords and thereby abolish their economy was imperative as the former groups constituted 20–30 per cent of the whole populace, while the poor and lower middle peasants made up 70 per cent (1977:231). These well-to-do middle and middle peasants were supported by the rich peasants and landlords. How did Mao phase out the rich peasant economy?

As noted above, before the full cooperativization drive could be implemented following the success of the revolution, the rich peasant economy was indispensable for the rehabilitation of the economic production of the peasantry; and thus the existence of the rich peasants had to be tolerated temporarily. Thus, the 1950 Agrarian Reform Law was characterized by the policy of protecting the rich peasant economy – a policy which was even more lenient than the pre-1949 land policy toward the rich peasants. Mao's policy (1977c:29) witnessed the change from requisitioning their surplus land and property to one of maintaining the rich peasant economy. This policy was designed to boost rural production which was essential to the development of a viable national economy as well as to isolate the landlords. This was because 'as the war has basically ended on the mainland and the situation is entirely different from that in the period 1946–8 when the People's Liberation Army was locked in a life-and-death struggle with the KMT ... and the issue had not yet been decided' (1977c:29).

Basically, the objective of Mao's collectivization scheme was 'to organize public and private labour, mobilize the mass production enthusiasm and increase labor efficiency ...', because, he (1976:75) argued, 'if labour forces of *all* peasants are organized for collective labouring in terms of mutual aid (and cooperativization)', capitalism would crumble due to the astronomical cementing effect of the masses. As a result, the mass line strategy would eliminate capitalist exploitation. In ensuring the realization of people's power, Mao injected into the peasantry a catalyst – the spirit of 'serving the people selflessly'. Further, in ensuring the success of the collectivization scheme, Mao introduced a state of egalitarianism where (theoretically) everyone was equal politically and economically. Mao's egalitarianism was a means but not an end in his battle against capitalism by involving all and making them united. He (1977c:254) considered it 'imperative to attain unity between the middle and the poor peasants, consolidate the co-operatives, expand production and achieve socialist transformation in the entire country'. This was 'to establish the dominant position of the poor peasants and the new lower-middle peasants in the leading body of a cooperative, with the old lower-middle peasants and the new and old upper-middle peasants as the auxiliary force' (1977c:254). This was because they were the majority. Thus, in his attempt to 'wipe out' capitalism, Mao was to realize astronomical power by winning over the majority of the people in carrying out economic production. With this policy, *all* Chinese could then become well off *together* and united against the powerful enemy or enemies outside China. The realization of an egalitarian peasantry following the completion of land reform was therefore a precondition for ensuring the achievement of Mao Zedong's scheme of collectivization.

In the urban areas, immediately after the takeover, the Communists nationalized the KMT-owned heavy industries – iron and steel, cement, electric power, petroleum, railroads and highways, and air transport. They also took over foreign-owned firms (1976a:212). Protection of industry and the commercial enterprises of landlords and rich peasants [Article 4 of the 1950 Agrarian Reform Law except where they were run by 'bureaucrat-capitalists and counterrevolutionary local tyrants'] were spelled out in the land reform program in the early 1950s. The provision governing this was spelled out in Article 12 of the 1947 Outline Land Law. According to the 1950 ARL, land reform was to pave the way for China's industrialization. The industrial and commercial enterprises of the landlords and rich peasants were complementary to the peasant economy for the early rehabilitation of China's economic production. Thus, on many occasions, Mao

(1967f:203) stressed the necessity for private industry and commerce run by landlords and rich peasants.

However, although Chinese private capitalists and businessmen were permitted to operate their own business, they were restricted in order to prevent capitalist development. Restricting the private capitalist economy was to improve 'the livelihood of the workers and other working people on the basis of increased production' (1977c:105).

The Five Antis Movement in 1952 was directed explicitly at law-breaking of capitalists, but its larger target was the national bourgeoisie as a class. This movement showed that the road that revolutionary China pursued was to socialism, not capitalism.[43] It was considered as 'the first preparatory step toward the socialist transformation of Chinese capitalists' (1966m:104). The result of the movement strengthened the state-controlled economy.[44] By the end of 1952, only a third of wholesale trade, a little more than half of retail trade, and barely a third of factory production remained in the hands of private enterprises (1966m:101–7). In 1955–6 'three million capitalist industrial and commercial enterprises were converted into joint state-private enterprises'.[45] This meant that the state invested in the enterprises and assigned personnel to share in the management together with the capitalists.[46] By 1956, most industries in China had been socialized. New cooperatives were formed by the amalgamation of wholesale, retail trade and handicrafts.[47] By September 1956, Zhou Enlai claimed that 99 per cent of formerly privately owned enterprises had entered into partnership with the state.[48] Socialist transformation of capitalist industry and commerce was basically completed by 1957. China now had only two types of ownership of the means of production, namely, socialist ownership by the whole people and socialist collective ownership.

Socialized Agriculture and the Realization of People's Power

Mao adopted the mutual-aid teams from the traditional Chinese peasantry as the basis of his cooperativization plan. This was to tap all available labor forces so as to realize the people's power. The collectivization campaign was completed in 1957, with one hundred million peasant households organized into 750,000 higher-level APCs. How did this come about?

Through cooperative arrangements among peasants in the form of small production teams, the MAT was adopted to achieve maximum production efficiency. It had been a simple informal work exchange system practiced by Chinese peasants throughout the centuries. The principle of this cooperative teamwork involved was that peasants helped each other for mutual benefit. During peak seasons, a peasant family was handicapped by a shortage of workers, and if laborers were hired they would be idle in the off-peak seasons. Mao argued that 'teams for the exchange and hire of labor were usually formed by peasants with insufficient land and that labor-exchange was a means by which the peasants adjusted labor power among themselves. Besides exchanging work among themselves for mutual aid, their members also hired themselves out collectively to families which were short of labor power' (1967e:160–1). Hiring was normally carried out by offering their own labor in return when the latter needed hands during peak seasons. Wong's research (1973:218) shows that ox-cooperatives were also 'promoted in order to overcome the scarcity of draft animals'.

Thus, the people's power conceived by Mao for 'wiping out' capitalism was to be realized by making everyone better off through cooperation for mutual benefit. In addition, supply cooperatives, credit cooperatives, and consumers' cooperatives were established to increasingly restrict the private economic opportunities of rich peasants and channel economic resources to the cooperative sector. To strengthen the ties between the urban and rural economies to guarantee the flow of commodities and capital between them, the 'relation contract' was initiated.[49] Furthermore, the local clans undertook construction and maintenance of communal projects such as waterworks through cooperative peasant teamwork efforts. As early as

1934, Mao (1969a:110–11) had already decided that, to abolish capitalism, cooperativization was the answer. This was because 'coordinated with the state enterprises', cooperative activities 'will become a tremendous force in our economy and will gradually prevail and assume leadership over the private sector' (1967c:144).

Socialized agriculture was active even in the CCP-held border areas in north China during the anti-Japanese war period; and MATs were used to tap available labor and other scarce resources in stepping up production for the increased war effort. With a tradition of rural cooperatives, these areas achieved impressive records of economic production. Mutual aid was developed after 1949 in both old and newly liberated areas. Mao organized MATs in 1950 and completed cooperativization within a short span of eight years. To ensure the success of Mao's cooperativization scheme, the various rectification campaigns and movements were also carried out to develop the 'proletarian consciousness'. The 'proletarian consciousness' was meant to 'unite all who can be united' against US imperialism and the looming Soviet 'revisionism'. Since 'wiping out capitalism from the face of the earth' entailed 'uniting all that can be united', Mao's project of changing human nature from selfishness to selflessness became more crucial. Mao thought that selfless people could be more easily united than selfish ones.

The Mass Line Strategy and Thought Reform

The principal objective of his rectification campaigns and movements to develop 'proletarian consciousness' and to correct deviant thoughts was to strengthen close ties with the masses. It is important to note that rectification of cadre work *style* was a major aspect in this scheme. Failings in cadre work style can be traced to 'vestiges of evil ideology of the oppressing class, namely, remnants of petty bourgeois individualism' (Mao, 1954c:56). Mao (1967e:48) referred to cadre shortcomings such as 'bureaucratism', 'subjectivism', 'sectarianism', and formalism in propaganda work. Other shortcomings were patriarchal despotism, authoritarianism, the sentiment of mountain stronghold and so forth. Mao (1960c:215) argued that the origin of all these failings in cadre work style could be traced to the attitude of arrogance and self-centeredness. All these would lead to divorce from the masses. It was in this context that Mao's rectification campaigns originated in the Yenan period were aimed to ensure the success of his mass line strategy.

Mao's approach for attitude change was primarily aimed at ridding cadres, Party and non-Party members of bourgeois attitudes and specific 'deviations', which were considered as obstacles to the realization of his Herculean scheme of 'uniting with all who can be united', from Party officials down to agricultural and industrial workers. The scheme carried out to generate people power for his anti-imperialist and anti-revisionist fight comprised the 1950 Rectification Campaign, Party Rectification and Party Building of 1951, the Anti-Bureaucratism-Commandism Movement of 1953 and the 1957 Anti-Rightist Struggle and Rectification Campaign.

In sum, by virtue of organizing and consolidating the whole Chinese population through his collectivization scheme, Mao devised his national united front policy against the new 'US-Soviet collusion at the disadvantage of the PRC'.

Conclusion

Treating the United States as the primary enemy and the USSR as the secondary enemy in Mao's tripolar worldview following the establishment of the PRC, Mao's foreign policy, strengthened by Zhuge Liang's 'international' order of tripolarity, was to collude with the latter against the stronger former from a weak position. However, in January 1954 he perceived the gradual 'US-USSR collusion to the disadvantage of the PRC'. The theme of the *Romance of the Three Kingdoms*, i.e., 'empires under heavens, long united, must divide, and vice versa', was confirmed with Mao's prediction in January 1957 that 'a flare-up of Sino-Soviet hostility would occur sooner or later'. Thus, his domestic policy of a national united front for China's defense against US imperialism and guard against the new 'US-USSR collusion' was devised. Mao's mass line strategy was to serve his collectivization drive aimed at 'uniting with all possible'. The drive was meant to ultimately lead to his defense-oriented communization goal, which will be discussed in the next chapter. All in all, Mao designed his political-cum-economic strategy to create a united population to fight US imperialism and 'US-USSR collusion'.

CHAPTER FIVE

1954–1964 Period of Tripolarity: The Sino-Soviet Break Up and Dismissal of the Soviet-backed Peng Dehuai

The previous chapter surveyed the bipolar order of 1945–50 to Mao's global order of tripolarity starting in 1950, with the United States as his primary enemy and the Soviet Union as his secondary enemy. I also dealt with Mao's collectivization drive, which preceded his defense-oriented communization initiative, in order to 'wipe out capitalism'. While the United States had always been China's primary enemy, the twin superpowers, starting in 1954, were found to be 'actively colluding to the disadvantage of China'. However, it is important to note that Mao had also perceived the Soviet-US hostility even before this same year. With the realization of his cooperativization efforts in about eight years, Mao launched his Great Leap Forward (GLF) and commune movements in the years of 1957 and 1958 respectively. With the anti-Japanese Yenan experience as model, his communization project was accelerated in response to US and Soviet pressures in this period. In Mao's tripolar consideration, this was disastrous in terms of Zhuge Liang's perspective. In this chapter and the next, we will consider that he aimed to 'concentrate astronomical power' to deal with the enemies 'one by one' respectively and that while the Soviet Union was transformed into Mao's primary enemy in his global order of tripolarity, the United States gradually became the secondary enemy. In this chapter, we will consider how the Sino-Soviet relations turned sour and how Khrushchev abrogated the Sino-Soviet agreements and withdrew Soviet aid and economic advisers and technicians in 1959 leading to intense Sino-Soviet dispute and then hardened into bitter hostility. I will also argue that the 1959 dismissal of the Soviet-backed 'right opportunist' Peng Dehuai was part of the Sino-Soviet acrimonious dispute. In the following, I will first deal with the international environment in terms of the Soviet-US hostility.

Starting in 1947–8, the Cold War already solidified when US aid provided under the Marshall Plan to Western Europe had brought those countries under American influence and the Soviets had installed openly communist regimes in Eastern Europe. In 1949, the United States and its European allies formed the North Atlantic Treaty Organization (NATO), a unified military command to resist the Soviet presence in Europe. A unified military among the Soviet-bloc countries, the Warsaw Pact, was formed in 1955, and West Germany was admitted into NATO that year. In November 1958, Khrushchev provoked a new crisis in Berlin demanding that the Allies withdraw from West Berlin within six months.

Immediately following his inauguration as president of the United States, John F. Kennedy increased the US defense budget by 30 per cent and approved the development of a strategic triad of weapons – the land-based Minuteman ICBMs, submarine-launched Porlaris missiles, and B-52 bombers.

In July 1960, Cuban President Fidel Castro invited Soviet aid and came to rely on it heavily after the United States curtailed Cuba's sugar import quota. Castro made Cuba into an immensely valuable Soviet satellite 90 miles from the United States.

Kennedy's first crisis stemmed from his endorsement of the CIA plan to unseat Castro. The landing at the Bay of Pigs in mid-April 1961, was a fiasco. The Soviets reaped a propaganda harvest and pledged to defend Cuba in the future.

In the mid-1961, Khrushchev evidently considered the young president to be weak and on the defensive and tried to intimidate him with a new ultimatum to turn over control of Western access to West Berlin to the East German government. Kennedy responded by pledging to defend West Berlin, but the hesitancy of the NATO allies limited the West to a reassertion of access rights to West Berlin.

In 1962, the Soviets began secretly installing missiles in Cuba that could be used to launch nuclear attacks on US cities. This sparked the Cuban missile crisis, a confrontation that brought the two superpowers to the brink of war before an agreement was reached to withdraw the missiles. The crisis hardened the Soviets' determination never again to be humiliated by their military inferiority, and they began a buildup of both conventional and strategic forces that the United States was forced to match for the next 25 years.

President Kennedy was assassinated on 22 November 1963, and Khrushchev was removed from the Politburo in October 1964, a victim of his own failures in foreign policy particularly in relation with the United States and China and agriculture and of the Communist Party's resistance to his attempted reforms.

As discussed above, Mao interpreted the theme of the historical novel *Romance of the Three Kingdoms* spelled out at the beginning of its first chapter and towards the end of its last chapter as follows: 'The empires under the heavens, long united, must divide; and vice versa. Thus it has ever been'.

Mao's conviction of its relevance to the Sino-Soviet relations was strengthened as seen in his 'An Anti-Revisionist Report' in September 1964 (1969:83, 578). Even as early as January 1957, as noted above, in his concluding remarks on the Provincial and Urban Committee Secretarial Meeting, he had already considered that 'a flare-up of the Sino-Soviet animosity would occur sooner or later'. During the period 1954–64, though the United States was treated as the primary enemy, Mao quoted the theme of the historical novel on a number of other occasions earlier as follows:

(1) In October 1955, he quoted the famous statement in the reception held to welcome legislative members of the Japanese Congress.[1]
(2) On an occasion soon after the period of the 'Three Bad Years' of 1959–61, still very bitter about the way Khrushchev abrogated the Sino-Soviet agreements and withdrew Soviet technicians, Mao referred to this same statement again.[2]
(3) In February 1964, he quoted the same statement while talking to the visiting North Korean Party Secretary Kim Il-sung.[3]

In the global tripolar situation, let us first consider the Sino-Soviet communist giants at loggerheads before their breakup.

1954–1964 Period of Tripolarity: The US as Primary Enemy and Sino-Soviet Breakup

As discussed above, following the Korean War, the new US foreign policy was aimed at further isolating the PRC, in addition to its encirclement activities in East Asia. I also discussed US Secretary of State Dulles' 1954 announcement of 'peaceful transformations' and the subsequent Soviet positivist response. This, which alarmed Mao, was taken as the beginning of 'superpower collusion at the disadvantage of the PRC'. I further discussed that the Chinese were outraged at Khrushchev's secret de-Stalinization movement in the Twentieth CPSU Congress in February 1956, which was considered detrimental to Mao Zedong Thought and his leadership. Two months later, the Chinese accused this CPSU Congress of 'postulating US-USSR friendly cooperation to dictate to the whole world', apart from 'combating Stalin's personality cult'.[4] The Chinese further claimed that 'the Twentieth Congress was the origin of the evils of Khrushchev's alignments with imperialism and oppositions against China'.[5] Thus, in July 1957, in his speech 'On the Correct Handling of Contradictions Among the People', Mao (1977c:411) began to denounce Soviet 'revisionism', which he described as 'a bourgeois trend of thought that is even more dangerous than dogmatism'. According to Mao, it was 'cowardly acquiescence to Western, especially US, domination'. Under their 1950 treaty of friendship, solidarity, and mutual assistance, Soviet technical aid flowed to Beijing to support China's five year plan after 1953. Thus, in mid-November 1957, following the Soviet launching of the first ICBM and space satellite, Mao attempted to verify if the Sino-Soviet alliance survived intact by virtue of trying to consolidate the alliance and the socialist camp with his estimate of the international situation that 'the forces of socialism were over-whelming superior to those of imperialism'. Mao's attempt was rebuffed. On 13 May 1958, the *People's Daily* referred to Mao's statement in his 'Contradictions' speech, with Khrushchev as the main target.

Further, the Chinese claimed that in order to carry out its maritime strategy for global expansion, the Soviet Union under Khrushchev changed its navel strategy from 'offshore defense' to 'attack in the distant seas' and that it 'frantically expanded nuclear submarines, built aircraft carriers and other warships for launching an offensive far from home waters'.[6] Soviet appropriations for expanding its navy increased from about 15 per cent of its defense budget during Khrushchev's rule, the Chinese continued.

Thus, it was not surprising that latent hostility between China and the Soviet Union was aggravated by 'Khrushchev's intention to control the Chinese coast from the autumn of 1958 onward through a common navy' as Mao revealed (1969:432). Mao later added that 'Khrushchev's arrival at the end of July was because of this' and implied that Khrushchev's request was rejected (1969:432). In my work *Mao Tse-tung's Purposive Contention with the Superpowers: The Theory of Ch'i* published in 1995, I argue that Khrushchev was not prepared to stand firmly by Mao's August 1958 Taiwan Straits offensive.[7] With great restrain to avoid direct confrontation with the US navy, Mao initiated the Taiwan Straits Crisis to discern how far Khrushchev would commit his new power in support of China's interests.[8] It is worth to reproduce my arguments here to give a clear picture of the crisis.

Mao's initiative of bombarding Taiwan's offshore islands of Quemoy and Matsu was aimed to resolve the following question: To what extent was the US committed to Taiwan in the event of the Chinese using force to 'liberate' it?

If Mao's suspicions of the 'US-USSR collusion at the disadvantage of China' were right, then it was unlikely that Khrushchev would stand firmly by Mao's 1958 Taiwan Straits offensive. And it would be likely that Khrushchev had been bluffing when giving the following warnings to the US:

(1) 'any power which threatened China is a threat to the Soviet Union also';
(2) 'in its just struggle China would receive necessary moral and material help';
(3) 'a counterblow against any new military adventure in the Far East would not be restricted to the Taiwan Straits, but would put an end to US imperialist aggression';
(4) 'an attack on China would be considered an attack on the USSR'.[9]

For, if we accept Mao's claim (1969:432) that 'from the autumn of 1958 onward, Khrushchev intended to blockade the Chinese coast, wanted to form a common fleet with our nation in order to control us, and that Khrushchev's arrival is because of this', then we may conclude that Mao would certainly not take Khrushchev's warnings to the US seriously. Judging from the causal way Khrushchev was received on his arrival in Beijing on 31 July 1958, which was hardly mentioned in the official press – although the *People's Daily* did carry news of his departure and of the 'Sino-Soviet Stand' on 3 August 1958[10] – we can conclude that the meeting between Mao and Khrushchev was far from cordial, and that Khrushchev did not get what he 'intended' on his Beijing trip. That was why only a few months later the Soviets aborted the Sino-Soviet agreements and withdrew all their technicians. Further, the lines in Mao's *Irregular Verses* to the tune of *Man Jiang Hong* entitled 'To Answer Comrade Guo Moruo': 'In Chang An leaves spill in the west wind, the arrowhead sounds in the air' clearly hinted at incipient Sino-Soviet hostility at the time of Khrushchev's arrival in Beijing. Mao composed this lyric in January 1963, five years after the Taiwan Straits Crisis and when the Sino-Soviet dispute was starting to loom large. Nevertheless, it was possible that Mao deliberately made use of Khrushchev's bluff to counter Dulles' bluff pretending that he was accepting Khrushchev's warnings to the US as genuine.[11] Mao may have taken a calculated risk in initiating the Taiwan Straits Crisis even without the Russian nuclear backing, for he was convinced that Dulles, being 'dangerously isolated from both Allied support and public opinion in the US,[12] dared not use nuclear bombs'.

If we reconstruct some of the moves in the Crisis between the US and the PRC after the shelling of Quemoy on 23 August 1958 with particular attention to the Chinese primary motive, we might come to an astonishing conclusion as follows:

On 4 September, China declared a twelve-mile coastal zone to be national waters,[13] the US sent naval vessels within three miles of the coast;[14] China was unwilling 'to fire on American ships'.[15] This indicated that China did not intend to engage in a direct military confrontation with the US.

Snow (1966:640) argued that 'The Taiwan crisis of 1958 was to provide the first clear test ... of how far Mr. K would commit his new power in support of ... China's interests ...'. However, this thesis argues that the outcome of Khrushchev's Beijing visit on 31 July before the Crisis on 23 August would have indicated Khrushchev's decision regarding the Soviet commitment to China's interests.

Having found the answers to the US stance on Taiwan in the event of Chinese using force to liberate it, and having seen that the situation was worsening, Zhou Enlai on 6 September, 'offered to reopen the suspended Sino-US ambassadorial talks (provided for by the Geneva Agreement) at Warsaw to seek a peaceful settlement'.[16]

In its contention with the US, China's bombardment of Quemoy and Matsu clearly showed where it stood in its anticipation of any plausible future contention with the US. The Crisis indicated that the US really meant business.

In his thesis 'Mao Zedong and the Bombardment of Quemoy' published in 2005, Commander Ye Fei (叶飞) recalls: 'Mao ordered that the target of bombardment be Chiang Kai-shek's warships but not the US navy'.[17] As Snow (1966:641) revealed in his celebrated *The Other Side of the River*: 'Khrushchev's quite gratuitous and maladroit tip-off to the US that the bomb would be withdrawn from Mao's hand if he followed through with an offensive to close down the Quemoy-Matsu bases'. In his book published in 2000, Khrushchev's son, Sergei Nikitich (2000:268), confirms that Khrushchev 'flatly refused to participate in military actions in the Taiwan Straits'. The Taiwan Straits Crisis demonstrated US determination to dominate Asia through its containment-of-China policy and the domino theory.[18] At the same time, a new enemy, the 'No. 1 accomplice of the US', was now confirmed witnessing Mao's new worldview as a result of the changing international kaleidoscope.

Khrushchev's 'ambition to blockade the Chinese coast', to borrow Mao's term, was plausible. For the Soviets needed to dominate the PRC, not only because of the US-Soviet detente, but to eliminate this potential threat to Soviet supremacy. In a meeting between Mao and Khrushchev in Beijing in August 1958, Khrushchev did not get what he 'intended' as mentioned above.[19] The Sino-Soviet relations turned sour and the Soviets aborted the Sino-Soviet agreements and withdrew all their economic advisers and aid a few months later. This culminated in the Khrushchev-Eisenhower Camp David Meeting in 1959. These events reinforced Mao's anxiety, though officially Sino-Soviet friendship was still intact.

In 1959 the Soviet sided with the Indians against the Chinese in the Sino-Indian border conflict. This was followed by a border arms buildup along the Sino-Soviet border in 1962. In addition, in November 1963, the Chinese claimed that after the Indians had initiated armed provocations against China in 1960, the Soviets began to supply India with military aid.[20] With the 1963 Sino-Soviet dispute came into the open, the accusation of the 'US-USSR collusion to rule the world' had become more direct: 'Even the US imperialists said that this type of Soviet aid 'is in harmony with our interests'. By assisting imperialism and new colonialism, Khrushchev has not lagged behind the old revisionism in its assisting imperialism and old colonialism. They stand on the side of the imperialists and colonialists against the liberation revolution of the oppressed peoples'.[21]

The Chinese considered that the Russian part in the signing of the June 1963 Test Ban Treaty with the US (and the UK) as a betrayal of the Sino-Soviet alliance, for not only did the Chinese need to develop their own nuclear capability,[22] but more importantly, they believed the growing US-USSR cooperation and détente was aimed at them. Allowing Chiang Kai-shek as a signatory to the treaty, the Chinese argued, meant that the Russians conspired with the US against them: 'This is a proof that the Russian leadership is trying to please the US by going along with the treacherous scheme of 'two Chinas', and is betraying its allies and the socialist camp, and the interests of the world's people'.[23]

By the middle 1960s, the Sino-Soviet dispute had hardened into bitter hostility with massive build-ups along their border.

In chapter three, I discussed that, stimulated by the theme of the novel the *Romance of the Three Kingdoms*, Mao formulated his own global order of tripolarity with his concept fundamentally involving the primary and secondary enemies to suit the contemporary world of his time. In response to the politics and actions of the twin superpowers as he saw it, Mao's worldview was transformed from 'friend' into 'enemy', from 'secondary enemy' to 'primary enemy' and vice versa. His scheme of collusion with the 'secondary enemy' or 'secondary enemies' against the 'primary enemy' was formulated in this manner. The Soviet Union had become the 'No. 1 accomplice of the US' in 1954, and Mao had no choice but try to collude with, or incite the third world nations against the superpowers or fan revolutionary movements in the third world. Understandably this link was weak. It proved difficult for Mao to carry out his anti-imperialist and anti-revisionist agenda. The pressures exerted on the PRC by the superpowers, both separately and collectively, intensified Mao's determination to rely on his mass line strategy *to consolidate the people* at home to fulfill his GLF plan, the first step of his communization goal with the anti-Japanese experience as model. Understandably, therefore, in the Fifteenth Supreme State Council Meeting on the international situation in early September 1958, Mao emphasized the importance of military training in the communes (1999a:412).

The Defense-Oriented Great Leap Forward and the People's Commune Movement

Disappointed with, and in defiance of, the Soviet-imposed development strategy during the spring and summer of 1958, the first year of the Soviet-dictated Second FYP, Mao launched the GLF in his own view on China's economic development. Goodman (1994:73) claims that Mao's GLF initiative was 'a significant ideological challenge to the Soviet Union's claims to be furthest along the road to communism'. This study goes further to argue that with the Soviet economic model abandoned, Mao's GLF program, which was aimed at achieving phenomenal progress on all fronts through the mobilization of peasants and workers, men and women, civilians and soldiers, to 'enter communism', was meant to be defense-oriented in the face of the external imperialist enemies. Military considerations thus underlay China's 'heavy industry first' policy. In the Fifteenth Supreme State Council Meeting on the international situation in September 1958, Mao (1999a:412) declared his communization objective 'to arm the whole population'. This study contrasts with Lardy's pure economic approach (1987:363) on Maoist policy particularly concerning 'Mao's firm belief in his mobilization of existing resources primarily labor within the rural economy to provide a breakthrough for more rapid growth'.

The problem the PRC faced in the formulation of the Second FYP was how to maintain the rate of industrial growth and, at the same time, improve agricultural performance. Mao was not prepared to divert investment resources from industry to agriculture, with a consequent decline in industrial growth. He (1977c:288–9) subsequently made clear that 'national defense is too indispensable; and we are being bullied and encircled by our enemies'. Lieberthal contends that the GLF was 'based on almost utopian optimism about what the CCP, with its methods of mass mobilization, could accomplish' (1987:294). Ignoring the importance of international politics, Cheek (2010:11) goes further to attack Mao's GLF as 'the single greatest crime' during his rule, which was 'disastrously flawed and ruthlessly implemented'. However, my argument is that Mao's domestic mobilization in the GLF was to unify the great masses of the people against possible attacks by China's external superpower enemy or enemies 'in collusion'. It was along these lines that his new development strategy was speeded up in the second half of 1958.

Under great pressure from the US and USSR superpowers, Mao argued for the need of a more productive steel industry. In the Fifteenth Supreme State Council Meeting concerning the international situation in early September 1958, he called for the GLF and industrialization to move quickly, an urgent issue at the height of the US pressure on China.

He (1969:69) noted that '(o)ur private industry is estimated to be only 1.7 billion yuan, that is, less than US$7 billion. With this little bit (of capital) how couldn't we be bullied? That the imperialists bully us is not without reason'. He argued that, with the availability of steel as a base, defense industries would be possible. According to Mao, 'we must firmly grasp the three-line construction. After we have established steel, defense, machinery, chemical industry, oil (fossil fuel), we will not fear even if war breaks out'. In early 1958, the NPC announced the GLF agenda for the next three years, with the aim of increasing steel production by 19 per cent, electricity output by 18 per cent of electricity and coal output by 17 per cent in 1958 (Hsu, 1995:654). It is not surprising that he had an obsession with steel as an indicator of collective strength, as evidenced on many occasions particularly during the GLF period, as can be seen in his speeches collected in the book *Mao Zedong Si Xiang Wan Sui*. The following are examples:

(1) If we can produce 11 million tons of steel next year, and 17 million the year after next, we will shake the world. If in five years, we can reach 40 million tons, then in 15 years, we will surpass the US (May 1958).
(2) We must achieve the production of 11 million tons of steel this year ... We must increase ++ tons next year in order to reach ++ million tons. A year of hard work will give us ++ million tons of steel, that is, we will rank third after the USSR and the USA (September 1958).

Even as early as in September 1950, Mao (1999:93) argued that US imperialism 'having an abundance of steel demonstrated its military advantages'. Understandably, the discovery of a major iron-ore site in southwest Sichuan province in the late 1960s led to Mao's personal instruction to build the Chengku Railway starting from the new city Panzhihua (攀之花市).[24]

In the industrialization drive, Mao took a further step toward socialist transformation by creating the people's communes. The Second FYP was abandoned in mid-1958 when the nationwide GLF and commune movements were launched. By November 1958, he had organized 26,000 people's communes convening 98 per cent of the peasants from the merger of 750,000 higher-stage cooperatives that combined industry, agriculture, trade, education, and military affairs with government administration and commune management. On average, each rural commune consisted of some 30 cooperatives of about 5,000 households or 25,000 people. With the slogan 'politics in command', the GLF was a landmark mass mobilization of labor for irrigation, reclamation, and flood control tasks designed to raise agricultural yields and output with minimum input of capital (Eckstein, etc., 1985:7). Mao relied on mass mobilization of China's astronomical manpower in his quest for an instant breakthrough on all fronts. In an attempt to consolidate the masses, Mao mobilized 90 million peasants to build backyard steel furnaces, with the neglect of expertise. The shoots of communism appeared in 1958 in the form of the multi-functional communes, which were meant to provide a transition from socialist collective ownership to ownership by all. Mao's strategy was to transform the narrow collective ownership of the land of the communes and capital goods into ownership by all the people in the full socialist form. In this way, social coherence was to be guaranteed and the mobilization of a united population to repel possible attacks by external enemies could be possible.

With the purpose of consolidating the entire population, the Rectification Campaign of 1957–8, launched following the Third Plenum, was related to the Great Leap Forward movement and people's commune movements (Teiwes, 1993:334, 337). The realization of GLF aims, the amalgamation of APCs and the development of the commune necessitated indoctrinating the masses once again with selfless communist spirit. To ensure the success of these movements, the dictum 'uniting with all possible' was applied as the theme of mass mobilization.

Mass mobilization, together with the GLF emphasis of maximum use of local resources, led to administrative decentralization. Characteristic of the rectification and improvement was the partial phasing out of the centralized bureaucratic economic apparatus in favor of decision-making autonomy for localities. Thus the *xia fang* or downward transfer of cadres was needed. First appearing in the early 1940s, the downward transfer of cadres to lower levels had been popularized since 1957. This was originally designed to change cadre attitudes through physical labor to break down the distinction between mental and manual work. Apart from serving as both administrative decentralization and strengthening local units, the downward transfer movement was aimed at bringing cadres into direct contact with the masses to overcome bureaucratism, and at avoiding their divorce from the masses through participation in labor. Moreover, efforts were made in the movement to bring intellectuals and workers and peasants together. This was 'to unite with all possible'.

Mao's economic strategy now was not that of the heavily industrial, capital-intensive, Soviet economic model, which allowed for agricultural stagnation. This Soviet model was not suited to the Chinese conditions of abundant labor, little capital, and little agricultural surplus for industrial capital. He instead initiated a policy of 'walking on two legs', which stressed agriculture and industry. Meanwhile the traditional and modern sectors were preserved in that medium and small-scale labor-intensive industries based on indigenous technologies were developed with the modern industrial sector (Meisner, 1977, 230).

The Defense-Oriented Communization Concept

In this section, based in part on my published work *Mao Tse-tung's Ch'i and the Chinese Political Economy With Special Reference to the Post-Mao Modernization Revolution*, I will discuss Mao's commune system as an organizational technique of tapping the power of the people to face China's imperialist enemies (Lam, 2000:159–67).

In order to 'wipe capitalism from the face of the earth', Mao organized the people to 'unite all that can be united'. This technique can be traced to the anti-Japanese war period, when Mao organized the anti-Japanese government in the Shen-Kan-Ning Border Areas. The political-economic-military principles that guided this process became crucial to the commune system Mao set up in 1958. In other words, the Border Areas *as a whole* became a prototype for this commune system. Mao's idea that the nation be organized as a 'combination of production and militia' therefore materialized in relation to communes as individual units.

During the period of revolutionary struggle against Japanese imperialism, militancy was the key to political organizations in the Border Areas. This principle applied to the 1958 commune drive to combat the 'US and Soviet collusion at the disadvantage of the PRC'. In the communes, all young men were expected to become soldiers. Men eligible by age and demobilized servicemen were organized into the militia underwent continuous military training.[25] In a speech delivered in Beijing on 30 September 1958, Mao stressed that the militia was both a military organization and a labor organization'.[26] Reflecting the Yenan experience, workers, peasants, traders, students and soldiers of the nation were systematically integrated into Mao's communes so that 'the broad masses of the people become workers when entering factories, peasants when going to the fields, and soldiers when taking up arms'.[27]

The consumption-related activities such as cooking, washing and child-rearing were shifted from the households to the communes, releasing female labor for work in farming activities (Lardy, 1987:365). These shifts toward increasing collective activities were to enhance Mao's dictum 'uniting all who can unite'. To further enhance the dictum, principles of income distribution were fundamentally changed, with a large share of net earnings distributed on a per capita basis to minimize the income differentials within the communes.

Further, in November 1958, Mao (1999a:434–5) asserted the importance of the production of commercial goods appropriate for exchange in the communes, in addition to those of self-sufficient production. According to him, commercial production served the cause of socialism in that it provided the state not only with goods, but with accumulated capital (1999a:440). Previously, in September 1953, Mao (1977c:112) had emphasized that state capitalism would transform capitalist industry and commerce. This would serve the nation's economy and raise the standard of living of the people (1977c:112). More importantly, Mao argued, this was 'to unite a few hundred million peasants' (1999a:437).

Evolved from the traditional cooperative system for organizing peasant labor forces, the commune model was developed in the early 1940s by Communists who organized production teams and combined the production systems with the local militia in each community unit (village) under a unified command. The organizational structure and management of the 1958 communes corresponded to that of the Shen-Kan-Ning Border Government model. Defined as 'both economic unit and basic unit of state power', the commune was organized to strengthen the control functions of the Party at the lower levels and to give new functions to the local governments such as the *xiang* (township) and the *xian* (county). Thus government decentralization at the higher levels was balanced by centralization at lower levels. Linkage between the political and economic administrations also made possible to tap the people's power from the whole populace. Judging from the MATs of the Yenan period developed in the post-liberation period into the basic agricultural producers' cooperatives, which in turn were developed into the advanced APCs, it is clear that the people's commune was, for Mao, the most logical way of tapping the people's power of the whole population to fight powerful external enemies.

The commune was a higher form of socialist organization with the structure roughly approximating a sub-unit or district within the county. It was essentially a township comprised of a market town (sometimes even several small towns) and its satellite villages. Within each large village or brigade were production teams made up of between 20 and 60 households, depending on the district. The mix of private and collective activities was shifted toward the latter. Private farming plots were eliminated under the commune system; households within certain sections of the village now worked the land as a team (Lardy, 1987:365). During the non-farming period, household members might serve on other brigade teams, work in commune industries or services. While the commune in 1958 typically was a township (*xiang*) comprised of a number of villages (*cun*), Mao's ideal commune also included gradual development into 'the federation of people's communes at a county level to become one with the people's council of that county'.[28] Mao's original 1958 commune was based on the idea of 'one *xian* one commune' system. The original form of the actual commune was a huge organization (5,500 households each), about 25 times the size of the higher-stage APCs formed in 1955–6 which took over the functions of the local government and claimed to have achieved 'communism' by providing 'to each according to his needs'. Thus the commune project revealed Mao's strategy that the task of China's socialization aimed at reaching ownership-by-all of the means of production and eventually a consolidated communist society.

Therefore, to eradicate capitalism and guard against possible imperialist intrusion through consolidated power generated by the masses of the whole nation, Mao organized the defense-oriented communes. With the notion of 'serving the people' as catalyst, Mao's communization plan served as a means to realize consolidated power by first 'wiping out capitalism' for his ultimate aim of fighting imperialism.[29] Thus we can see that Mao's method of acquiring this power had been at work since the Yenan period. This phenomenon persisted throughout the decades in his anti-feudal, anti-capitalist and ultimately anti-imperialist tasks.

The Moral Incentive of Selflessness and Astronomical Power of the Whole Population

In this section, I will elaborate how Mao furthered his commune system to consolidate the entire population by introducing the moral incentive of 'serving the people selflessly'.

The principal objective of Mao's commune system was to promote 'proletarian consciousness' so that close ties with the masses could be strengthened. First, all bourgeois thought and culture were to be suppressed. In addition, individual interests were to be subdued to the common interest, private property renounced, the ethical education of all carried out by the state. This was reminiscent of the Yenan anti-Japanese imperialist 'unified leadership' through which public enterprises, peasant cooperatives, a collective self-reliance economy, education, the choice of rank and possession, and the arts and literature were all placed under the exclusive and absolute control of the state. Based on Mao's idea that social life must be the collective life, this consummation of his ideal of justice was to be attained by a system of communism and the common education by the state. Furthermore, the system incorporated into a nation's whole structure would enable astronomical power to become generative *vis-a-vis* powerful external enemies.

To Mao, egalitarianism meant social coherence, mass participation, and serving the people – a vision that could be fulfilled only when individuals first served others. Its complete antithesis, the pursuit of private profit, would produce social individualism and thus divisiveness rather than social coherence. On this view of the nature of man, one owes a responsibility not merely to oneself, but to one's neighbor. This was Mao's approach to realizing consolidation of the great majority of the people. This social coherence was to be guaranteed by establishing a commune system in China. This rationalized Mao's hyperbolical ideal of 'the will of each thinking in terms of all' – an effective method of consolidating 'all possible' to produce an astronomical result. In response to Marx's call for the selfless brotherhood of communism, Mao put the notion of egalitarianism into practice. Heir to Marx, Mao envisioned a cohesive society where each would live to 'serve the others' and no rights to private property would be asserted. In order to implement this concept effectively, Mao saw that as vanguard of the proletariat, the party system was vital with effective leadership. Thus China was to become a conglomeration of communes where people elected their own leadership.

The realization of Mao's communist ideal necessitated indoctrinating the masses with selfless communist spirit. Division of labor had had a drawback from Mao's viewpoint with respect to his mass line philosophy. By creating an egalitarian society, he applied the moral incentive of 'serving the people' in order to win over the majority. Social cohesion, as Mao saw it, could only result from collective contribution, not competition for individual gain.

An important factor hindering this desired social coherence, Mao explained in 'Dialectical Materialism', was 'idealist philosophy', or the 'reactionary ideology of the ruling classes'. This ideology, according to Mao, was rooted in the material process of production with the technical and social division of labor. With the development of the productive forces of society, Mao argued, 'the division of labour saw the emergence of persons elevating themselves entirely and exclusively to intellectual labour' who 'became the exclusive privilege of the ruling class, while manual labour became the oppressed classes'.[30] Thus, it was difficult to 'unite with all possible' to eradicate capitalism in order to fight imperialism effectively. Thus, to eliminate the distinction between manual labor and intellectual labor was one of the pre-conditions for eliminating capitalism.

To make his commune system effective in the long-term in generating astronomical power to eradicate capitalism, 'minimizing or abolishing the difference between town and city, between rural worker and factory worker, between manual and mental labour' was needed. This was to make the feudal peasant educated, literate and scientifically-minded – the counterpart of an educated, literate, technical factory worker.[31] Therefore the social organization of the future communist society was to be centered in the commune and designed to be at once city and countryside, trade market and production center.[32] This meant that the commune would take over all local government functions, and would be the instrument for elimination of private ownership of the means of production. Each commune would thus become a small individual state whilst in addition to being united to all the others by cultural, economic, political and military bonds.[33]

In sum, Mao's grand strategy was the formation of the basic unit on which to build the structure of a nation and through which Herculean power could then be generated for the purpose of fighting imperialist intrusion, similar to the Yenan model designed for dealing with Japanese imperialism.

Mao's Communization Model Challenged: The Soviet-Backed Right Opportunism

In 1959, 'right opportunists' led by Peng Dehuai were found opposed to Mao's defense-oriented communization agenda, and their opposition was encouraged by the Soviets. This was an age of 'US-USSR collusion' against China as Mao perceived it. Mao was thus under great pressures both externally and internally. In the following, I will deal with his dismissal of the 'right opportunist' Peng, which was part of the Sino-Soviet acrimonious exchange.

The 1959 dismissal of Soviet-encouraged 'Right Opportunist' Peng Dehuai

Barme argues that Peng at the July 1959 Lushan Conference submitted to Mao to call 'for a rethinking of the Great Leap in light of the devastation the policies had already visited on the nation' and that 'deeply suspicious that it was a ruse that disguised an insidious plot against him and party policy, (he) turned on Peng and his associates'.[34] Teiwes argues that the country descended into accelerated crisis, because Mao, who interpreted Peng's critique of the GLF as a personal challenge, insisted on the latter's dismissal.[35]

The 1959 dismissal of the 'right opportunists' on the surface revolved around policy differences over the 'three red banners'. However, this campaign – a 'rectification of the whole Party' – was a major effort to combat widespread opposition led by Peng Dehuai over the CCP's economic policies. More importantly, this widespread opposition was backed by 'revisionist' Khrushchev as Mao implied in his letter to the editors of *Shikan*, Zang Kejia and Yuan Shuipai, on 1 September 1959.

Mao's astonishing economic plans, together with unfavorable weather conditions, first caused disaster to agriculture and then severely curtailed the supply of agricultural raw materials to industry. The economy took a serious leap backward starting in 1959. 'Right opportunists' then launched their anti-Mao attack.

With the Soviet backing, the 'right opportunists' led by Peng attacked Mao's policies of the GLF and people's communes as 'left adventurist' errors. However, as early as February 1959, having noted the 'leftist wind of communism' after the establishment of the commune system in the autumn of 1958, Mao (1999b:12) warned that this 'leftist wind' or 'communist style' of 'robbing the peasants' in terms of 'equal distribution, moving the ownership of certain properties of the production teams upwards without compensation, and reclaiming banking loans from the peasantry', which was detrimental to his mass line strategy, had to be stopped. The 'right opportunists' ignored Mao's warning prior to the Lushan Conference.[36] In late June of 1959, on his way to the conference, Mao called for the ignoring of unrealistic targets set by higher levels leadership and identified comprehensiveness and balance as critical issues.[37] The 'right opportunists' disregarded Mao's statement and charged that the GLF was a scheme of 'petty-bourgeois fanaticism', as Peng put it, based on a 'pitch black' general perspective.[38] Mao was aware that this opposition was detrimental to his strategy of uniting all of the people – crucial to his 'three red flags' – he needed the spirit of single-mindedness of the masses if his schemes were to succeed. He argued that through pouring cold water on the 'revolutionary zeal' of the Party and hundreds of millions of people, Peng's challenge would have had a negative effect on Mao's defense-oriented plans.[39] Mao's real concern was de-emphasis of the mass line through promotion of capitalist elements to the masses. With the view of collective production as excessively rigid and detrimental to the productive enthusiasm of peasants, the 'right opportunists' advocated measures to promote 'small freedoms' and individual production. The result, the Maoists argued, would be a 'retreat to scattered individual labor' and the danger that capitalism would be restored in the peasantry.[40] The emergence of the Russian 'revisionism' had inspired the 'right opportunists' to challenge Mao's 'three red flags'. Thus, in a Hangzhou meeting in November 1959, Mao warned that Dulles' agenda had seeped through the very foundation of socialism, referring to Dulles' three talks of 1954 on US-proposed 'peaceful transformations'.[41] Importantly, that year was the beginning of the US-USSR collusion against the PRC, as Mao saw it.

Further, Peng was accused of following a revisionist military policy even before 1959. According to Chiou, Peng was charged with trying to

(1) put the army before the Party,
(2) counterpose regularization and modernization against proletarian revolutionization of the army,
(3) substitute the system of one-man leadership for the collective leadership of the Party committee in the Army, and
(4) place military technique in the first place in the Army building.[42]

Peng, according to Chiou, was also accused of over-emphasizing the importance of nuclear weaponry and seeking the Soviet umbrella.[43] According to Chiou, since taking over the PLA in 1954, Peng had tried very hard to modernize the Army along the pattern of the Soviet Red Army and to make it into a less politicized professional armed force.[44] It is important to note that this was the age of 'US-USSR collusion against China', according to Mao.

It became quite obvious that what Mao actually objected to was: firstly, 'right opportunists' colluding with the Russians to oppose his 'three red flags'. The harmful effect of the bourgeois 'expertise' of the 'right opportunists' to Mao's 'redness' and 'mass line' strategy was considered great. Further, the revolutionary fervor of the masses, without which Mao's 'three red flags' and hence his socialist revolution would collapse, would be extinguished. The effect would be extremely detrimental as it would involve hundreds of millions of people, thus weakening his anti-imperialist stance. Thus Mao's struggle against the 'right opportunists' began with a call for opposing bourgeois ideas and for increased efforts to achieve the 'three red flags' goals. Since the plenum, the press had been filled with denunciations of 'right opportunist' views such as 'bourgeois anti-socialism' and 'criminal activities against the building of socialism'. The 1959 rectification campaign was an effort to stop the danger of 'right opportunist ideology' spreading throughout the nation. The campaign showed that Mao was determined to wipe out capitalist thought at any price and, more importantly, the detrimental external influences of the Khrushchev-backed 'right opportunist' Peng.

Mao's view on high treason

According to Teiwes, during his 1959 spring tour to the Soviet Union, Peng Dehuai 'expressed misgivings' regarding Mao's GLF and commune schemes to Khrushchev. Khrushchev in turn 'allegedly encouraged Peng to return to China to oppose Mao' and subsequently 'attacked the Chinese communes in a speech in Poland'.[45] Mao's outrage at Peng's unprincipled behavior described as 'treason' was understandable.[46] Undoubtedly Mao regarded what Peng did as 'most despicable', likening it to 'a family member who eats at home but crawls outwards' (吃里爬外). The international situation in 1959 was crucial when the Soviet Union was confirmed as the 'No. 1 accomplice of the US primary enemy' in Mao's worldview. Mao (1969:94) considered Peng's 'collusion' with the Russians an attempt to 'push over Mt. Kunlun' as an act of high treason. He even branded Peng and associates 'rotten eggs (王八蛋) who ignore the eight virtues of filial respect (孝), respect for elder brothers (悌), patriotism (忠), honesty (信), good manners (礼), fraternity and justice (义), moral cleanliness (廉), and shame (耻)'.[47] To the Chinese, this abusive language is always used in very serious situations. Therefore Peng's fate was sealed as a result of the 1959 rectification campaign against 'right opportunism'. The case against Peng and his supporters such as Zhang Wentian, Zhou Xiaozhou, Huang Kecheng resembled that of Gao Gang and Rao Soushi in 1954. In his 'speech at the second plenary session of the Eighth Central Committee of the CCP' on 15 November 1956, Mao (1977c:340) denounced Gao's high treason as 'having illicit relations with foreign countries' (里通外国). In September 1959, in his talks 'On the Central Military Committee's Extended and External Meetings', Mao (1969:97) reminded those present about the danger of having 'illicit relations with foreign countries'.

During the months of August and September 1967, an article was published three times in a row in the *Beijing Review* that accused Peng of carrying out 'his heinous crimes' of anti-Party activities particularly with respect to the GLF and communization movements.[48] To appeal against some of the charges against him particularly those of having secret ties with the Soviet Union and organizing an anti-Party clique, Peng wrote a letter to the Central Committee and Mao during the period of 'the wind of reversal of verdicts'. This period involved re-examination of wrongful verdicts and the rehabilitation of individuals found falsely charged in the 1959 anti-rightist struggle.[49] Mao responded that rehabilitating Peng was out of the question.[50]

Mao referred to many acts of treason committed in ancient China. For instance, the overthrow of Zhou Wang (纣王) of the Shang dynasty (sixteenth century B.C.–1066 B.C.), according to Mao, was a result of the treacherous Shang minister Wei Zi's (微子) 'illicit relations with the foreign Zhou (周) dynasty', and betrayal by other traitors such as Bi Gan (比干) and Ji Zi (箕子).[51] With his critical appreciation of the ancient text *The Various Kingdoms of the Eastern Zhou Dynasty* (东周列国) written by Feng Meng Long (冯梦龙), Mao talked about the 'overturning of a country with treason'.[52] Mao's comments on this issue occurred around December 1959 after the Lushan Meeting. This meeting focused on the anti-'right opportunism' struggle against Peng Dehuai, described as 'ganging up with Khrushchev' against Mao's commune system.[53]

Mao's psychological insight can be seen in his great reverence for the patriotic Yue Fei (岳飞) (1103–41), the celebrated general of the Song dynasty (960–1279), who is considered as China's preeminent national hero. I discovered that Mao's calligraphy of Yue's lyric *Man Jiang Hong* (满江红) is displayed in the gallery beside Yue's tomb in the Hangzhou city of Zhejiang province (浙江省).

Conclusion

The fundamental causes of the Sino-Soviet split must be traced to contradictions in the Soviet roles as leader of the Communist movement and the Soviet Union. The independent economic approach in China was a disaster for the USSR, for Mao would inevitably refuse to play the role of a subordinate. Upon the completion of his anti-capitalist cooperativization plan in 1957, Mao accelerated his communization endeavors. Based on the Yenan model as a prototype, this was meant to 'unite with all possible' in response to pressures from the United States and the Soviet Union. Mao's economic-cum-defense strategy was a solution for China's survival in the hostile international environment. Inspired by the theme of the *Romance of the Three Kingdoms*, which he interpreted as 'a flare up of the Sino-Soviet animosity sooner or later', he tried but in vain to collude with the

United States against the Soviet Union, which was being developed into Mao's primary enemy. The 1959 dismissal of the 'right opportunist' Peng Dehuai was part of the Sino-Soviet acrimonious dispute. He considered Peng's 'collusion with the Russians to oppose the three red flags' an act of high treason.

CHAPTER SIX

1965–1969 Period of Tripolarity: Cultural Revolution as Part of the Sino-US Hostility

In the last chapter, I surveyed how Mao increased his communization endeavors amid 'revisionist' objections at home and abroad, with the 1959 dismissal of the Soviet-backed 'right opportunists' as part of the Sino-Soviet acrimonious dispute. In this chapter, I will consider that with the US to begin its deep involvement in Vietnam in 1965, Mao took the opportunity to launch his Cultural Revolution against Liu Shaoqi and others as part of the Sino-US acrimonious exchange. In mid-1966, Zhou Enlai announced PRC's support to North Vietnam. Only a year later, the United States began to be transformed into Mao's secondary enemy from the twenty-years-long primary enemy. I will consider how this came about.

Tripolar International Environment: 1960–1969

As discussed in the preceding chapter, in the late 1950s, in Mao's perspective, the Soviet Union became a confirmed 'devil' while the US was still seen as the primary enemy. The bipolar conflict between the American and the Soviet blocs in the early 1950s had already given way to a more complicated pattern of international relationships in which the world was no longer split into two clearly defined opposed blocs. I considered how in the late 1950s the Sino-Soviet relations turned sour and how Khrushchev abrogated the Sino-Soviet agreements leading to Khrushchev's attack on Mao at Bucharest in 1960. While claiming to be the leader of international Communist movement, in 1961, the PRC charged that the Soviet policy of 'peaceful co-existence' was induced by fear of the US nuclear arsenal. The Sino-Soviet relations then worsened, exacerbated by a series of disputes between the two communist giants. This included the Sino-Soviet border arms build-up in 1962,[1] and finally the 1963 Sino-Soviet intense dispute hardened into bitter hostility.

On the basis of the theme of the historical novel as well as the antagonistic US-Soviet relations as briefed above, Mao dropped hints about his wish to collude with the United States against the Soviet Union on two occasions as follows:

(1) In February 1959, Mao told American correspondent Anna Strong that he had always swum across the Yangtze and other Chinese rivers and that he would like to try the Mississippi River.[2]
(2) In October 1964, he referred to the same wish to Edgar Snow.[3]

This was Mao's style of expressing his wish of improving China's relationship with the United States with the ultimate aim of colluding with that superpower against the Soviet Union. Unfortunately, none of the Westerners took his hints. However, only on the occasion of China's National Day on 1 October 1970 Premier Zhou Enlai led Edgar Snow and his wife to stand at Mao's side on Tian An Men that Kissinger later realized the importance of the incident: 'The inscrutable Chairman was trying to convey something ... Eventually I came to understand that Mao intended to symbolize that American relations now had his personal attention', he recalled. '(W)e had missed the point when it mattered', he continued. 'Excessive subtlety had produced a failure of communication', according to Kissinger (Kissinger, 1979:699).

In April 1965, the Chinese accused the new leadership of the CPSU of following Khrushchev's 'general line of foreign policy to uphold peaceful co-existence' and 'US-Soviet collaboration for the solution of the problems of the world' and that the Twentieth Congress of the CPSU 'was the first and the most significant sign of the emergence of Khrushchev revisionism'.[4] In the same year, a new Soviet book entitled *The USSR and the USA – Their Political and Economic Relations* 'lavishly praised the Soviet government's perfidious activities of colluding with the US', the Chinese argued, which were not only 'in accord with the interests of the Soviet and American peoples', but were 'vitally necessary for the destiny of all mankind'.[5] The Chinese criticized that with the abolition of the dictatorship of the proletariat behind the camouflage of the foreign policy of upholding peaceful co-existence, Soviet leadership under Khrushchev paved the way for the restoration of capitalism.[6] The Chinese were concerned about 'US-Soviet collusion' against them.

In these circumstances, in which the PRC seemed to stand in opposition to the world's strongest powers combined, had no alternative but to initiate resistance to the 'colluded' superpowers by relying on Mao's people's war. In the influential 'Problems of Strategy in Guerrilla War against Japan' (first published in May 1938 by Mao), the *Beijing Review* of 27 August 1965 republished Mao's theory of the people's war. The ideas expounded in the article, the editor hinted, 'played a great guiding role' in China's possible war against the United States, which had 'colluded' with social imperialism. It particularly pointed out 'the important strategic role of guerrilla warfare'. The article elaborated that '(t)oday it is very clear that the theory of a people's war found in Comrade Mao Tse-tung's article is of vital practical importance for the Chinese people ... against US imperialism and its lackeys'. The pressures exerted on the PRC by the superpowers, both separately and collectively, intensified Mao's determination to rely on his mass line strategy *to consolidate the people* at home to fulfill his GLF plan, the first step of his communization goal with the anti-Japanese experience as model. Mao had clung to his communization drive the entire time. However, Mao perceived Soviet-US hostility in his tripolar worldview as follows:

As noted in the preceding chapter, Cold War solidified after the Second World War, climaxing in the nuclear brinkmanship of both superpowers in the Cuba Crisis in 1962. The Chinese argued that the US-USSR contention focus had always been in Europe.

Intensified US-USSR superpower contention for hegemony had always been focused on Western Europe since the eve of the World War. For years, the Soviet Union deployed in Europe a conventional armed force far surpassing that of the West. In Eastern and Central Europe the Soviet bloc's airfields for highly manoeuvrable fighter planes and other military airfields had greatly out-numbered those of the West. However, on its part, the United States began large-scale renewal of its tactical nuclear weapons deployed in Western Europe to cope with the Warsaw Pact's superior conventional forces, and at the same time reduced non-combatant forces there while increasing and strengthening its combat troops. Both sides engaged in massive nuclear expansion. 'Détente' in words was designed to camouflage intense rivalry for hegemony in deeds. In addition, striving for hegemony in Europe both had also been bitterly contending over Europe's flanks – the Middle East, the Mediterranean and the Balkan area. In their view, the one who controlled these regions could influence developments in Europe.

In the following, I will consider the US debacle in Vietnam.

Guided by the principle of containment, which enveloped the globe, the United States expanded its treaty commitment far beyond the Organization of American States (OAS) founded in 1948 in binding the American alliance and the North Atlantic Treaty Organization (NATO). After the collapse of French forces in Indochina in 1954, US Secretary of State John Foster Dulles was instrumental in assembling the Southeast Asia Treaty Organization (SEATO), which was intended both to support existing treaty obligations with Taiwan, Japan and Korea, and to arrest Communist control of all Indochina by safeguarding US commitments in Southeast Asia from falling state by state, like a row of dominoes. Even before Kennedy's assassination towards the end of November 1963, US involvement in Indochina overshadowed its long-standing confrontation with the PRC. American troops were present in South Vietnam to share the fighting against its internal enemy, the Vietcong, which was abetted by the North Vietnamese. As South Vietnam's President Ngo Dinh Diem lost his grip on the country, a series of successors failed to provide a stable government, let alone wage a successful war against the enemy. Thus President Johnson dispatched a massive US military infusion. The Tonkin Gulf Incident, in which two American destroyers had reportedly been attacked by North Vietnamese torpedo boats, opened the way for the dispatch of more than half a million US troops within four years.

Soon after his inauguration in January 1965, US President Johnson sent American combat troops into Vietnam, followed by massive bombing of North Vietnam a month later. In mid-February the same year, the *Peking Review* editorial celebrated the 15th anniversary of the signing of the Sino-Soviet Treaty of Friendship, and Mutual Assistance with the aim of 'struggling to safeguard Sino-Soviet unity'. This was attempt to pursue the new Soviet leadership to 'condemn US aggression in Vietnam' with the aim of neutralizing the 'US-USSR collusion at the disadvantage of China'. However, the Soviet policy on the question of Indochina was of 'disengagement'.

Nevertheless, the Soviet Union reacted to American escalation by trying to bring pressure to bear on the United States to submit to the peaceful reunification of Vietnam. The PRC bluntly refused to encourage a negotiated settlement, however. In mid-April 1966 when the United States sent massive reinforcements to South Vietnam and extended its bombing of North Vietnam, Premier Zhou Enlai announced China's support to the North Vietnamese, while the new leadership of the Soviet Union continued Khrushchev's policy of 'disengagement' on Vietnam.

Womack (2006:176) reported China's support for Vietnam in its war against the United States as follows:

> China figured the total cost of its support for Vietnam at twenty billion dollars, and it sent 320,000 military-related personnel in 1965–69, primarily for transformation construction and repair and manning anti-aircraft batteries .... China suffered casualties of 1,100 killed and 4,200 wounded. China's general support of the basic economy was just as important as military aid. Overall China provided 5 million tons of food, the equivalent of Vietnam's total food production for one year. In 1966 China provided 500,000 tons of food, 10 percent of Vietnamese production that year.

In October 1964, Khrushchev was removed from power by the Politburo, a victim of his own failures in foreign policy and agriculture and of the Communist Party's resistance to his attempted reforms. Leonid Brezhnev, who had replaced Khrushchev as Party leader in the Soviet Union, was focusing on domestic problems. A campaign against dissidents of every kind began with the trial in September 1965 of Andrei D. Sinyavsky and Yuli M. Daniel, arrested for publishing ideologically objectionable books abroad. This campaign resulted in a protest to the Twenty-third Party Congress the next spring by a group of prominent Soviet scientists and intellectuals.

Both Soviet problems at home and US involvement in Vietnam brought the Chinese some relief in the international arena and gave Mao a lot of leeway to launch his Cultural Revolution against the 'No. 1 power holder in the Party taking the capitalist road' at home.

The 'Capitalist-cum-Revisionist' Liu Shaoqi, 'China's Khrushchev'

Ignoring the crucial international factors, MacFarquhar writes that 'after 1950, overall, Mao's rule was disastrous' and that 'the negative appraisal of the Cultural Revolution and of Mao's culpability is widely accepted in the West'.[7]

However, the development policy of the Liuists was identified as US capitalist motivated and Soviet 'revisionist' oriented. It was opposed to Mao's defense-oriented communization agenda. This was an age of 'US-USSR collusion' against China in Mao's tripolar perception. To account for the purge of Liu Shaoqi, the 'No. 1 power holder in the Party taking the capitalist road' during the Cultural Revolution, I must first deal with (a) the origins of the Liuist pro-Western economic approach, which was considered to hinder to Mao's collectivization scheme, and (b) the Three Bad Years of 1959–61 and the aftermath.

Origins of the 'Rightist' and 'Revisionist' Economic Approach

The origins of Liu Shaoqi's pro-Western economic approach can be traced back to his 'oppose rash advance' (反冒进) campaign against Mao's collectivization scheme in the early 1950s. This was in the midst of the period starting after the Second World War in which, in Mao's worldview, China's primary enemy was the United States, with the Soviet Union as its *de facto* enemy. He considered imperative to consolidate the great masses of the Chinese population by accelerating the process of his collectivization scheme *vis-à-vis* the 'US-USSR collusion at the disadvantage of the PRC'. This scheme, however, motivated the Liuist 'rightist' onslaughts on a number of occasions. Further, Mao considered the Liuist-led rightist movement in 1957 detrimental to the scheme and the Party leadership.

The 'Rightist' Liu's 'oppose rash advance' onslaughts

Liu Shaoqi consistently adhered to his pro-Western economic approach, without paying attention to the crucial international environment characterized by the gradual 'US-USSR collusion at the disadvantage of the PRC' starting in 1954 as Mao perceived it. In the early 1950s, Mao's determination to speed up the process of collectivization led to onslaughts by the 'rightists' as follows:

First, in the early 1950s, the completion of land reform witnessed a new trend in the peasantry. By the end of 1952, three-fifths of all peasant farms were still privately owned, while the remainder 'had joined seasonal MATs with only a very small share belonging either to permanent MATs or to APCs'.[8] According to Mao, in the 'oppose rash advance' campaign led by Liu Shaoqi in the spring of 1953, the rightists attempted to 'sustain private ownership' and practice the 'four big freedoms', which were to 'facilitate the growth of a small number of rich peasants and follow the capitalist road' (1977c:139). As a result, many peasants had sold their land to the rich peasants and the renting and leasing of portions of land and farm capital to the poor by the rich peasants had become common, since all this was allowed by the 1950 Agrarian Reform Law (Article 6). The development of the rich peasant economy was thus uncurbed and rural capitalism was resurgent.

According to Mao, mutual-aid teams by themselves were not enough to stop peasants from selling their land, but only cooperatives and big ones of one or two hundred households could do so and could eliminate the need of peasants to rent out land (1977c:132–3). Mao argued that cooperativization could make his anti-imperialist mass line strategy workable. Therefore, by October 1953, he had curtailed the rights of the rich peasants with the intensification of his cooperativization drive, and agricultural cooperation had been developed in 60 to 70 per cent of the old region and 20 to 25 per cent of the new region (1999:296).

Secondly, by the mid-1953, according to Mao, the 'rightists' led by Liu Shaoqi had 'firmly established new democratic program', which inhibited his socialist transformation (1977c:93). According to Mao, 'this new Liuist social order hindered the progress of the socialist cause' of 'burying the capitalist system and all other systems of exploitation once and for all'. Therefore, Article 4 of the PRC Constitution published in the *People's Daily* on September 1954, was to ensure that 'through socialist industrialization and socialist transformation, gradual annihilation of the exploitation system to establish socialist society in China (would be) guaranteed'.

Thirdly, criticizing the rightists' campaign of 'oppose rash advance' in opposition to the cooperatization scheme in the spring of 1955, Mao (1977c:242) as editor of the book *Socialist Upsurge in China's Countryside* wrote: '(The rightists wanted) the resolute contraction of cooperatives'. Mao's objection (1977c:248) to the rightists' campaign was that 'the well-to-do and fairly well-to-do middle peasants, who constituted 20 to 30 per cent of the rural population, are quite strong' in that 'behind the well-to-do middle peasants were landlords and rich peasants who gave them support'. Mao considered that the rightist attitude encouraged the growth of capitalism. According to Mao, the Liuist-led 'oppose rash advance' movement in 1956 'dampened the enthusiasm of the masses' which could jeopardize the mass line strategy and his anti-imperialist task (1977c:243–4). In the international realm, this was the time of the 'US-USSR collusion' against the PRC as Mao saw it.

In April 1956, Mao called for increased efforts into his scheme, with the emphasis that 'man definitely can defeat heaven (nature)' (人定胜天). However, together with Liu Shaoqi, Chen Yun and others, Zhou Enlai, who was branded 'almost a rightist', was opposed to Mao's call. Zhou claimed that, as premier, his 'oppose rash advance' stance was guided by conscience, arguing that Mao's 'rash advance' could jeopardize material supplies, which would result in more difficulties in the peasantry.[9] Zhou, though not a rightist, obviously disregarded the importance of the international environment in which the 'US-USSR colluded at the disadvantage of the China'. He was criticized in the various conferences in Nanning (11 January 1958), Hangzhou (19 January 1958), Chengdu (9 March 1958) and elsewhere.[10] Mao was even 'mad at Zhou' on a number of occasions.[11] Mao's cooperativization scheme called for the spirit of single-mindedness of the leadership and the masses. He argued that the rightist opposition was likened to pouring cold water on the 'revolutionary zeal' of the Party and the masses.[12] In autumn 1957, he claimed that the 'oppose rash advance' movements encouraged more rightist attacks.[13]

However, Zhou admitted his 'erroneous' stance, in attempt to avoid a Party split.[14] Further, towards the end of 1957, he revised Mao's grand plan of 'catching up with the Great Britain in 15 years' into 'catching up with the Great Britain in 15 years or a bit longer'.[15] He also deleted the words 'or a shorter time' in Mao's plan of 'fulfilling China's overall agricultural development in the next ten years or a shorter time'.[16] It seemed that Zhou had not fully considered the crucial importance of Mao's concept of 'world order of tripolarity', which, in principle, took priority over all other issues.

The collapse of the economy resulted in Mao's realization that 'capable generals are indispensable when a country faces the invasion by hostile forces; a virtuous housewife is badly needed for a poverty-stricken family'. He admitted that 'it was Enlai and Chen Yun who put the economy in order (during the three bad years)'.[17] 'Certainly', Mao continued, 'Zhou was credited for bailing me out' during the three bad years of (1959–61).[18]

With China's abundant labor, scarcity of capital, and technologically undeveloped condition, Mao could forgo mechanization before agricultural collectivization was realized *for the sake of uniting the masses.*[19] He argued that if China's agriculture 'could not make a leap from small-scale farming with animal-drawn farm implements to large-scale mechanized farming, then the contradiction between the ever increasing need for commodity grain and industrial raw materials and the generally low output of stable crops' could not be resolved (1977c:19–17). Liu Shaoqi condemned Mao's policy as a 'rash advance' toward full collectivization before the realization of the stage of agricultural mechanization.[20] However, Mao argued that Liu's policy of mechanization based on the Soviet experience as a guide could not make full use of the available population by mobilizing all human forces (and even animal forces) in the crucial drive for cooperativization.[21] According to Mao, the production and use of agricultural tractors and other farm machinery should only be considered on the basis of an agriculture where large-scale cooperative farming prevailed (1977c:197). He (1977c:197) criticized the Liuists for failing to see that China was now carrying out a revolution not only in the social system, a change from private to public ownership, but also in technology, a change from handicraft to large-scale modern machine production, and that the two revolutions were interconnected. Further, according to Mao, they failed to realize the link between the large funds, which were needed to accomplish both national industrialization and the technical transformation of agriculture, and the fact that a considerable part of these funds had to be accumulated through agriculture (1977c:197). Mao also argued that the large-scale expansion of light industry required the development of agriculture as well as of heavy industry and that only socialist cooperative agriculture could give peasants far greater purchasing power than they now possessed.

The important point Mao (1977c:198) emphasized was that by 'taking the stand of the bourgeoisie, the rich peasants or the well-to-do middle peasants with their spontaneous tendencies towards capitalism', the Liuists thought 'in terms of the few' and 'failed to think in terms of the interests of the whole country and people'. In his February 1957 thesis 'On the Correct Handling of Contradictions among the People', Mao (1977c:411–12) criticized the Liuists 'who vainly hope to restore the capitalist system' and whose 'right-hand men are the (Soviet) revisionists'. It is important to note that from then on Mao identified the Liuists with the 'capitalists' as well as the Soviet 'revisionists'.

The 1957 Rightist Onslaught

Nineteen fifty-seven was the crucial year when the advanced APC was set to be transformed into the commune. His 'three red banners' – the Party's general line for socialist construction, the Great Leap Forward and the people's commune were considered crucial to defense against the external aggressors. Thus the 1957 Anti-Rightist Struggle and Rectification Campaign was launched to safeguard the 'three red banners'. He was anxious about the rightist opposition to the Party leadership led by the Liuists through their various 'anti-rash advance' movements.

Starting from 1956, the intellectuals were given a degree of academic freedom. They were also allowed to criticize officials in order to improve the bureaucracy. Goldman (1987:242) contends that launching a new attempt in industrialization required the support of the intellectuals and professionals, while Harrison argues that Mao appeared to have wanted the intellectuals to 'educate' the Party cadres in strengthening their ties with the masses. Thus, starting from 1956, the intellectuals were given a degree of academic freedom. In addition, they were allowed to criticize officials in order to improve the bureaucracy. Zhou Enlai proposed certain reforms in order to arouse their enthusiasm. It was in this context that the Hundred Flowers Campaign was initiated in May 1956 to invite the people to criticize the ruling elite freely. According to Mao, 'as scientific truth, Marxism fears no criticism' and Marxists should suppress bourgeois tendencies not by force but by argument, using the slogan 'long-term co-existence and mutual supervision'. In consolidating the unity of the whole population, Mao made his 'Contradictions' speech at the end of February 1957, stressing the continuation of contradictions under socialism and 'certain contradictions existing between the government and the masses', although these, according to him, were primarily 'non-antagonistic' and 'among the people'.

However, the intellectuals and professionals began to call for more access to Western publications and ask for the London 'Hyde Park' type of free speech forums. Some pro-Western economists even questioned the relevance of Marxist economic theories in the PRC. In early June, Party leaders found that criticism was being directed against the guiding policies and leadership of the Party – a direct response to the growing student unrest. Moreover, the 'democratic' parties demanded that they be allowed independence from the CCP. In May 1957, Mao (1977c:411) warned that the inner Party 'revisionists' and the 'right-wing intellectuals outside the Party acted in concert' and that the anti-Party 'revisionists' inspired by Soviet 'revisionists' were 'more dangerous than dogmatism'. The 'rightists' were accused of 'paying lip-service to socialism, but actually admiring capitalism and Euro-American type of government'.[22] The PRC was being encircled by the United States. As Mao saw it, by sheer accident, the 'blooming and contending' campaign had led the anti-Party elements to expose themselves. Top CCP leaders decided that the 'blooming and contending' campaign was unacceptable if left unchecked. The period of free criticism was suspended and Mao (1977c:411) launched the Anti-Rightist Movement against 'bourgeois liberalism' in the public media. This certainly shattered the assumption of united national support for the Party. Mao criticized the bourgeois rightists, such as Zhang Bojun (章伯钧), Luo Longji (罗隆基) and the leaders of the Democratic Alliance and the Peasants-Workers Democratic Party as 'bourgeois reactionaries'. In his September 1957 'Report of Rectification' to the Third Plenum, Deng Xiaoping (1957:7) attacked the 'bourgeois rightists' for arguing that 'laymen cannot lead experts, and that Marxism is dogmatism, and that socialist countries are inferior to capitalist countries'. Reflecting bourgeois ideology and opposing centralism and Party leadership, the 'revisionists' were considered inspired by the Soviet 'revisionist' enemies.

In the realm of international relations, China's primary enemy was the United States, and Mao could not afford to let the 'rightists' undermine the Party leadership. This movement was primarily aimed at the bourgeoisie and intellectuals in the urban areas and members of the democratic parties. The

Anti-Rightist Campaign showed Mao's increasing concern that educated youth, China's future generation of leaders, had insufficient revolutionary consciousness. The campaign purged about half a million intellectuals, who were sent to the countryside and factories for reform.[23]

Zhou Enlai admitted that shortcomings had been pointed out earlier and declared that they were recognized by the highest leadership, who called for continued efforts to handle correctly 'contradictions among the people' and to overcome 'subjectivism, bureaucratism and sectarianism' which could not 'unite with all possible'.[24] Therefore, the 'rectification and improvement' movement was launched in September 1957 to replace the Anti-Rightist Campaign.[25]

Teiwes (1993:288) argues that official statements had interpreted that the aim of the 'rightists' was to overthrow the existing system and restore capitalism, and that the rightists were proposing institutional change including rotating democratic parties in power, establishing a genuine coalition government of all parties. However, I argue that it was not merely this which caused Mao's anxiety. The 'rightists' were hardly in a position to achieve their aims. It would be more likely that Mao was more concerned about the impact the 'rightists' would make, particularly through the press, on the society at large. The primary enemy's containment activities were in full swing. The year 1957 was a crucial year when the advanced APC was to be transformed into the defense-oriented commune. By mid-summer of 1957, it was reported that the events of the Hundred Flowers Campaign had adversely affected the rural situation, and criticism of the Party by 'bourgeois rightists' had encouraged landlords, rich peasants, and counter-revolutionaries to engage in anti-Party activities.[26] Equally important, the inner-Party 'revisionists were more dangerous than dogmatists'. All this threatened Mao's dictum of 'uniting with all possible' against the external primary enemy.

Thus, as articulated in his revised version of his 'Contradictions' speech, Mao's 'Anti-Rightist Struggle' focused on the theme of 'uniting with the people but not dividing them', in other words, to 'unite with all possible'.[27] In addition, in July at the Qing Dao Conference Mao called on Party members to carry out a rural socialist education movement to combat 'individualism, departmentalism and absolute egalitarianism' among cadres and to correct 'right opportunist' ideas within the Party.[28]

Understandably, Mao's rectification and improvement movement launched in September 1957 on the eve of the transformation of the advanced APC into the commune was aimed at uniting the great masses to counter the external pressure from US imperialism and Soviet 'revisionism'.

To sum up, first, Mao's collectivization scheme led to the Liuist 'rightist' onslaughts on a number of occasions, second, he felt that the 1957 rightist attack would dangerously undermine his scheme and the Party leadership. Thus, the anti-'rightist' purge was aimed at consolidating the whole population to face the external pressures of US imperialism and Soviet 'revisionism'.

Three Bad Years of 1959–1961 and the Emergence of 'Capitalist-cum-Revisionist' Economy

In the initial stage of the Great Leap Forward, differentiated and incentive rewards were increasingly replaced by an egalitarian wage system, causing a negative effect on labor productivity (Eckstein, 1975:287). At the same time, the approach of modern industrial technology and large-sized plants emphasized in the Soviet-dictated First Five-Year Plan was turned to indigenous production methods and small plants, which turned out to be detrimental to the economy (Eckstein, 1985:11). Harmed by a succession of agricultural setbacks starting in 1959 due primarily to unfavorable weather conditions that lasted for three years ('the worst in the century') and by the sudden withdrawal of Soviet advisers and technicians, agricultural output significantly declined, the economy was badly disrupted. As farm output worsened in 1960, Mao's mass labor mobilization plans were abandoned and the GLF discontinued (Eckstein, 1975:280). This resulted in a sharp decline in commercial crop output for light industry and subsequently a fateful blow to heavy industry. As a result, sources of investment funds dissipated (Chao, 1985:555). The winter of 1960–1 witnessed the worst food, agricultural and economic crises in the PRC since it came to power. Economic development was virtually brought to a standstill.

During the 'difficult period of 1959–61', a series of natural disasters exacerbated by the disastrous GLF led to a liberalization of agricultural policies and Liuist 'revisionist' policies were officially carried out. Measures were taken to increase material incentives through the '*san zi yi bao*' system, which allowed private plots and free markets, increased the number of small enterprises responsible for their own profits, and in some cases allowed peasants to leave communes to engage in private farming. The average size of the communes was also reduced through the transfer of much decision-making authority from the communes to production brigades and teams. Research works of Skinner and Richman confirm that by 1964 there was a re-appearance of former economic patterns based on material incentives for China's peasantry, while Hoffmann's study reveals the re-appearance of free markets in 1959 and the small private plots in 1960,[29] which created links between individual effort and compensation (Gurley, 1976, 215). At the height of international hostility, this 'revisionist' economic policy, which threatened the mass line, was certainly not acceptable to Mao. Further, at two enlarged Party and Central Committee work conferences in January–February 1962, Liu Shaoqi criticized the economic problems that resulted from Mao's GLF (Gurley, 1976, 215). Liu Shaoqi had partially 'reversed the verdicts' of the anti-rightist struggle and GLF, restoring Party positions to those dismissed. Thus, the 'struggle between two lines' flared up at both conferences. At the first conference Mao emphasized the need for continued 'protracted, complex and at times ... violent class struggle' because of the persistence of bourgeois ideology, and for guarding against a 'capitalist restoration' such as had been occurring in the USSR (Harrison, 1973:485).

The Great Proletarian Cultural Revolution of 1966–1969

For four decades Mao had been continuously combating the basic human defect of individualism – petty bourgeois thought – and more importantly, revisionism, in order to consolidate the Chinese masses against the external enemies. This culminated in his Great Proletarian Cultural Revolution of 1966–9. The basic aim of this movement was to break the Liuist political-economic apparatus with great power. The Liuist approach could not 'unite all who can be united' in the face of the threats of the twin superpowers.

Overtures of the Cultural Revolution can be traced back to 4 June 1958 in the *People's Daily* editorial entitled 'Modern Revisionism Must Be Fought to the End' in which the Maoists declared their 'fight against modern revisionism represented by the program of the Communists of Yugoslavia'. In their accusation of the 'Yugoslav revisionism' as product of US imperialist policy, they aimed at 'revisionist' Liu. They claimed that the so-called 'self-management of enterprises' carried out by the Tito government was fundamentally based on Western economic principles. The Maoists also claimed that in Yugoslavia the socialist planned economy had practically been abolished and state-owned factories and every enterprise of the national economy arbitrarily determined the output, variety and prices of its products according to the supply and demand situation in the market. In July 1961, the Maoists attacked 'the self-management of enterprises of the Tito clique of Yugoslavia', which were placed under 'independent' management of the so-called 'workers collectives' in the enterprises concerned (through the 'workers' councils' and 'administrative committees'). They aimed at Liu's 'revisionist' economic approach.[30] Under the Tito rule, the Yugoslav economy was subjected more and more to the economic system of the capitalist world. The 'revisionist' approach stressed 'material incentives' and encouraged capitalist methods of management.

In August 1962, Mao openly attacked the Liuist 'revisionists' at the Central Committee work conferences in Beidaihe. Bolstered by improved agricultural conditions, he curbed some particularly liberal features of the Liuist 'revisionist' policy established during the difficult period. At the

Tenth Plenum of the 8th Central Committee, held in September 1962, having secured the adoption of resolutions to halt the decentralization and liberalization of the communes, Mao renewed his emphasis on 'politics in command' under the slogan 'never forget class struggle'. His Socialist Education Movement of 1962–6 was launched in the rural areas to curb excessive emphasis on material incentives as understood in Liuist 'revisionist' policies (Harrison, 1973:485). Steps were taken to restrict 'small freedoms' including prohibiting the division of land among households, cutting back on excessive private plots, and tightening control over free markets and private speculative activities.

The Socialist Education Movement proceeded in several stages.

Firstly, from the winter of 1962 to mid-1964, the Party attacked errors in commune operations, especially basic level cadre corruption and the neglect of the mass line. This stage emphasized the 'four clean ups' campaign to rectify politics, ideology, organization and the economy (Harrison, 1973:486–7).

Secondly, Mao's 'first ten points' plan of leadership by 'poor and lower-middle' peasant rural work associations adopted by the Central Committee work conference in May 1963 had been revised by Liu at the September conference to emphasize lower-level Party leadership and material incentives. In the December 1964 Central Committee work conference, Mao's 'twenty-three points' were utilized to attack the Party's handling of the Socialist Education Movement for misinterpreting Mao's techniques of 'investigation' and the mass line (Harrison, 1973:488). The 'twenty-three points' were described as measures against Liuist 'spontaneous capitalist tendencies' prevailing in rural areas.

Thirdly, the movement to study of Mao Zedong Thought, initiated in August 1965 and directed at cadres and the masses alike, stressed 'self-reliance' and 'self-sacrifice' as well as the importance of collective interests.

Fourthly, the movement of 'criticism and self-criticism' was carried out from mid-October 1965 to March 1966 to rid *xian* Party secretaries of their 'mandarin-like work styles' and 'negative behavior of looking for stability' which had arisen from 'selfishness' and 'conservatism' thus disenabling them to 'unite with all who can be united'. It was in this period of Mao Zedong

Study movement and of emphasis in politics to 'take command' that the Socialist Education Movement merged into the Cultural Revolution.

In his major work *Maoism in Action: The Cultural Revolution*, Chiou (1974:47) compiled different interpretations of the Cultural Revolution and various schools and thought concerning its origins as follows:

First, the editors of the *Monthly Review* challenged Barry Richman's 'bets' against the workability of the Maoist classless society that the Cultural Revolution espoused. Second, Ellis Joffe, Benjamin Schwartz, Tadao Ishikawa, Kikuzo Ito and others of this school all contended that Mao was 'the guiding spirit and guiding hand of the campaign' to aim at 'eliminating his political opponents'. Third, Neale Hunter and later Chiou concurred with this group's pro-Mao argument that 'the Cultural Revolution was Maoism in action'. Chiou elaborated that Mao had to resolve China's basic or 'impossible problems' before it could become a nation that was not 'another revisionist Soviet Union or another capitalist modern nation'. Fourth, Chalmers Johnson and Richard Pfeffer argued that Mao initiated the campaign but 'unintended consequences diverted his forces from their long-term goals into emergency salvage operations'.

Apart from Chiou's argument, none of the other arguments above consider the crucial external factors related to Mao's movement. I argue that these schools of thought were meaningless without taking account of the importance of national defense in the face of 'collusion of US imperialism and Soviet revisionism at the disadvantage of China', which first emerged in January 1954.

The official explanation described the Cultural Revolution as a crucial battle in a long-term struggle between two lines: the Maoist line and the 'revisionist' line of 'China's Khrushchev', the 'No. 1 power holder in the Party taking the capitalist road, head of state and Mao's heir apparent Liu Shaoqi'. Liu was accused of being a 'traitor' and 'lackey of imperialism and modern revisionism'. The Great Proletarian Cultural Revolution of 1966–9 thus witnessed displacement of the 'leading persons in authority (who are) taking the capitalist road' and reinstatement of the fervor of popular revolution, mass participation and self-reliance. Most scholars agree that Mao launched the Cultural Revolution to forestall a 'capitalist restoration' in China, and eradicate ideological degeneration within the CCP.

However, I argue that Mao's Cultural Revolution to combat 'economism' or 'capitalistic backsliding' which deviated from a true Marxist-Leninist-Maoist path was, equally important, also to tap the people's power. Mao objected to Liuist 'revisionism' and 'capitalist restoration' because, as noted above, they could not 'unite all who can be united' to face the ferocious superpowers singly or in unison. The importance of national defense, to reiterate, first emerged in January 1954 in the face of the combined US imperialism and Soviet 'revisionism'.

Therefore, towards the end of January 1967, the *People's Daily*'s editorial called for 'the proletarian revolutionaries to form an alliance and launch an all-embracing mass struggle on a nationwide scale to seize power from those capitalist roaders in authority'.

I argue that the origins of Mao's Cultural Revolution can be traced back to Liu's consistent onslaughts on Mao's collectivization initiative starting in 1950. During the Cultural Revolution, Liu was accused of opposing labor-exchange teams, multi-aid teams and the development of collective economy.[31] Mao's acceleration of the process of his defense-oriented collectivization led to the onslaughts of the 'rightists' led by Liu Shaoqi on a number of occasions as discussed above.

Mao therefore avowed that the GPCR was merely the first of many such cultural revolutions – one of a continuing series of ideological rejuvenations needed to keep the communist spirit free of cancerous capitalistic poisons, which prevented the functioning of 'uniting with all possible'; these were the revolutions, which would constantly refresh China's true Marxism-Leninism-Maoism by re-affirming anti-economism, anti-elitism, and anti-intellectualism. Mao felt that even in a classless society 'restoration of capitalism', revisionism and 'the emergence of a new class' might hamper the dictum of 'uniting all who can be united'.

Mao's rectification campaigns launched virtually one after another over a period of forty years were primarily aimed at combating bourgeois attitudes and approaches. This showed Mao's determination to promote a selfless communist man and to unite the populace. These campaigns showed that Mao was obsessed with eradicating capitalist thought at any price, as bourgeois culture and approaches were detrimental to his strategy of uniting with all.

Mao's rectification campaigns launched virtually one after another over a period of forty years were primarily aimed at combating bourgeois attitudes and approaches. This showed Mao's determination to promote a selfless communist man and to unite the populace. These campaigns showed that Mao was obsessed with eradicating capitalist thought at any price, as bourgeois culture and approaches were detrimental to his strategy of 'uniting with all possible'. Mao thus did not aim just to create a communist man *per se*. My argument is that Mao endeavored to make a selfless man to defend against a potential imperialist-'revisionist' intrusion.

Mao's main objection to the economic strategy of Liu Shaoqi and associates during the three-year difficult period was to their advocacy of material incentives such as private plots, bonus payments, specific material rewards and free marketing. In 1959, the Liuist-styled decentralization of the Maoist commune organization took place. In the summer of 1960, as a result of the failure of the GLF, the so-called 'three-level management' was modified to 'three-level ownership', with the production brigade as the basic unit of authority for production management. In early 1961, the production brigades were made independent of the commune and were able to plan their production, while the communes were left with control only over its own enterprises. The production teams also were given specific guarantees to stabilize their position within the framework not of the communes but of the production brigades. Communes still had at its disposal a small labor force engaged in commune-owned industries but had no right to conscript labor from the brigades or teams as it had been in 1958 (Lethbridge, 1963:101–2). To Mao, these changes were characterized by divisiveness that severely undermined his dictum of 'uniting with all possible'. After 1962 Liuist measures were taken to stimulate agricultural recovery so that the patterns of production and distribution virtually reverted back to the advanced APC stage, with the commune providing only an overall administrative framework. In that year, another development catalyzed the downward shift from the brigade to the production team as the basic accounting unit in the countryside, a further decentralization of administrative power, thus neutralizing Mao's dictum further. This development meant that the production team virtually assumed full responsibility for organizing production, showing a slip back to the 'old' MATs and the elementary cooperatives (Lethbridge, 1963:105).

Liu Shaoqi's well-known material-oriented development theme appeared as early as 1949 in his 'Tienjing Talks'. During the Cultural Revolution, Liu was accused of advancing the idea of welcoming capitalist exploitation and developing capitalism, since the founding of the PRC.[32] In the years of 1956 and 1957, his industrial policy stressed private capitalism as expressed in his speeches such as 'Admitting Private Capitalists to Establish Factories for the Support of the Socialist Economy'. This philosophy was further advanced in his 1959 speech 'The Use of the Old-Styled Capitalism to Develop Commodity Economy' and his 1964 speech on 'Learning from Capitalism in Organizing Socialist Production'.

Mao's objection to Liu's pure economic policy was that it failed to take into account the crucial international situation. Although Liu's tightly structured and hierarchically centralized Party apparatus did play an important role in revitalizing the nation's fragile economy in the 'three bad years', his bureaucratized elitist Party machinery based on technocratic 'expertise', centralism and a 'careerist' professional cadre undermined Mao's revolutionary 'redness', 'democratic centralism' and revolutionary cadre approach (Chiou, 1974:47). Mao argued that Liuist economic policy would create a gulf between the masses and the Party and, in the long run, a capitalist trend of exploitation of the majority by the minority, thus hindering the 'uniting all who can be united'. This made counteracting potential imperialist intrusion impossible. China was confronting the 'US-USSR cooperation'. Without considering the grave international situation China faced, Liu's pure economic strategy was aimed at 'liberating and developing the productive forces' as advocated in his work 'National Industrialization and Raising the Levels of the People's Livelihood'. As early as February 1957, in his 'Contradictions' speech, Mao criticized Liu who 'vainly hoped to restore the capitalist system' with the 'Soviet revisionists as his right hand men'.

Uniting with the great majority of the people necessitated the inculcation of proletarian culture and attitudes among the masses. However, characteristic of Liu's bourgeois approach, which was at variance with the socialist economic base, was the factor of bureaucratization in his Party organization. Mao considered that this would inevitably lead to revisionism, for bureaucracy bred 'bureaucratism' owing to its inherent hierarchical, elitist, 'expertist', 'careerist' 'professional' and 'centralist' (rather than 'democratic centralist') elements. These elements, which would lead to competition, inequality and hence exploitation, could not unite with the majority of the masses. In contrasting Mao 'redness' with Liu's pro-Soviet revisionist 'expertise', the latter was designed for the minority and could not help amass the power of the people needed for his anti-imperialist and anti-'revisionist' endeavors. However, 'redness' was designed for 'uniting with all possible' with one mind. This called for Mao's approach of 'politics in command'.

However, Mao believed that 'redness' and 'expertise' can coexist but that the former could enhance the latter in order to reap positive results. Mao evidently argued that with the approach of 'redness' and 'politics in command', science and technology would only be effective on a large scale if 'all' united. This was because Mao's mass line approach was initiated to raise not only the living standard for everyone at the same time, but also the long-term well-being of the collective, a crucial anti-imperialist and anti-'revisionist' tool. The element of collective selflessness needed to be promoted to encourage Mao's mass mobilization.

The Cultural Revolution witnessed the adoption of a Maoist guerrilla military style even further. For instance, soldiers were assigned the work of running farms and helping communes (Robinson, 1970:32). It was in this context that Robinson wrote: 'The old guerrilla tradition, that the Army is fish swimming in the waters of the people, is cherished more than ever' (Robinson, 1970:32).

The Second Purge of 'Right Opportunist' Peng Dehuai

In the midst of the Cultural Revolution, the mid-August 1959 'Resolution of the Eighth Plenary Session of the Eighth Central Committee of CCP Concerning the Anti-Party Clique Headed by Peng Teh-huai' reappeared in the mid-August 1967 issue of the *Peking Review*. This was aimed at purging 'Khrushchev-supported revisionist' Peng for the second time. In the *Peking Review* issue that followed, the Maoists claimed that Peng's 'anti-Party activities had not only Liu Shaoqi – "China's Khrushchev" – as behind-the-scenes boss, they were also supported and encouraged by the Soviet Union's Khrushchev'.[33] The struggle against the Soviet-backed 'Right Opportunism' was carried out in the second half of the year 1959 as discussed above.

Deng Xiaoping: The 'No. 2 Capitalist Roader'

Finally, in the following section, I will consider Deng Xiaoping's position during the Cultural Revolution.

Our discussion above has shown that Mao launched the Cultural Revolution primarily to circumvent the 'rightist-revisionist' policy of Liu Shaoqi who, beginning in 1950, had consistently and systematically opposed Mao's political economic policy. In addition, Liu had planned to put the future of Mao's communization project in jeopardy. Therefore Liu's fate was sealed right from the beginning. Although Deng was 'the No. 2 capitalist roader', there was hardly any evidence to show that he had systematically tried to jeopardize Mao's general political and economic policy.

It is my belief that Deng (1994:115) honestly disagreed with Mao's GLF and the commune, which could not effectively develop or could undermine the productive forces. His disagreement might not have taken into consideration the international perspective as the primary issue. All this could not be considered as 'treasonous'. He was 'treated differently' compared with Liu Shaoqi, 'the Chinese Khrushchev' or with Peng Dehuai who was opposed to Mao's GLF with 'Khrushchev's encouragement'. Therefore Mao would have considered Deng Xiaoping's 'attempt to reverse correct verdicts' of the Cultural Revolution from a different angle.

Deng's staunch Marxist stance was well known even long after the Cultural Revolution. For instance, he persistently emphasized the domination of public ownership in the national economy, which was integrated with the post-1971 budding market economy. Deng adopted Mao's mass line strategy for the four modernizations scheme. Furthermore, in his attempt to raise the living standard of the people, Deng consistently promoted a 'non-capitalist' stance to prevent the growth of capitalism. This was because, according to him, capitalism would lead to the polarization of wealth. Although given the 'cap of a capitalist roader', Deng saw the capitalist economic approach as a solution to the mass famine, as shown in his statement: 'What did it matter', asked Deng once, 'whether the cat was black or white – as long as it caught the mouse?' Although the capitalist economic measures of Liu Shaoqi enabled the Chinese economy to recover from the disastrous conditions partly created by the GLF, Liu's Soviet approach with his emphasis on the primacy of the Party as organization implicitly denied Mao's 'redness', his revolutionary cadre policy and so forth. This Liuist approach, in the long run, had detrimental effects on Mao's basic policy for 'uniting all who could unite'. The crux of the matter was that in 1954 the Soviet 'revisionists' emerged and began to collude with the United States against the PRC threatening its survival. 'Revisionism' means the 'liberalization' of economic policies and the application of capitalist methods such as over-emphasis on 'expertise' and material incentives to run the economy (Chiou, 1974:48). On the surface, Mao considered the Soviet approach to be a betrayal of the Marxist principles. However, more importantly, Mao's real concern was the implications of this 'revisionist' approach. This was because the Soviet Union 'co-existed with the US-led West' and was the 'No. 1 accomplice of the US' against China. Understandably, Deng, who had never been considered 'treasonous', was 'capped' with the name of 'capitalist roader', and banished to Nanchang in Jiangxi province but was rehabilitated after the Cultural Revolution. The point is that Mao considered Deng's 'political attitude is strong'.[34] In March 1973, Deng's Vice-Premiership was restored. In addition, in January 1973, he was made Vice-Chairman of the CCP, Vice-Chairman of the Central Military Committee as well as Chief-of-Staff of the PLA. In March 1973 Deng's Vice-Premiership was restored. In addition, in January 1975, he was made Vice-Chairman of the CCP, Vice-Chairman of the Central Military Committee as well as Chief-of-Staff of the PLA. On the other hand, as 'China's Khrushchev', the 'treasonous' Liu, was critically different.

US Love Signaling and China's Response

I discussed above Mao's prediction of, as well as the break-up of, the Sino-Soviet relations. I also mentioned that none of the Westerners took his hints about his wish to improve the PRC's relationships with the United States, before he launched his Cultural Revolution in 1966.

Back to January 1965, in answering Edgar Snow, who had asked if there was any hope for improved Sino-US relations, Mao had said 'yes'. He implied that the major threat to China came from the Soviet Union and that there were corresponding prospects for Sino-US cooperation (Li, 2001:306). Further, understanding that the US-Soviet conflict was the paramount global contradiction, on two occasions, in January 1964 and mid-September 1965, he told visitors 'this contradiction can never be resolved' (Li, 2001:296).

Meanwhile, the United States unavoidably slid into the Vietnam quagmire. Anti-war dissent grew and spread. President Johnson's attempt to prevent the war from disturbing his own domestic program was in vain. The Tet Offensive, though carried out at a terrible cost to Communist strength, turned itself into a psychological defeat for the United States. Instead of ordering a counterattack, Johnson removed himself from the 1968 presidential campaign. In 1968, Vietnam finally forced Americans to face the limits of their resources and will. There was increasing domestic opposition to the War particularly by young people, who dominated anti-War demonstrations in the United States. Protests began in the spring of 1965 and grew in intensity as the numbers of young men sent to Vietnam increased. Whoever succeeded, Johnson would have little choice but to find a way to get out from Vietnam. With further relief, Mao was able to dismiss the 'No. 1 power holder in the Party taking the capitalist road' by launching the Cultural Revolution.

Washington's prolonged Vietnam War had incurred heavy financial and human losses and produced a profound social and political crisis. This compelled the United States to re-evaluate its foreign policy in relation to China. In an article in the October 1967 issue of *Foreign Affairs* entitled 'Asia after Vietnam', Nixon wrote: 'efforts to contain China should not become a permanent policy leaving the PRC to live in angry isolation'. In his *Memoirs*, he (1978:347) also wrote: 'The most pressing foreign problem I would have to deal with as soon as I became President was the war in Vietnam'. To manage its Vietnam problem, the US would have to deal with China, because China provided crucial support to Hanoi (Nixon, 1978:384).

Responding to the new Kissinger-Nixon Doctrine, which called for gradual withdrawal of the US from Northeast and Southeast Asia, Mao saw a golden opportunity to normalize the Sino-US relations in the face of the Soviet threat. Therefore, encouraged by the theme of the historical novel: 'the world under the heavens, long divided, must unite', which he interpreted as 'the Sino-US relations, long divided, must unite', Mao initiated the so-called 'ping-pong (table tennis) diplomacy', which led to Kissinger's secret mission to Beijing in the year 1971. With President Nixon's China visit in 1972, this unavoidably led to the decisive changes of China's relations with the superpowers in Mao's global order of tripolarity. I will deal with the new Sino-US relations in more details in the next chapter.

Conclusion

In the international perspective, Mao perceived not only 'Soviet-US collusion' against the PRC, but also Soviet-US hostility in his tripolar worldview. Inspired by the theme of the *Romance of the Three Kingdoms*, which he saw as 'the US, long divided, must unite' with China, he tried, though in vain, to befriend her at the expense of the Soviet Union during the period 1959–69. However, in addition to Soviet problems at home and US-Soviet contention in Europe and their brinkmanship in the Cuba Crisis, the Soviet disengagement and American quagmire in Vietnam brought relief to the PRC. It was good timing for Mao to launch his Cultural Revolution as part of the Sino-US acrimonious exchange. The PRC supported North Vietnam against the United States in the Vietnam War.

Liu Shaoqi's strategy, which was of purely Western economic origin, neglected the crucial, realistic power politics. In his capitalist approach, which Mao considered dangerously detrimental to his mass line, Liu ignored the simple fact that the Soviet Union had emerged as the *de facto* enemy since 1945 and become 'No. 1 accomplice of the US primary enemy' since 1954 in Mao's worldview.

Mao's Cultural Revolution would have been delayed or his decision to launch the movement could even have been changed, if the United States had grasped the meaning of his hints 'to swim in the Mississippi River' in the mid-1960s. However, it was towards the end of the 1960s that a golden opportunity for the normalization of the Sino-US relations appeared, and stimulated by the theme of the historical novel with the US as the non-antagonistic secondary enemy in his global order of tripolarity, Mao staged his 'ping-pong diplomacy' in 1971, which I will consider in the next chapter.

CHAPTER SEVEN

1969–1976 Period of Tripolarity: Sino-US Courtship and Mao's Modernization Initiatives in Western Economic Style

The previous chapters surveyed Mao's defense-related development model initiated to counter the US imperialist threat or the 'US-USSR collusion against China'. In this chapter, I will consider that in response to US President Nixon's new foreign policy of the late 1960s with the relatively less hostile US attitude towards the PRC, he personally initiated ping-pong diplomacy in March 1971, leading to President Nixon's visit to China the following year. These developments made China's quest for modernization possible. Mao's modernization scheme, which adopted elements of Western 'individualistic' economic style, was initiated to befriend the United States at the expense of the Soviet Union in his global order of tripolarity. All this showed the valid application of the famous theme emphasized at the beginning of the first chapter and towards the end of the last chapter of the *Romance of the Three Kingdoms*, which Mao often referred to: 'empires under the heavens long divided must unite and vice versa'.[1] First of all, let us consider the international environment of the period 1969–76.

The USSR as Primary Enemy and the US as Secondary Enemy: 1969–1976

In Mao's global order of tripolarity, his perception of the Soviet Union as primary enemy and the US as non-antagonistic secondary enemy began to come into focus as early as 1969 as a result of Soviet President Brezhnev's hostile new policy, which was not officially acknowledged until 1 October 1972.[2]

As discussed above, Sino-Soviet relations worsened throughout the 1960s as the Soviets reinforced their forces along the Sino-Soviet and Sino-Mongolian borders and signed a treaty of friendship and cooperation with Mongolia. This suggested a military alliance directed against China.[3] Sino-Soviet relations clearly took a new turn in August 1968, with the Soviet invasion of Czechoslovakia. While other elements remained roughly the same as in 1965, the Chinese worldview from 1968–9 gradually shifted, with the Soviet Union replacing the United States as the primary enemy. It was not merely the Russian invasion of Czechoslovakia, but, more important, the Soviet announcement of the Brezhnev Doctrine of Limited Sovereignty in November 1968 that accelerated the Chinese perception of possible Russian military action against the PRC. This underscored the Chinese fear that the Indo-Pakistani War was taking place, as the Soviets claimed, 'in direct proximity to the border of the Soviet Union',[4] and therefore 'involve(d) the interests of Soviet Union'. According to the Chinese, this was the sort of Japanese argument which had led to the Japanese invasion of North China before the Second World War. Similarly it was also the Russian argument that justified the Russian invasion of Czechoslovakia in 1968.[5] Obsessive Chinese fear of Soviet nuclear attack resulted in the construction of vast, fully-stocked 'underground cities' in Beijing, Shanghai, Canton and other major population centers. This was followed in mid-1969 by what the Chinese perceived as a Soviet revival of John Foster Dulles' containment policy of the 1950s – the practice of an 'Asian Collective Security System'. As a result of the skirmish on the Sino-Soviet border in 1969, a massive military concentration in the Soviet Far East and Outer Mongolia was established, and this seemed to confirm the intentions of the USSR as advanced in the Brezhnev Doctrine. The Chinese argued that Brezhnev's Asian collective security system was designed to 'edge out' US influence and establish Soviet hegemony in Asia. After attempting to foster military alliances with the PRC's neighbors similar to its agreement with India in 1971, the Russians increased their military and political pressure in Asia. It thus became increasingly clear that the USSR had replaced the US as the 'most ferocious' primary enemy of China. In mid-September 1969, the PRC government declared to the world that it was prepared to fight a nuclear war against the Soviet Union.

The Chinese believed that the Russians were aiming at establishing hegemony over the Eurasian landmass, though China in the East and the Atlantic alliance in the West were obstacles to this ambition. The Chinese argued that the USSR's strategic plan was to establish an entire ring of pro-Soviet nations around China's borders, with naval bases and a fleet operating from the Soviet Union stretching from East Siberia through the Soviet Western Asian region, and joining the nations fringing the Indian Ocean, from Asian Minor to Southeast Asia. Thus Mao needed to re-orient his foreign policy with respect to the two superpowers, in order to combat the Soviet threat as China's primary concern. Facing China's two-front threat, Mao sought to reduce Sino-US tensions and enhance the international united front against Soviet hegemony.

In the following section, I will first argue about the shift in Chinese perception of the US superpower from primary enemy to secondary enemy.

Towards the end of the last chapter, we mentioned that, back to January 1965, in answering Edgar Snow, who had asked if there was any hope for improved Sino-US relations, Mao had said 'yes'. He implied that the major threat to China came from the Soviet Union and that there were corresponding prospects for Sino-US cooperation.[6] In addition, understanding that the US-Soviet conflict was the paramount global contradiction, on two occasions, in January 1964 and mid-September 1965, he told visitors 'this contradiction can never be resolved'.[7]

The Chinese argued that the struggle between the two superpowers to 're-divide the world' was bound to become ever more violent. Their struggle for hegemony, they continued, reached every corner of the world. However, according to the Chinese, Europe was the focus of their rivalry. And striving for hegemony there, both bitterly contended over its flanks – the Middle East, the Mediterranean and the Balkan area. In the view of the superpowers, the Chinese argued, the one who controlled the region could influence developments in Europe.

Washington's prolonged Vietnam War had incurred heavy financial and human losses and produced a profound social and political crisis. This compelled the United States to re-evaluate its foreign policy in relation to

China. In an article in the October 1967 issue of *Foreign Affairs* entitled 'Asia after Vietnam', Nixon (1978:347) wrote: 'efforts to contain China should not become permanent policy leaving the PRC to live in angry isolation'. In his *Memoirs*, he also wrote: 'The most pressing foreign problem I would have to deal with as soon as I became President was the war in Vietnam'. To manage its Vietnam problem, the US would have to deal with China, because China provided crucial support to Hanoi (1978:348). In response, on November 26, 1968, Beijing proposed to the United States a resumption of ambassadorial-level talks in Warsaw. Three days later, Johnson, the outgoing President, encouraged by president-elect Nixon, accepted China's proposal. Although the actual resumption of the talks was delayed, this was the first sign of détente in Sino-US relations. In his inaugural address on 20 January 1969, Nixon again signaled his interest in improving relations with the PRC: 'We seek an open world, a world in which no people, great or small, will live in angry isolation'.[8] In his work *White House Years*, Kissinger (1979:685) wrote that US leaders now understood the importance of having 'contact with ... one quarter of humanity'. On 21 July 1969 the United States cancelled certain sanctions against the PRC and relaxed limitations on travel to China (Li, 2001:314). In August 1969 Nixon lifted the travel and trade ban, allowing his Secretary of State William Rogers to signal interest in opening a dialogue. Crucially, in November 1969, he also terminated regular Seventh Fleet patrols in the Taiwan Straits (Foot, 2001:286).

Therefore, grasping the full significance of the above statements and events, Mao made the following two crucial moves:

First, On 1 October 1970, Mao received Edgar Snow on the Tiananmen rostrum and had his photograph taken with Snow at his side. The photo appeared on the front page of the *People's Daily* along with Mao's statement that 'people from all over the world including the people from the US are our friends'.[9]

Second, on 21 March 1971, after six years of absence, China entered the Thirty-first World Table Tennis Championship Competition in Nagoya, Japan. According to his nurse Wu Xujun (吴旭君), the decision was made by Mao himself who subsequently instructed a team member Zhuang Zedong (庄则栋) to skillfully invite the American team members to visit

China (Wu, 2005:346–53). Therefore Mao initiated the so-called 'ping-pong (table tennis) diplomacy', which led to Kissinger's secret mission to Beijing that year. This unavoidably led to the decisive changes of China's relations with the superpowers in Mao's global order of tripolarity, with President Nixon's China visit in 1972.

These moves, which led to the normalization of the Sino-US relations, Mao told Wu, were considered from the standpoint of his concept of the global tripolarity of the United States, Soviet Union and China; and his aim was to collude with the United States in isolating the Soviet Union as well as in Western capital and technology transfers (Wu, 2001:346–53). This was confirmed by W. A. McDonald (2002:871). The rapprochement with the United States brought twenty years of confrontation and mutual suspicion to an end and eventually reduced the US military presence in the Asia Pacific region. Importantly, it promoted the normalization of bilateral relations and paved the way to improved relations with other Western countries and Japan. These developments made China's quest for modernization possible, while helping to contain Soviet expansion. This initiative seemed to further the establishment of trade relations with the United States, Japan and Europe, and, importantly, a gradual adoption of the elements of the Western 'individualistic' liberal economic model (Gurley, 1976:224). Mao was eager to acquire Western capital and modern technology for his modernization initiatives.

However, the previous chapters surveyed Mao's dismissal of the 'right opportunist' Peng Dehuai in 1959 as acrimonious dispute with the Soviet Union and his purge of the 'capitalist-cum-revisionist' Liu Shaoqi during the Cultural Revolution period 1965–9 as acrimonious exchange with the United States. First, 'Right Opportunist' Peng Dehuai was opposed to his defense-oriented communization agenda. His widespread opposition was encouraged by the Soviets. Second, Mao's determination to wipe out capitalist thought and prevent the 'restoration of capitalism' associated with the US primary enemy was hindered by the Liuist 'revisionist' economic approach. Mao perceived that starting in 1954 the twin superpowers 'colluded at the disadvantage of the PRC'. His attempt to consolidate the great masses of the Chinese population by accelerating the process of his collectivization scheme motivated the Liuist 'rightist' onslaughts on a number of occasions. In addition, during the 'difficult period of 1959–61', the Liuist 'revisionist' agricultural policies were carried out. Liu Shaoqi's purely economically-oriented strategy neglected the crucial realistic power politics. His 'revisionist' approach was considered dangerously detrimental to Mao's mass line strategy. Liu's 'rightist-cum-revisionist' plans and his opposition to Mao's communization endeavors inevitably led to Mao's launching of his Cultural Revolution.

Sino-US rapprochement was needed by both sides in the face of the threat of expansionist Soviet Union, their respective adversary. In mid-February 1973, during a meeting in Zhongnanhai, both Mao and Kissinger confirmed that their countries 'face(d) the same danger' and that their 'target (was) identical' (Gong, 2001:357). Clearly, in the first half of the 1970s, Soviet expansionism was Mao's principal concern, superseding the Taiwan issue. Mao told Kissinger in 1972: 'The small issue is Taiwan, the big issue is the world' (Kissinger, 1994:726). With the United States also now relegated to the secondary position, the Soviet Union became China's primary enemy.

The Sino-Soviet border talks, which lasted more than a year and a half, failed, and the prospect that Sino-Soviet hostility might be relieved, faded.[10] The period 1972–6 witnessed the Chinese attempts to break out of the 'Soviet containment' ring as follows:

The Chinese elevated the Second Intermediary Zone, vitally comprised Europe and Japan, into the Second World as evidenced in Mao's (1999b:441) conversation with Zambia's President Kaunda in February 1974 on the question of the 'Three Worlds'. Europe and Japan appeared to be considered the primary areas of potential Soviet weakness, where the PRC could disrupt the Soviet containment ring *from the outside* before it could be successfully established. In this light, it was clear that the Chinese attack on 'superpower hegemony' in Europe was primarily meant to incite Western Europe to stand up against Russian hegemony. Similarly, the Chinese incitement of anti-Soviet feeling in Japan was understandable. Second, Deng Xiaoping's speech in the United Nations in April that year under the cover of anti-superpower hegemony aimed to win over as many nations of the First and Second Intermediary Zones as possible. The Chinese scheme was aimed at not only persuading West Europe and

Japan to go against the Soviet Union, but also the 'friendly' Africans to exert more pressure on the Soviet southern flank, thus posing a threat to the Russian Black Sea maritime outlet.

The Chinese also tried to persuade the relevant Third World nations to defuse the Soviet strategic points along its containment ring. This explained why the PRC, since entering the United Nations, had aligned itself firmly with the Third World by stressing coordination of economic and armed struggles, and 'setting up, or taking over, international conferences and organizations to institutionalize this economic and geo-political warfare' (Adie, 1974, 36).

Mao's new concept of the 'Three Worlds' (三分天下), was inspired by the famous theme of the historical novel *Romance of the Three Kingdoms*, which he interpreted as: 'Empires under the heavens long divided must unite, and vice versa.' As noted above, he often referred to the theme. At the Sixth Special Session of the UN General Assembly in April 1974, Deng Xiaoping referred to Mao's skilful new concept of the Three Worlds as follows:

(1) The First World, which consisted of 'the imperialist United States and the hegemonic Soviet Union',
(2) The Second World, which belonged to the advanced Western European industrialized nations, Japan and the Oceanic nations, and
(3) The Third World, in which China was the leading developing nation.

The focus of Mao's 'Three Worlds' was his global order of tripolarity of China and the First World. This was a revised version of Zhuge Liang's 'international' order of tripolarity, with the realistic conditions of the contemporary world of his time.

Mao's concept of the 'Three Worlds' was fundamentally formulated to contend with the primary enemy of the First World, i.e., the hegemonic Soviet Union, while aiming to collude with the secondary enemy of this First World, i.e., the imperialist United States. In addition, his contention with the Soviet primary enemy was carried out actively, whether directly or indirectly, through inciting the Third world nations or even Second World nations to unite against the Soviet Union. For instance, the period 1972–6 witnessed the Chinese attempt to break out of the Soviet containment by trying to win over as many nations of the Second and Third Worlds as possible, as exemplified by Deng Xiaoping's appeal to the United Nations in April 1974, as mentioned above.

Mao's 'Three Worlds' strategic concept was crystal clear as shown in Deng Xiaoping's (1983:158) statements that 'Comrade Mao formulated the strategy ... to usher personally in a new stage in Sino-American relations.; (and) by so doing he created new conditions for the development of the worldwide struggle against hegemonism and for the future of world politics'. He continued to argue that 'China should ... try to win over the second-world countries for a concerted effort against hegemonism, and establish normal diplomatic relations with the United States'.

While the Chinese established their counter-containment ring, the Soviets began to reconcile with the NATO nations. By the mid-1970s, they had strengthened their cooperation with the French and validated the Soviet-West German Treaty, the West Berlin Agreements, the Polish-West German Treaty, and the East-West Germany Basic Relations Treaty, etc. With great effort, they had taken part in the preparatory talks of Helsinki's European Security and Cooperation Conference and Agreements, and of Vienna's European Arms Reduction Conference. This indicated that the Soviets had tried to relax tensions in Europe. The Chinese considered that easing tensions between East and West in Europe would enable the Russians to pay more attention to their eastern front, however. Nixon's Year of Europe, that is, his doctrine of self-sufficiency of 1973, was designed to establish a new Atlantic Charter of self-reliance within the EEC while the ongoing US-USSR detente would assure West Europeans that the Soviet threat to their security would be minimal. But the Chinese tended to see the desired new Atlantic Charter as a rationale for US withdrawal. They feared that the achievement of a true US-USSR detente in Europe would leave the Russians free to concentrate their military might along the Sino-Soviet borders. Thus, the Chinese encouraged West Europeans to resist the US-imposed Year of Europe, wanting the NATO alliance to counter-balance Russia's western front. In the East, moreover, the Soviet threat to Chinese borders was real. Therefore, Chinese land troops, bomb shelters, population decentralization, and so on were prepared for this eventuality.

In East Asia, with the urgent need to counteract the Soviet 'Asian Collective Security System', China needed to acquire Japan's acceptance of an anti-hegemonic clause as a basis for Sino-Japanese reconciliation. This explained why 'the PRC intimated that she preferred maintenance of Japan's security arrangements with the US' (Deng, 1983:158). It was an attempt to resist the USSR's plan of containment of China through Japan. The new Sino-Japanese communique repeated the anti-hegemonic clause in the Nixon-Zhou statement in Shanghai was an indication that China, Japan and the United States now came to accept the new terms of international relations in the Asia Pacific region.

Even in Eastern Europe, beginning in the early 1970s, the Chinese had begun to strengthen their already cordial relations with Albania, and to improve their relations with Yugoslavia, Romania, and others. This was aimed at disrupting the Soviet control of the East European communist nations so as to puncture the Soviet containment ring throughout that part of the world. Since the visits to Beijing by Romania's Ceausescu and the Foreign Minister of Yugoslavia in the summer of 1971, the Chinese had attempted to intrude, diplomatically, in the Warsaw Pact states. This was to encourage revival of the idea of regional Balkan cooperation, which without doubt was to weaken the cohesion of the Soviet bloc. From the beginning of 1973, the Chinese started to improve their relations with Bulgaria, Hungary, East Germany, Poland, Czechoslovakia, and others.[11]

It should be noted that, generally speaking, although Mao's maneuvers did not help much in isolating the Soviet Union, China's role in the tripolar relationships was crucial.

By 1972, the Nixon administration not only had reversed the American China policy, but also reached a détente with the Soviet Union. Nixon's visit to Beijing led to fuller diplomatic exchanges, in an apparent effort to form a counterweight to Soviet power. His trip to Moscow three months later produced economic and military results. A massive US grain deal was completed with the Soviet Union. The need to repair the Soviet image in the wake of the Prague Spring and the chronic Soviet need for agricultural imports and access to superior Western technology were all powerful incentives for seeking détente. In 1973, Soviet Party leader Leonid Brezhnev visited the United States, where he and President Nixon signed a nuclear non-aggression pact.

Further, American initiatives with the Soviet Union helped maintain peace in the Middle East until 1973. After war broke out again, the United States and the Soviet Union re-imposed a ceasefire between Israel and its Arab neighbors through the United Nations. A treaty, ending America's long war with North Vietnam concluded in January 1973, was built on the tacit support of China and the Soviet Union. During his first three years in office, Carter continued a policy of détente with the Soviet Union, though the US administration discontinued its campaign to urge the ratification of the SALT II nuclear arms limitation treaty, an accord that had been signed by President Carter and Soviet leader Brezhnev in Vienna in June 1979.

Dictated by the new international environment, China now treated the Soviet Union as its primary enemy with the United States seen as a non-antagonistic secondary enemy. Chinese maneuvers in the Second and Third worlds were aimed at disrupting Soviet containment of China and establishing a counter-containment ring. More important, Mao was now in a position to advance his new economic strategy in line with the Western economic model. While aiming to open up China to the outside world to tap capital and science and technology from the US-led Western world for his modernization initiatives, he also adopted the Western liberal 'individualistic' economic approach to 'improve the livelihood of the people' overall. Equally important, the adoption of these Western economic features was a gesture of friendship towards the West. The new international environment made all this possible. In the next section, I will delve into Mao's new development strategy.

Western Economic Approach to 'Befriend' the US

With the new international environment conducive to his scheme of opening up his country to the outside world, Mao initiated relaxed economic policies to improve the livelihood of the people. His economic approach was to 'befriend' the US-led Western countries.

As far back as April 1945, Mao (1967e:252) had already argued about the importance of industrialization as follows: 'Without industry there can be no solid national defense, no well being for the people, no prosperity or strength for the nation'. Clearly, Mao argued about the importance of the modernization of China's agriculture and industry. This was the same view of Marx that the growth of natural science had enabled modernization, through industry, to transform the life of man. Following this reasoning, with the influence of science and technology, Marx envisaged the true emancipation of mankind. In the following, I will first deal with Mao's original plan of the mid-1950s for transforming the lives of the people, a quarter of mankind, through the modernization of agriculture and industry.

In February 1957, in discussing China's path to industrialization, Mao stressed the importance of agriculture to the growth of heavy and light industry. This was because: 'As China is a large agricultural country, *with over 80 per cent of its population in the rural areas*, agriculture must develop along with industry, for only thus can industry secure raw materials and a market for building a powerful heavy industry' (1977c:419) (emphasis added). However, in his celebrated paper 'The Situation in the Summer of 1957', Mao urged the Chinese to 'build a modern industry and modern agriculture and the way is to seek truth from facts and *follow the mass line*'. (Emphasis added). This was because, according to him, 'without good relations between the Party and *the masses*, the socialist system cannot be established or, once established, be consolidated' *for the very purpose of defense against the primary enemy* (1977c:477). In the summer of 1957, the United States remained China's primary enemy but the Soviet Union had begun to emerge as the 'No. 1 accomplice of US imperialism'. Mao had to concentrate his efforts on his political mobilization to realize his communization scheme.

In December 1959, with the basic purpose of 'improving the livelihood of the people', Mao initiated his plan of socialist transformation based on 'the four modernizations' of industry, agriculture, science and technology, and defense.[12] In March 1960, stressing the importance of the peaceful and stable international situation for 'China's modernization of agriculture, industry, scientific culture and defense', he (1999b:152) urged the Chinese to 'strengthen scientific reform and technological revolution' as he put it. In December 1963, he (1999b:351) argued that without science and technology, the production forces will not be developed. As noted above, prior to 1971, Mao's plan could not have been put into practice, owing to the hostile international environment. During the period 1953–70, Mao made the commune system a priority in his defense-oriented national development.

With the new international environment favorable to the PRC in the early 1970s, Mao was in a position to launch his modernization efforts to aim at 'improving the livelihood of the people' in the real sense. His modernization initiatives were meant to open up China to the outside world in order to tap capital inflow and science and technology particularly from the US-led Western world. A characteristic of 'improving the livelihood of the people' with science and technology of the US-led Western world was a hallmark of Mao. This was the spirit that drove Mao to 'strive for the Four Modernizations with one mind to remove Mt. Tai'.[13] This was the same spirit the post-Mao leadership exhibited when urging the people to 'remove China's two mountains of economic and technological backwardness'.[14] This spirit was important to Mao and the post-Mao leadership, because it not only stimulated their visions to realize their modernization scheme, but also provided the theoretical base to acquire the astronomical power to carry out the plan. This meant that only in a peaceful and stable international environment could the 'mountains of economic and technological backwardness' be uplifted with the Western economic principles and the advanced science and technology of the world especially the US-led Western countries. Deng Xiaoping (1994:190, 358) called this 'ning ju li' (凝聚力), that is, 'concentrated power' or 'astronomical power'.

It has been argued unceasingly that Mao's political campaigns and movements carried out since 1950 to 'wipe out capitalism from the face of the earth' led to the neglect of effective economic development. In addition, it is argued, too much national time was spent on class struggle, which aimed at changing human nature to embrace selfless communism. This school of thought has also argued that since 1957 there had been very little improvement in economic performance in both rural and urban areas and that very low rural living standards persisted thirty years after the CCP had seized power with peasant support. Despite the egalitarian Maoist policy, it goes on, inequalities persisted. This school of thought has often argued about the 'ten lost years' and even the 'twenty lost years' caused by Mao's Cultural Revolution. It has also contended that compared with the modernization of other countries in the region particularly Japan and the Four Little Dragons, China's progress had been marginal and that the Cultural Revolution helped lay the foundation of change that began in December 1978. This school of thought has often referred to riotous disturbances in Beijing in April 1976 to illustrate social disappointment with leftist Maoist policies. Bernstein (1993:45) writes that what disturbed the post-Mao leadership were 'immense imbalances, inefficiencies and poor results', which 'included disparities in growth rates among the three major sectors of heavy industry, light industry and agriculture, and the neglect of services, which sharply lowered the quality of life'. Yuen Chen (1985:155) writes that the Marxist central planning and management are naturally inefficient and production was incommensurate with the needs of society under Maoist leadership.

This is a distorted picture, however, neglecting the importance of the hostile international situation, which deprived Mao of his priority of improving the livelihood of the people, as argued above.

With the perceived change of the international environment, the Fourth FYP of 1971–5 witnessed Mao's new policy of opening up the country to the Western world to tap foreign capital and science and technology. To be in tune with US-led Western economic principles, the Maoist economic model in the Fourth FYP stressed relaxed policies providing individual and material incentives, for instance, for individual labor as well as decentralized production, which encouraged local self-reliance.

Thus, starting in 1971, Mao's Fourth FYP stressed the improvement of 'the people's livelihood' overall, with commune members now allowed to farm small plots for their personal needs, to engage in limited sideline production at their households, and in pastoral areas to keep a small number of livestock for their personal needs.

The Maoist new economic model during the Fourth FYP period stressed the following relaxed characteristics, adhering to the mass line strategy for the purpose of uniting the entire population against possible external enemies:

(1) Foreign capital inflow was now allowed. This meant the opening up of the country to the outside world.
(2) For the first time, the Maoist leadership gave priority to the livelihood of the people allowing individual farming plots and individual labor. Dictated by international politics, this strategy was considered in tune with the US-led Western economic model and was allowed, provided that self-interest did not lead to exploitation.
(3) Economic development of rural areas featured communes and small industries.
(4) Decentralized development encouraged local self-reliance.
(5) Egalitarian characteristics still dominated in the short-run. The policy was to raise the living standard of the people overall avoiding the exploitation of the majority by the minority.

After 1969, Gurley (1976:223, 310) observes, the Chinese economy had made large gains on a broad front through a balanced development program that emphasized both agriculture and industry, large and small enterprises, self-reliance, and individualist and collective incentives, among others. Gurley also writes that 'substantial progress has also been made in the urban areas in both heavy and light industry, high levels of employment, good rates of output growth' and that the country experienced no recession, inflation, or energy crisis in the first half of the 1970s.

Clearly the characteristics of the FFYP demonstrated the typical Maoist approach to encourage the growth of astronomical power from the very participation of the whole population in developing national economy, while still paying attention to defense. The relaxed policy regarding individual and material incentives was meant to be in tune with the Western economic model. Although the mass line strategy and egalitarian characteristics were still intact, they were eventually to give way to the Western economic approach in terms of self-interest.

Under this pretext, Mao announced his new economic strategy of 1971. This new model featured small industries in the communes, while also encouraging local reliance in decentralized development. This paved the way for the application of the Western principles, not only of individualism, but of material incentives as well. Mao was well aware that this would eventually lead to the abolition of his communes, with the spirit of individualism injected into his new economic endeavor. He realized that this was logically practical. This was because in the changing international political environment, the capitalist Western world was now no longer a menace to China's survival. Thus Mao's previously sacrosanct tenet of selflessly serving and uniting with the collective had to begin to incorporate the Western capitalist concepts of liberal individualism and material incentives. This would eventually make his egalitarian objectives redundant. Marxist 'class struggle', which had made 'selflessness' effective in unifying '98 per cent plus' of his people to weed out 'class enemies', had to eventually die a natural death. Selflessness as a mass line strategy, which was devised to unite the masses effectively against imperialism, would also eventually and unavoidably become redundant.

The economic-political-social change was that *collective* farms were to eventually give peasants individual family holdings, linking output to remuneration. The new economic conditions would inspire the appearance of a kind of 'market economy' that would integrate with the world economy dominated by the US-led West. This meant that the ideological polarization of the capitalist and communist systems that had existed previously in China would be phased out over time. This was necessary with the occurrence of the new international political order.

Mao understood that the means of generating growth would be to open up the country to foreign investment, with the foreign management practices and innovative technologies especially those related to information and communication. His new foreign investment policy would encourage not only inflows of foreign direct investment into every industrial and service sector, but eventually the establishment of foreign invested enterprises in China.

In 1973, with the implementation of the balanced National Economic Plan in which the new pro-Western Maoist economic strategy was introduced, the Chinese economy made large gains on many fronts (Liu & Wu, 1986:384). This program emphasized agriculture and industry, large and small enterprises, self-reliance, individual and collective incentives, among other elements. With the import of complete sets of equipment and new technology, industrial production began to pick up (Liu & Wu, 1986:384). Total output value of industry and agriculture in 1973 was 9.2 per cent higher than the previous year, while foreign trade increased dramatically. The total volume of imports and exports amounted to US$10.98 billion, an increase of 34 per cent over the same period Liu & Wu, 1986:384). This rate of growth, Liu and Wu posit, was the highest since the First FYP. I attribute this increase for the most part to the favorable new international political situation, which made Mao's new economic efforts possible.

The 1975 Constitution contained provisions regarding nonagricultural individual laborers and people's commune members, allowing them to farm small plots for their personal needs and to engage in limited household sideline production. This was demarcated from Liu's recommended 'fixing of farm output quotas for individual households with each on its own and the abolition of farm plots for personal needs'.[15] The spirit of dedicated selflessness still prevailed, but it was not considered the most critical element. This contradicts Gurley's argument that the Maoist leadership was 'persistent in encouraging collective endeavors that return benefits to the group and in promoting hard work partly through revolutionary fervor rather than entirely through promises of material gains' (1976:311).

Conclusion

Stimulated by the theme of the historical novel, Mao staged his 'ping-pong diplomacy' that led to President Nixon's China visit in 1972. In the early 1970s, with improved Sino-US relations, he began to view the Soviet Union as his primary enemy and the United States as the non-antagonistic secondary enemy in his global order of tripolarity. In 1974, inspired by the well-known theme of the novel as well as Zhuge Liang's tripolar concept, Mao created his new concept of the 'Three Worlds' primarily to contend with the primary enemy, the Soviet Union, while aiming to collude with the secondary enemy plus the Second and Third World nations. Although Mao's global order of tripolarity did not help much in isolating the Soviet primary enemy, China's crucial role in the tripolar relationships was confirmed. As the international environment was now conducive to his plan of opening up China to the outside world, Mao began to adopt a more relaxed economic policy in 1971. His four modernizations scheme was initiated to promote the acquisition of US-led Western capital and modern technology along with the capitalist economic principles. This was not only to befriend the US-led West at the expense of the Soviet Union, but also to improve the livelihood of the people. It was in this context that in the next chapter I will consider Deng Xiaoping's 'good-neighborliness' policy and the collapse of the Soviet Union both which will eventually lead to the collapse of Mao's global order of tripolarity.

CHAPTER EIGHT

1979–1990 Period: The Collapse of Mao's Global Order of Tripolarity

In December 1978, two years after Mao's death, the Third Plenary Session of the Eleventh Central Committee of the Chinese Communist Party adopted Vice-Premier Deng Xiaoping's proposal to shift the focus of the entire Party's work to 'socialist modernization' starting from the year 1979. With 'the essence of holding high the great banner of Mao Zedong Thought', the so-called 'socialist modernization' was translated into the 'four modernizations of agriculture, industry, defense and science and technology'. The PRC adopted Deng's policy of economic reforms and formally opened up China's economy to market forces and foreign investment. Since then, the Chinese government has committed itself to moving away from a rigid centrally planned economy to a relaxed planned-cum-market economy initiated by Mao in 1971. Deng called it 'socialism with Chinese characteristics'.[1] Along with Western economic principles, the post-Mao modernization revolution naturally brought about political change, thus rendering irrelevant the ideological fervor, class struggle and mass political campaigns of the Maoist era. The Chinese claimed that this Herculean national task was based on 'the theory of building socialism', which Party Chief Jiang Zemin attributed to Deng Xiaoping as its principal founder and called the 'Deng Xiaoping Theory'. Jiang, however, declared that 'Deng Xiaoping Theory is a continuation and development of Mao Zedong Thought'.[2] In the following, let us first survey the post-1979 international environment related to China's modernization drive.

The International Political Environment in 1979–1985

The post-1979 international environment continued to be favorable to Deng Xiaoping, enabling him to carry out Mao's four modernizations revolution. By opening up the PRC to the outside world, Deng aimed at tapping science and technology as well as foreign capital from the US-led West for China's economic reform. Inheriting Mao's modernization initiatives, the post-Mao global strategy focused on the *maintenance* of normalized relations with the United States, Japan, and other advanced Western industrialized countries in a peaceful and stable international environment.[3]

I argued above that, in the first half of the 1980s, based on the international reality of the time, Deng continued to treat the Soviet Union as the primary enemy of the First World, while the United States was its secondary enemy.[4] The Sino-US Normalization Communique was signed in 1978. This perception placed Japan and other US-led advanced Western industrialized nations in the Second World. China now aimed at 'colluding with its secondary enemies' against 'hegemonism' of its 'primary enemy'.

Soviet expansionism and hostility toward China was the main external threat during the period. Chinese propaganda asserted that the Soviet Union was the source of the next world war. Moscow had deployed up to a third of its total strategic nuclear forces, including more than 160 SS-20 medium-range, triple warhead missiles, in the Far East over the decade 1977–86. The Soviets invaded Afghanistan in 1979. A year earlier, the Soviet-supported Vietnam had invaded Cambodia to overthrow the Chinese-backed regime.

Although Soviet expansionism and hostility towards the PRC posed the main external threat during this period, the international environment remained relatively stable for the PRC's economic reform and open-door policy. This was in contrast with the period 1959–69 when the United States was China's primary enemy, and the Soviet Union was the 'the No. 1 accomplice of the United States'.

Deng's Global 'Friendliness' Policy and Economic Development

In adopting Mao's new economic strategy, the Dengist policy of attracting foreign investment and funds was associated with its need for foreign technology. Achieving its goals of quadrupling its 1980 GNP by the end of the twentieth century depended on increasing capital and labor inputs, but more importantly, on advanced science and technology to enhance productivity. Thus, technology transfer was crucial to upgrading its technological levels and eventually to improving its competitiveness in the global markets.

As mentioned above, Deng's open-door policy was to facilitate technology transfer through international trade. Thus, special economic and technology zones were initiated along the PRC's coastal regions not only to facilitate its foreign trade, but also to attract joint ventures and foreign investments. A joint venture law was also promulgated in 1980. Initial contact with world markets was mainly through the four special economic zones of Shenzhen, Zhuhai, Shantou, and Xiamen. Deng's concept of the Special Economic Zones (SEZ) was so successful that the central government in 1984 extended this scheme to fourteen coastal cities and Hainan Island for foreign investments. The fourteen coastal cities are: Dalian, Qinhuangdao, Tianjin, Yantai, Qingtao, Lianyungang, Nantong, Shanghai, Ningbo, Wenzhou, Zhangjiang, Fuzhou, Guangzhou, and Beihai. In 1985, it further opened up three special regions of the Zhujiang Delta, the Changjiang Delta and the Minnan Delta, which included Xianmen, Quangzhou and Zhangzhou as special areas. The central government also accelerated the development of Shanghai's Pudong New Area.

Starting from the early 1980s, foreign investors were invited to these special economic zones. The most successful part of the initiative was attracting wealthy overseas Chinese investors, particularly from Hong Kong through whom massive capital was transferred to the cities in the Zhujiang Delta laying the foundation for the PRC's successful export policies. In the

Delta, by far the most successful was Shenzhen, which grew within ten years from a village of 20,000 to an industrial metropolis of two million.[5]

In the early 1980s, stimulated by the Asian economic miracle, which had swept across the continent, Deng formulated the 'good-neighborliness' policy which was compatible with the peaceful and stable international environment. The policy was aimed to be part of the development miracle of the Newly Industrialized Economies (NIEs). Spelling out this policy in December 1982, he promised that, first of all, China would continue its efforts to develop relations with Southeast Asian nations 'on a long-term basis'.[6] Deng aimed to strengthen Western Pacific economic cooperation particularly with its economically advanced neighbors. Beijing now began to scale down its military support for Southeast Asian insurgents. The object was to win over not only the Little Economic Dragons, but also the wealthy Chinese in Southeast Asia to invest in the PRC with much needed technology transfers.

In adopting the Maoist foreign policy strategy, in August 1985 Deng Xiaoping (1994:133) aimed to promote a 'peaceful international environment ... to absorb as many things as possible from other countries'. The Dengists were eyeing the US foreign direct investment and sophisticated technology. Deng's 'good neighborliness' policy was subsequently extended to include Western Europe and elsewhere. The post-Mao leadership can therefore be said to have inherited Mao's spirit through its open-door policy eventually aimed at inducing the whole world to help modernize China. It was to lead a quarter of mankind to 'uproot the mountains of economic and technological backwardness', as the Dengists put it.

In the rural areas, starting in 1979, with Mao's Western-oriented 'individual' economic principle, Deng broke up the collective farms in order to give farmers individual family holdings and linking output to remuneration. Based on Mao's relaxed economic strategy of 1971, this scheme, called the household responsibility system, was implemented among the Chinese peasantry. The restructuring of the rural economy understandably saw the modification of Mao's defense-oriented and highly centralized people's commune system. Under the new system, the lowest level of the former commune system, i.e., the production team, was abolished, and the former brigade became the village committee. This meant that ownership of the land remained with the village or township thus featuring both centralized and decentralized management. The function of the village committee was now to contract land out to families, collect tax and effect payment to finance collective undertakings such as irrigation, and to administer sales of produce to the state (Beinstein, 1993:49). With Mao's new material incentives and the Western-oriented principle of self-interest serving as catalyst, Deng's (1994:152) new strategy aimed to 'invigorate our domestic economy'. The reform effort transformed the majority of individual households into basic productive establishments.

Building on the success of the rural reform, a comprehensive urban restructuring scheme was initiated in May 1984. With Mao's 1971 new strategy emphasizing local control, the post-Mao era witnessed a broad range of structural economic reforms to free enterprises from state and Party control. The separation of government administration from enterprise management was to reduce the political and administrative interference from the Party (1994:152). Thus, a gradual transformation of existing industrial enterprises occurred with the simplification of administrative procedures, while structurally market forces were introduced to direct and regulate economic activities. This meant that greater autonomy was given to individual enterprises to introduce their own production plans, scheduling their daily operation processes as well as setting their own prices (1994:152). All this was based on the principle of Deng's new self-responsibility system. It served to revitalize the Chinese industrial enterprises by giving them decision-making powers, while promoting technological transformation of the enterprises. This was a new 'enterprise responsibility system' in which 'township and village industrial enterprises' were set up as joint ventures with foreigners and wholly owned foreign and private enterprises. They were given the responsibility for their own profits or losses, and managers of these enterprises were given greater decision-making authority. Further, small-scale private businesses were promoted to stimulate production and absorb unemployed labor (Kau & Marsh, 1993:342).

In attracting advanced technology and capital from the West for their modernization revolution, the Dengists continued to apply Mao's strategy of opening up the country to the outside world and carry out his Western-oriented economic reform. This was feasible with Deng's global strategy based on maintaining normalized relations with the international community, particularly the US-led West, and on his new 'good neighborliness' policy in helping promote a peaceful and stable international environment. It is important to note that Deng's initiative of 'good-neighborliness' policy was designed to induce the whole world to help modernize China, which was eventually to include the Soviet Union under Gorbachev.

Characteristic of the period 1979–90 was China's vigorous efforts to promote regional and global peace and stability conducive to its economic modernization endeavors. In this section, I will argue that the gradual collapse of the Soviet Union made the international environment even more favorable to China's modernization drive. The transformation of Mao's global order of tripolarity began in the early 1980s when Deng Xiaoping introduced his 'good-neighborliness' policy and launched his modernization program through China's Sixth FYP of 1981–5. Deng launched the second stage of his modernization program through China's Seventh Five-Year Plan (1986–91), which was similar to the Sixth FYP. In the following, I will show the gist of Deng's twin FYPs.

The first priority of the Sixth FYP was to 'improve the people's livelihood' with the aim of furthering the modernization process. This meant an increased output of agricultural produce, textiles and other light industrial goods as well as other consumer goods industries to raise the per-capita consumption level. With new confidence and experience gained from the Sixth FYP and a relatively stable and peaceful international environment conducive to its modernization program, China launched its Seventh FYP for national economic and social development in March 1986. This was Deng's second-stage modernization program, with the continuation of the Maoist development strategy in agriculture, light industry and heavy industry, while the Outline of the Ten Years Plan continued to emphasize agriculture and industry to further improve the people's livelihood. With the Maoist material incentives and self-interest serving as catalysts, Deng's socialist planned market economy was to invigorate the economy and improve the people's livelihood for carrying out the four modernizations more effectively. With the international environment conducive to Deng's and subsequently Jiang Zemin's opendoor policy, the PRC aimed at acquiring modern technology and foreign investment funds from the advanced Western countries and the four economic 'dragons'. In the following, I will consider how Deng's 'good-neighborliness' strategy induced the whole world to help modernize China further.

The Transformation of Mao's Global Order of Tripolarity and the Collapse of the Soviet Union

With the accession to power of the Soviet leader Mikhail Gorbachev in March 1985, the transformation of Mao's international order of tripolarity accelerated. This had important implications for Deng's global strategy of inducing the whole world to help modernize China. First, the expensive arms race with the US and the enormous foreign aid program had been a drain on the Soviet power. The rigid Soviet economic policy inevitably led to severe economic recession and material shortages. As a result, the Soviet leader began to carry out a program of significant changes. By adopting Western economic principles, his new strategy aimed at attracting foreign capital to enhance productivity and efficiency. Gorbachev also made a radical shift in Soviet military and defense policy by adopting the so-called 'reasonable sufficiency' strategy. In essence, his new approach called for a reduction in the size of the army and defense expenditure, while keeping reliable security. Furthermore, discarding the self-serving and coercive foreign policy, he formulated a new strategy, which stressed global security, non-interference in the internal affairs of other nations and a curtailment of foreign aid. Gorbachev's new foreign policy called for withdrawal of Soviet troops deployed in foreign nations. In dealing with the West, clearly the Soviet leader pursued detente, which emphasized disarmament, the avoidance of military confrontation, and the resolution of existing problems through political means. As a result, a new situation evolved in which security issues between the Soviet Union and the United States had come to focus on arms control rather than on military competition.

In December 1987 Gorbachev and Reagan signed the first major disarmament pact of the nuclear age in Washington, that is, the Intermediate-Range Nuclear Force Treaty. This was an important step to ease the threat of nuclear war.[7] In February 1988, Gorbachev announced the Soviet unilateral withdrawal of all the troops from Afghanistan. In that year, he announced the abandonment of the Brezhnev Doctrine of limited sovereignty that the Soviet Union was ready to use military force to stop undesirable political developments in the Socialist bloc. In his speech in the United Nations General Assembly in December that year, Gorbachev proposed a cut of the Soviet armed forces by 500,000 troops in two years, and the withdrawal of 10,000 tanks, 8,500 artillery pieces and 800 combat aircrafts from East and Soviet Europe. This would reduce Soviet conventional superiority in Europe. He also decided to withdraw the forces deployed in Mongolia and Soviet Asia.[8]

The unprecedented international changes since the autumn of 1989 had been the transformation of East Europe, the significant reduction of Soviet conventional forces in Europe, the disintegration of the Warsaw Pact, the re-unification of East and West Germany, which the Soviet Union sanctioned, and finally the collapse of the Soviet Union itself. These changes represented the most dramatic developments in international politics since the end of the Second World War.

Soviet and US foreign policies regarding Asia

In his Vladivostok speech on 28 July 1986, Gorbachev announced the Soviet initiative of establishing a new international order in the Asia-Pacific region through cooperation. Evidently he was convinced that the peace and stability of Asia should be based on economic rather than military terms. Understanding that economic strength can produce political and strategic power, the Soviet leader strove to find a viably peaceful international environment in which to build Soviet economic and hence strategic strength. In another speech at Krasnoyarsk in September 1988, Gorbachev attached great importance to the economic development of Eastern Siberia.

Certainly the Soviets were eyeing the technology and capital of Japan and the newly industrialized countries in the Far East.

The shift in Soviet foreign policy led to its application of pressure to Vietnam to withdraw its troops from Cambodia. The mammoth military aid to Vietnam had been a drain on the Soviet strategic capability; and about two-thirds of this aid was to be curtailed. The withdrawal of Soviet troops from Afghanistan and Soviet pressure on Vietnam led to a cessation of hostilities in the Indian Ocean and the Asia-Pacific region. In 1988 Mikhail Gorbachev offered to close down the Soviet bases in Vietnam in exchange for the US withdrawal from Clark Air Base and Subic Naval Base in the Philippines.

However, the US Asian policy emphasizes Asia's importance to itself, and the cooperation and shared leadership with all Asian countries in the pursuit of common interests there. Thus the United States continual military presence in Asia aimed at maintaining peace and stability of the region as vital for business investment and economic growth, although its presence there was to be eventually reduced. Major US economic interests had been and still are at stake in the Far East. For instance, its 1988 annual trade turnover in the Asia-Pacific region alone was about 37 per cent of the total worldwide, that is, about US$300 billion, and this was far more than that for the Trans-Atlantic trade for the same year which was about US$186 billion.[9] The US overseas investment shifted to the region with an average annual growth of about 12 per cent, surpassing that of other regions.[10] The United States was the second largest trader and investor in ASEAN after Japan. Nevertheless, the United States had already felt the Soviet leader's sincerity.

Sino-Soviet relations and Deng's 'good-neighborliness' policy

In July 1986, Soviet leader Mikhail Gorbachev announced the Soviet troop withdrawals from Afghanistan and Mongolia on China's northern border and called for closer ties with the PRC. This showed much prospect of a detente of the two communist giants. At the end of July of the same year, Gorbachev expressed Soviet willingness to discuss the establishment of neighborly relations with PRC; and in 1987, Gorbachev agreed to press Vietnam to withdraw its occupying troops from Cambodia. In February 1989, Foreign Minister Eduard Shevardnadze announced the Soviet reduction of the quarter of a million troops stationed along the Sino-Soviet border. This pullout reduced the Soviet threat to China. Gorbachev's efforts including the Soviet troop withdrawal from Afghanistan and Mongolia and Soviet pressure on Vietnam to withdraw its troops from Cambodia led to Deng's acceptance of a Sino-Soviet summit meeting in Beijing in May 1989. This meeting, which heralded the complete Sino-Soviet normalization of relations, marked the end of their thirty-year-old military confrontation. As a result, the Soviet Union in Deng's worldview was relegated to the position of secondary enemy and quickly transformed into a 'friend', following Party Secretary Jiang Zemin's visit to Moscow. In October that year, both parties discussed the establishment of a 'non-military zone' along their border, where troop withdrawal had already begun. In May 1991, Jiang Zemin reciprocated Soviet leader Gorbachev's visit to Beijing, and this marked the first visit to the USSR by a party chief of the People's Republic of China since 1957. Prior to Jiang's departure to Moscow, both sides had declared that they no longer posed a threat to each other. During his visit, the Sino-Soviet eastern border accord was signed.

As a result of the collapse of the Soviet Union, Deng's 'good-neighborhood' policy was extended to Russia. Deng's global strategy, which was aimed at attracting foreign capital and advanced technology from the US-led Western world, could now be applied to the world at large. The collapse of the Soviet Union confirmed the final collapse of Mao's global order of tripolarity. Thus, In April 1990, Premier Li Peng signed a series of agreements with the Russians in Moscow on cooperation in the fields of trade and the economy, science and technology.[11]

Conclusion

Deng's 'good-neighborhood' policy, which was designed to induce the whole world to help modernize China, now vitally included Russia, as a result of the collapse of the Soviet Union. Deng's policy helped maintain a peaceful and stable international environment. Thus, ironically, the policy marked the end of Mao's global order of tripolarity. The collapse of the Soviet Union confirmed the final collapse of Mao's global order.

CHAPTER NINE

Concluding Remarks

Mao told Edgar Snow in 1936 that he 'believed he was much influenced by the historical novel read at an impressionable age'. Therefore the theoretical foundation of the concept of Mao's concept of a global order of tripolarity can be traced to the following:

First, Cao Cao's *qi* inspired Mao to look at the world in its totality.

Second, the theme of the novel consists of two major components:

(a) 'Partition of the world into three', a concept initiated by Zhuge Liang, the Shu state's architect of war. Premier Zhuge Liang of the newly formed Shu state created the Chinese 'international' order of tripolarity to fight the powerful Wei state through colluding with the Wu state at all costs.
(b) 'The world phenomenon under the heavens, long united, must divide, and vice versa'. Mao interpreted the ambiguous theme as 'empires, long united, must divide, and vice versa', however. He considered it 'dialectic'. Inspired by the historical novel's retelling of the Shu-Wu split, which results in the battle at Yiling, he argued that 'a flare up of the Sino-Soviet animosity would occur sooner or later'.

Third, the battle at Chibi, described in details in the novel of the *Romance of the Three Kingdoms*, and the historical texts *Records of the Three Kingdoms* and *Zizhi Tongjian*, convinced Mao of the possible victory of battles won by outnumbered and inferior forces over superior forces in a tripolar situation. Mao commented on it on a number of occasions.

However, Mao considered Zhuge Liang's staunch anti-Wei Shu-Wu collusion as disastrously rigid. Thus, in reality, he made the fundamental principle involving the positions of the primary and secondary enemy in a tripolar situation flexible. This was to 'concentrate the astronomical power' to aim at defeating the primary enemy effectively by colluding with the secondary enemy. Mao obviously considered that his flexible exchange of the positions of the primary and secondary enemies would have resolved the Shu's geographical problem in relation to the Shu-Wei combined forces against the Wu, and would nullify the problem of an imperfect Shu-Wu alliance.

Zhuge's concept of tripolarity strengthened Mao's conviction to initially collude with the Soviet Union in an international communist brotherhood to fight the powerful United States immediately following the establishment of the PRC in October 1949. However, his plan did not work out as he intended, as Stalin successfully schemed to involve the powerful US and the new PRC in the Korean War which he instigated North Korea's Kim Il-sung to start.

In January 1954, Mao perceived the 'US-USSR collusion to the disadvantage of the PRC'.

Ignoring the crucial tripolar international perspective, Dikötter's new book *Mao's Great Famine: The History of China's Most Devastating Catastrophe 1958–62* considers the GLF as 'a result of Mao's personal competitiveness with Khrushchev' and 'an attempt to catch up with and overtake Britain in less than fifteen years', while Cheek's most recently edited work *A Critical Introduction to Mao* provides us with the following critiques:

(a) Barme argues that 'deeply suspicious of a ruse that disguised an insidious plot against him and party policy, Mao turned on Peng Dehuai';
(b) Teiwes contends that 'China descended into accelerated crises' as a result of Mao's 'interpretation of Peng's critique of GLF as a personal challenge and his insistence on Peng's dismissal'; and
(c) Cheek attacks Mao's GLF as 'the single greatest crime during his rule', which was 'disastrously flawed and ruthlessly implemented'.

However, I argue that Mao considered Peng's 'collusion with Khrushchev to oppose the three red flags' an act of high treason. The 1959 dismissal of the Soviet-backed 'right opportunist' Peng was part of the Sino-Soviet acrimonious dispute, likened to the Shu-Wu split. During the period 1959–69, the Soviet Union shifted from secondary to primary enemy in Mao's tripolar worldview.

In Cheek's edited book, MacFarquhar writes that 'the negative appraisal of Mao's Cultural Revolution and of Mao's culpability is widely accepted in the West'. However, I argue that as part of the Sino-US acrimony, apart from China's provision of support to North Vietnam, Mao's Cultural Revolution was aimed at purging the 'rightist-cum-revisionist' Liu Shaoqi whose pro-Western economic strategy neglected to take into account crucial, realistic international power politics. In his 'revisionist' approach, which was considered dangerously detrimental to Mao's mass line and opposed to Mao's defense-oriented communization agenda, Liu ignored the simple fact that the Soviet Union had become 'No. 1 accomplice of the US primary enemy' in Mao's tripolar worldview during the crucial period of 1954–69.

Understandably, thus, external and internal pressures that Mao had faced in the 1950s and 1960s forced him to adopt radical measures to prevent the country from falling apart. Mao's domestic policy of a national united front was devised, and his mass line strategy, which was to serve his collectivization drive, was aimed at 'uniting with all possible'. Mao's drive, with the Yenan model as its prototype, was meant to ultimately realize his defense-oriented communization goal for a united population to fight the imperialist and 'hegemonic' superpowers 'one by one'.

Inspired by the well-known theme of the *Romance of the Three Kingdoms*, Mao tried, though in vain, to form an alliance with the United States against the Soviet Union on two occasions in February 1959 and October 1964.

However, at the beginning of the 1970s, a golden opportunity for the normalization of the Sino-US relations appeared. Inspired by the theme of the novel, i.e., 'empires, long divided, must unite', Mao staged the 'ping-pong diplomacy' that led to President Nixon's China visit in 1972. In Mao's global order of tripolarity, the Soviet Union became the primary enemy, while the United States became China's non-antagonistic secondary enemy. In 1974, inspired by the theme of the historical novel as well as Zhuge Liang's tripolar concept, he created his new concept of the 'Three Worlds' primarily to contend with the primary enemy through aiming to collude with the secondary enemy, as well as with the second and third world nations. Mao contemplated the value of an American counterweight to the Soviets. Equally important, he sought technology resources for China's four modernizations program.

As the international environment in 1971 was conducive to his plan of opening up China to the outside world, Mao began to adopt a more relaxed economic policy. He initiated his four modernizations scheme to promote the acquisition of US-led Western capital and modern technology along with the capitalist economic principles. This was not only to befriend the US-led West at the expense of the Soviet Union, but also to improve the livelihood of the people.

Although Mao's global order of tripolarity was not especially effective in isolating the US or the Soviet primary enemy during the relevant periods, China's crucial role in a global tripolarity was confirmed.

In attracting advanced technology and capital from the West for China's modernization revolution, Deng Xiaoping applied Mao's strategy of opening up the country to the outside world and continued to carry out the latter's Western-oriented economic reform. Deng's policy of 'good-neighborliness' was designed to encourage other countries, including the Soviet Union under Gorbachev, to help modernize China. This policy helped maintain a peaceful and stable international environment. Ironically Deng's policy marked the end of Mao's global order of tripolarity. The collapse of the Soviet Union confirmed the final collapse of Mao's global order.

Epilogue

In the preceding, I considered Mao Zedong's global order of tripolarity. In the following, I will deal with the post-Cold War great power interactions in terms of the Sino-US and Sino-Russian relations during the period between the collapse of the Soviet Union at the end of 1989 and the beginning of the new century. First of all, I will consider the Sino-US relations in terms of the regional perspective.

The Sino-US Relations

Since the late 1970s, Deng Xiaoping's global strategy had been based on 'flexible pragmatism' to maintain normalization of relations with the United States, Japan, and other advanced Western industrialized countries. This was intended to help create a peaceful and stable regional environment vital to China's open-door policy of attracting foreign capital and advanced technology for its economic reforms and 'four modernizations' program. However, inheriting Mao Zedong's conception of the Three Worlds and based on 'international reality', the Chinese leadership continued to treat the Soviet Union as the primary enemy of the First World throughout the first half of the 1980s, while treating the United States as the non-antagonistic secondary enemy. This neo-Maoist perception placed Japan and other advanced Western industrialized nations in the Second World.

However, since the end of 1990, with the call for establishing a new international order 'devoid of hegemonism and domination by the First World countries', the predominantly regionally oriented Dengist foreign policy attempted to form a united front with Third World nations to counteract 'US and Japanese hegemonism'.[1] The Chinese leadership openly emphasized Mao Zedong's concept of the Three Worlds, with its perception of the emergence of a new world order dominated by 'a rich-nations club'.[2] With the collapse of Mao's world order of tripolarity, the Dengists perceived China as being positioned in a world moving towards 'multipolarity', with the growing prominence of Japan and a re-unified Germany.[3] This meant that with the demise of the Soviet Union, the United States had become the sole superpower, while Japan, which belonged to the Second World in Mao's worldview, had transformed into a First World nation together with re-unified Germany. Thus, in the First World, the United States was now treated as the primary enemy (though the Sino-US contradiction remained non-antagonistic), and Japan and Germany were viewed as secondary enemies. Other advanced Western industrialized countries had remained in the Second World. China's perception of the new world order reflected its fears; first, that as a result of the collapse of the Warsaw Pact, the world would be dominated by the United States, and second, that Japan's high-level economic development would likely be associated with a resurgence of Japanese militarism.

At a secret meeting held by the State Council representatives of the general office of the Chinese Communist Party Central Committee in mid-January 1991, the Dengists considered that the Persian Gulf War was a 'struggle between global and regional hegemonisms', and that 'a new world order' had already taken shape. This was because the US objective, they continued, was 'first, to teach Saddam Hussein a lesson, and then, dominate the world'.[4] The Chinese contended that 'this new world order' would not be realized so long as the 'club of wealthy nations' continued to dominate and control world affairs.[5] They implied that they were determined to destroy this budding world order starting at the regional level. The major members of the 'club' they referred to were clearly the United States and Japan. China's new worldview was that the United States was the primary enemy and Japan the secondary enemy, both in the First World. Using Lenin's 'Theory of Imperialism', the Chinese attacked the 'wealthy nations' for hegemonic contention over the Third World: 'There is a key difference between the competition described by Lenin and the present competition: the imperialists of Lenin's era fought primarily over colonies and semi-colonies, while the developed Western nations of today are not only locked in fierce battles over third-world countries, but are also vying for each other's markets'.[6]

Thus, in an attempt to win over Third World nations against 'power politics in any form', the Chinese leadership formulated its own new world order based on 'respect for the independence and sovereignty of every nation, regardless of size, wealth, or military power'.[7] This 'new world order', they argued, was 'markedly different from the old order (in which the exploitative West) harms developing countries'. They perceived the rise of 'American expansionism' particularly in the region. The Chinese based their anti-US argument on the following: first, the US decision to reduce its troop presence in Japan, South Korea, and the Philippines by only 10 per cent was to improve its military quality and efficiency, and this was a response to US budgetary constraints.[8] Secondly, of the three US armed services, the navy, which was a major force in the Pacific, would be least affected by budgetary cuts (Polomka, 1990:7).

Amidst all this, Beijing desired to form a regional united front with neighboring nations with the aim of curbing US influence in the region and curtailing a 'rising Japanese re-militarist tendency'.[9] Although, in reality, China could not count on the cooperation of all the neighboring countries in its anti-'club of wealthy nations' movement, it worked on the logic that more 'friends' mean less 'enemies'. The Dengists knew that while these Third World nations might not contribute towards an anti-hegemonist alliance, they might stand neutral in the equation. This new perception witnessed the most significant shift in China's foreign policy since the late 1980s. The new Chinese strategy was meant to go hand in hand with the diplomacy of good-neighborliness.

With the collapse of the Soviet Union, a reduction in the US presence in the Asia-Pacific, the importance of China as a political and military power had increased. Chinese manoeuvres to curb US influence in the region can be seen in the following light. First, exploiting anti-US sentiments in the Philippines, Premier Li Peng 'guaranteed' in mid-December 1990 that China would not pose a threat to nations in Asia even if the US military bases in that country were dismantled.[10] Secondly, during President Yang Shangkun's visit to Malaysia in mid-January 1992, the Chinese President pledged China's 'full support' for the Malaysian proposed East

Asian Economic Caucus, a concept opposed by the Bush Administration.[11] Thirdly, the Sino-Malaysian anti-US stance was clearly expressed in terms of the agreement by the two sides that 'the rights of the individual should not be allowed to destabilize the country', and that 'a balanced application of human rights should take into account our values'.[12] Fourthly, Yang's pledge, which came a few days after President Bush's visit to Singapore, seemed to imply its objection to the US plan to relocate its Seventh Fleet logistical command from Subic Bay to Singapore.

Despite its pull-out of all nuclear arms from the Korean peninsula and its precipitous withdrawal from the Philippines, America's Asian policy emphasized Asia's importance to the United States and the cooperation and shared leadership with all Asian countries in pursuit of common interests. America's continued military presence in Asia, therefore, aimed to maintain the peace and stability of the region, which was vital for a business environment and economic growth. Major US economic interests were (and still are) at stake in the Asia-Pacific. In recent years, the US overseas investments pouring into the region had had an average annual growth of about 12 per cent, surpassing that of other regions.[13] With the exception of Japan, the United States was (and still is) the second largest trader and investor in the ASEAN states. Because of US determination to remain a Pacific power, its withdrawal from the Philippines would not affect its overall interest in, and commitment to, the stability and security of the region. US Secretary of State James Baker assured the Southeast Asians in July 1992 that 'although the form of the US presence had changed, the substance of our commitment is firm'.[14] He stated that US military bases in Japan, South Korea, and Guam, and its new access to other Southeast Asian nations would ensure that the US navy 'remained fully capable of achieving its missions'.[15]

Rapid global changes have resulted in a basic shift in perception of governments in the post-Cold War Asia-Pacific region towards an expanding Japanese political and security role. With its reduced commitment to the region, the United States could not but allow Japan to assume some sort of military role commensurate with its economic might. Japanese economic interests and significant naval capability would likely make it a major power in the region.

According to the Chinese, it has recently become more and more apparent that the Japanese have sought the rank of a major power by assuming more global and regional responsibilities following the collapse of the old world order. Even since the early seventies, the Chinese had already argued that Japan's economic expansion was 'bound to bring about military expansion which could not be restrained by treaties'.

China seemed aware of the following Japanese military developments: Japan was steadily building up its naval forces. Its Maritime Self-Defense Forces had more destroyers and frigates than China, and Japanese naval chiefs were arguing the need for helicopter carriers. In December 1990, the Japanese government approved a US$172 billion program for the build up of national defense over a five-year period beginning in fiscal 1991.[16] The program was to contribute towards increasing costs from 39 percent in 1991 to about 50 per cent by 1995.[17] Japan's military budget increased by 5 per cent annually in real terms during the decade of the 1980s.[18] Being in a position to engage in the militarization of outer space, in September 1986 the Japanese government announced that it would participate in research for the US satellite-based missile defense system, the Strategic Defense Initiative (or Star Wars).[19]

Understandably, therefore, the US presence in the Asia-Pacific is widely perceived as serving to dissuade Japan from taking too autonomous a regional and international role. In a post-Cold War policy statement, the Pentagon urged the US Administration to prevent the emergence of a vacuum so as to pre-empt Japanese rearmament.

In the mid-1990s, ties between the PRC and the United States came under further strain. Apart from the issues of Taiwan, human rights abuses and intellectual property right violations, the case of nuclear proliferation in 1994 regarding the *Yinhe* incident, in which the United States accused the PRC of selling M-11 missiles to Pakistan, aggravated the already worsened Sino-US relations. During that year, a number of US congressmen even opposed the Chinese bid to host the 2000 Olympics. The mid-term elections in the United States in late 1994 brought several long-term anti-China right-wing congressmen into the foreign relations committees of both the Senate and the House of Representatives. Since then, according to the Chinese, the Republican-dominated Congress had passed many anti-China resolutions applying great pressure on the Clinton administration.[20] Further, in October 1995, the Chinese accused anti-Chinese US strategists of proposing to restore the Southeast Asia Treaty Organization (SEATO) with the Cold War policy of containing China.[21] The United States was certainly fearful of how the Sino-Russian cooperation in consolidating their commercial ties and in building 'a strategic partnership for the twenty-first century' could undermine US strategic advantage as the world's only superpower. Its defense analysts considered that China's purchases of Russian missiles and warships during the 1996 tension off the Taiwan Straits could threaten the US military presence in Asia.[22] As the No. 1 customer for Russia's arms industry, China had access to the most advanced missile, thermonuclear and aerospace systems the Russians could sell. In January 1999, the US Congress intended to include Taiwan in its Tactical Missile Defense (TMD) system. Inherited from the Dengist predominantly anti-US regional model, the Jiangist perception of the regional hegemony of the 'US-Japan club' further reflected China's fear that Japan would be associated with the US anti-missile forces of the TMD system. According to the Chinese, this system was to supply military technology to Japan and even more so to Taiwan. This plan, which was to form an actual military alliance between the United States, Japan and Taiwan against the PRC, would nullify the potential of China's own 700 or so medium-range missiles aimed across the Taiwan Straits. Moreover, in April 1999, the Sino-Russian governments joined forces to oppose the proposed missile defense system of the United States and warned that a new arms race could threaten global stability.[23] With United States as the dominant international power, China setting on a pattern of growth and Russia attempting to compensate its decline from its former superpower status, both found common cause in trying to set up a balance to the US.

However, the anti-China strategists and movements in the United States were not effective owing to the following crucial factors:

(1) Both countries have shared common views regarding the issues of preventing proliferation of weapons of mass destruction, maintaining regional stability in the Asia-Pacific region, promoting international trade, improving the ecological environment.

(2) The global multi-polarized tendency called for resolving international and regional problems through cooperation of the major powers vitally including the United States and China.
(3) With the process of economic globalization, the acceleration of technological innovation and economic interdependence on each other enhanced the sphere of Sino-US economic cooperation. By September 1994, China had set up 5 special economic zones, 32 economic and technological development zones and 52 national-level new and high-tech development zones.

In mid-March 1998, following the footsteps of the European Union, the US government declined to propose to the Congress to go against the PRC at the United Nations Human Rights Conference in Geneva. More importantly, with the aim of building the Sino-US 'constructive strategic partnership', Clinton visited Beijing in June the same year, the first visit by an American President in nine years. In May 1999, the US-led NATO bombed the Chinese Embassy in Yugoslavia. With Clinton's apology, the Chinese government reacted in a restrained manner thus resolving the conflict by dialogue.

After President George W. Bush took office in January 2001, his tough policy toward the PRC defied his predecessor's aim of building a 'strategic partnership' with it and redefined it as the 'strategic competitive rival of the US'. With the mid-air collision of Chinese military aircraft and US navy spy plane in April 2001, this policy gave rise to tension in bilateral relations. Furthermore, the Department of Defense of the United States began shifting the US military strategic focus from Europe to East Asia, with President Bush's National Missile Defense system vitally including Taiwan.

However, the terrorist attacks on New York and Washington D.C. on 11 September 2001, which shocked the world, ushered in the new phase of Sino-US bilateral ties of 'constructive cooperation', with China's anti-terrorist stance. Since then, Bush has considered the PRC a friend of his country. Further, the Shanghai Summit in mid-October 2001, China's admission to the World Trade Organization (WTO) as a formal member in November that year and its victory in July the same year for the 2008

Olympic bid all paved the way for the sound development of bilateral ties in the new century. Moreover, in October 2002, the Sino-US Summit took place at President Bush's private ranch known as the 'White House in Texas'. Bush considered the PRC as an ally of the United States in its fight against global terrorism. Both sides began the resumption of military exchanges, which were to bring about their strategic stability. US strategists realized that without China's cooperation, there would be no peace in Asia. Apart from China's anti-terrorist stance, the US needed the PRC's cooperation on the issue of security of the Korean Peninsula. Both China and the United States have shared common views on the issue of preventing proliferation of weapons of mass destruction (Jiang, 2006:527).

Both countries needed each other, particularly in economic and trade exchange. The PRC's modernization drive needed funds, technology, management expertise and a huge market that the United States could provide. The United States saw the potential of China.

The PRC mainly sold to the US labor-intensive products such as textiles, garments, shoes, toys and household electrical appliances. In 2000, Chinese exports to the United States were 21 per cent of its total exports and over 5 per cent of China's GDP.[24] The US mainly sold to China capital- and technology-intensive products such as aircrafts, machinery, chemical machinery, power generation equipment, electronics, telecommunications equipment, and agricultural products. In 1997, China was the biggest buyer of US aircraft. In 2002, jobs created by the US exports to China numbered 400,000 compared with 200,000 in the early 1990s.[25] The US exports to China achieved a 17 per cent growth in 2001.

The PRC is also one of the largest creditors of the United States. In 1999, China held US$51.3 billion in US treasury bonds, 4 per cent of all US treasury bonds purchased by foreign countries.[26] It acquired more than US$200 billion worth of treasury securities over 2004.[27]

As mutual dependency between both economies increases, the economic and trade relationship became a stabilizer for bilateral relations. At their meeting in Shanghai in October 2001, Presidents George W. Bush and Jiang Zemin agreed to build a constructive partnership cooperation to provide a direction for future development of bilateral relations.

In the long run, China's rapid economic growth and its WTO entry will provide an even broader space for future development of its economic and trade cooperation with the US, which will introduce more capital, technology and management know-how conducive to its further development. China is already home to a growing number of US-owned factories, many of them exporting back to the United States, and an even greater number of factories that are suppliers to US companies.[28] In 1995, the US Department of Commerce ranked the PRC first among the top ten rising markets. More business opportunities particularly in information technology, communications and financial services would be provided to US businesses after further improvement of China's commercial environment and further opening up of the market.

Sino-Russian Relations

In the first half of the 1980s, I argued above, based on the international reality of the time, Deng Xiaoping continued to treat the Soviet Union as the primary enemy of Mao's First World, while the United States its secondary enemy. This perception placed Japan and other US-led advanced Western industrialized nations in his Second World. The PRC now aimed at 'colluding with its secondary enemies' against 'hegemonism' of its 'primary enemy'.

I also discussed above that in July 1986, calling for closer ties with the PRC and announcing the Soviet troop withdrawals from Afghanistan and Mongolia on China's northern border, Soviet leader Mikhail Gorbachev's speech in Vladivostok foreshadowed the prospect of a détente of the two communist giants. Thus, in February 1989, Soviet Foreign Minister Eduard Shevardnadze announced the Soviet reduction of troops stationed along the Mongolian and Manchurian borders. This pullout reduced the Soviet threat to China. Govbachev's efforts including the Soviet troop withdrawal from Afghanistan and Mongolia and Soviet pressure on Vietnam to withdraw its troops from Cambodia led to Deng's acceptance of a Sino-Soviet summit meeting in Beijing in May 1989. This meeting, which heralded the complete Sino-Soviet normalization of relations, marked the end of their thirty-year-old military confrontation. As a result, the Soviet Union in the Dengist worldview was relegated to the position of secondary enemy.

The Soviet Union, China as well as the United States all believed that peace and stability in Southeast Asia was crucially based on the political settlement of the twelfth-year-old Cambodian problem. All these parties also realized that in finding a political solution to this problem, tripartite cooperation between them was crucial. Mikhail Gorbachev's initiative to establish a new international order good for the Asia-Pacific region was based on cooperation. Thus, the Soviet pressure on Vietnam to withdraw its troops from Cambodia was inevitable. In September 1990, the Chinese and Soviet foreign ministers agreed in Harbin to suspend military aid to all the warring factions in the Cambodian conflict. Encouraged by the PRC, the three factions in the Cambodian resistance coalition reached an accord in Beijing to take part in working out the highest-level central committee for the Jakarta conference on troop withdrawal of the warring factions under direct UN supervision. With tripartite efforts, a political settlement of the Cambodian problem was eventually worked out bringing a formal end to thirteen years of civil war in Cambodia.

As a result of the collapse of the Soviet Union, Deng's 'good-neighborhood' policy was extended to Russia. His global strategy, which was aimed at attracting foreign capital and advanced technology from the US-led Western world, could now be applied to the world at large. In April 1990, Premier Li Peng signed a series of agreements with the Russians in Moscow on cooperation in the fields of trade and the economy, science and technology.[29]

In mid-December 1992, the visiting Russian President Boris Yeltsin and Chinese President Yang Shangkun issued a 'joint statement on mutual relations between the PRC and the Russian Federation' in Beijing. In September 1994, President Jiang Zemin who succeeded Yang signed with President Yeltsin the second joint statement and the 'joint statement on mutually not using nuclear weapons against or aiming strategic nuclear weapons at each other'.[30]

Toward the end of April 1996, Boris Yeltsin revisited China for the creation of an Asia-Pacific regional security association which was aimed at promoting Russia-China commercial ties and building a 'Strategic Partnership for the 21st Century'. According to Yeltsin, cooperation with China was 'helpful to Russia's economic reform, the economic development of its Far East region'.[31] China's economic reform inspired Russia; and Yeltsin proposed to consolidate the commercial ties. Yeltsin's visit highlighted the signing of the first such treaty in Asia by the presidents of China, Russia and three former Soviet Union republics of Tajikistan, Kyrgyzstan and Kazakhstan. The treaty to demilitarize their common border was hailed as a significant boost to peace and stability in the Asia-Pacific region. The accord marked the apex of the ties of the Sino-Soviet alliance, which had collapsed in the 1960s. This had been the most important treaty to reduce border tensions in Asia and make economic cooperation possible since the Cold War. The treaty was unlikely to change the balance of power in Asia or the world, with the ending of the Cold War and the United States remaining the sole superpower. During the Cold War period, the agreements would have been viewed as the two communist giants colluding against the United States. Yet the treaty was of great symbolic significance in that it formally marked the end of an era in which Russian strategic thinking had posed as a massive military threat to Asia.

During Yeltsin's visit, both countries signed fourteen agreements ranging from trade deals to nuclear energy cooperation. Perhaps the biggest deal reached was the joint development of a pipeline to bring gas from the Siberian fields to the Yellow Sea. In mid-July 2001, visiting Chairman Jiang Zemin and Russian President Vladimir Putin signed a good-neighborly treaty of friendship and cooperation, with the aim of maintaining the global strategic balance and stability.[32] Although Russia's trade with Japan was only marginal and the value of two-way Russian-Chinese trade amounted to less than two per cent of China's total in 1995, Russia was now to attempt transform its centuries-old policy of military expansion into one of peaceful commercial exchange.

Notes

Prologue

1 'Chairman Mao on the Sino-Soviet Treaty and Agreements', *People's Daily*, 13 April 1950, 1.
2 Edgar Snow, *The Other Side of the River* (London: Victor Gollanez Ltd, 1966), 640.
3 *Ibid.*
4 'Mao's Talk to Chinese Students in Moscow', *People's Daily*, 19 November 1957, 1.
5 Chen Jin (陈晋), ed., *Explaining Mao Zedong's Reading Notes* (毛泽东读书笔记解析), *Vol. II* (Shenzhen: Guangdong People's Press, 1996), 1463.
6 *Mao, Mao Zedong Si Xiang Wan Sui* (Beijing: 1969), 179, 189; Snow, *The Other Side of the River*, 95.
7 Mao, *Mao Tse-tung Xi Xiang Wan Sui*, 179.
8 Mao, *Mao Zedong Si Xiang Wan Sui*, 131.
9 *Ibid.*, 144.
10 *Ibid.*, 501.
11 Minford, J., trans. & ed., *Strange Tales from a Chinese Studio* (Penguin Books, 2006), xiii.
12 Mao, *Mao Zedong Si Xiang Wan Sui*, 290.
13 Snow, *The Other Side of the River*, 95.
14 *Ibid.*
15 Chen, *Explaining Mao Zedong's Reading Notes, Vol. I*, 314.
16 Xu Zhongyuan (许中远), *Mao Zedong's Comments on Five Classical Novels* (毛泽东读评五部古典小说) (Beijing: Chinese Language Press, 1997), 305.
17 Chen, *Explaining Mao Zedong's Reading Notes, Vol. II*, 1617.
18 *Ibid.*, 1619.
19 Xu, *op. cit.*, 308.
20 Xu, *Mao Zedong's Comments on Five Classic Novels*, 306.
21 *Ibid.*
22 Minford, *Strange Tales from a Chinese Studio*, 91–4.
23 Xu, *op. cit*, 307; He Qifang (何其芳), *Complete Works of He Qifang* (何其芳文集), *Vol. III* (Beijing: People's Literature Press, 1983), 127.
24 *Ibid.*
25 *Ibid.*
26 Xu, *op. cit.*, 305–6.

27 Chen, *op. cit.*, 1625; see also Mao, *Mao Zedong Shuxin Xuanji* (毛泽东书信选集) (Beijing: People's Press, 1983), 576.
28 Mao, *Selected Works of Mao Zedong's Foreign Diplomacy* (Beijing: People's Press), 489.
29 Mao's conversation with Wu Zhipu (吴芝圃) on June 22, 1959; see 'Documents of Party' (党的文献), fourth edition (Beijing: 1959).
30 'Documents of the Party', fifth edition (Beijing: 1994).
31 Chen, *op. cit.*, 1441.
32 Teiwes, F. C., *Politics and Purges in China*, second edition (New York: M. E. Sharpe, Inc., 1993), 311, 328.
33 'Resolution of 8th Plenary Session of 8th C.C. of CPC on the Anti-Party Clique Headed by Peng Teh-huai', *Beijing Review* (Beijing: August 18, 1967), 8; 'Peng and His Behind-the-Scenes Boss' (25 August 1967), 6; Li, Hsin-K., 'Peng's Heinous Crimes of Usurping Army Leadership and Opposing the Party' (1 September 1967), 12.
34 Xu, *op. cit.*, 203.
35 *Ibid.*
36 Yu, A. C., trans. & ed., Journey to the West (Chicago & London: University of Chicago, 1977), 151–2.
37 Wu Cheng-en, *Monkey*, trans. Waley, A. (London: The Folio Society, 1968), 75–6.
38 The *People's Daily* did not mention Khrushchev's arrival in Beijing on 31 July 1958, but only carried very brief news about his departure three days later. This suggested that relations between the leaders of the two countries were far from 'friendly'.
39 Zhuang Zi, 'Flying Freely', Watson, B., trans., *The Complete Works of Chuang Tzu* (New York: Columbia University Press, 1971), 29.
40 'Moscow Test Ban Treaty', *China Reconstructs* (Beijing: April 1976), 5.
41 'Chao Kai Killed by a Poisonous Arrow', *Peking Review*, 27 February 1976, 11.
42 'Song Jiang was a capitulationist-revisionist', *The Chinese Youth* (中国青年报), 24 September 1988.
43 'Song Jiang's Capitulationist Line', *Peking Review*, 27 February 1976, 11.
44 *Ibid.*
45 *Ibid.*
46 'Khrushchev's Capitulationist Line of Peaceful Co-existence', *Beijing Review*, 30 April 1965, 15.

Chapter One

1 Snow, Edgar, *Red Star Over China* (New York: Grove Press, 1961), 133.
2 Li, Rui (李锐), *The Schooling Life of MaoZedong in His Early Age* (毛泽东早年之读书生活) (Liaoning People's Press, 1992), 26.

3 Mao referred to this concept on a number of occasions. The important ones are:
(a) See Dong Zhixin (董志新), *Mao Zedong Du Sanguo Yanyi* (毛泽东读三国演义) (Shenyang: Wan Juan Press, 2009), 54–66.
(b) Soon after the 'Three Bad Years' of 1959–61, still very bitter about the way Khrushchev abrogated the Sino-Soviet treaty and agreements and withdrew Soviet technicians, Mao referred to the statement again. See Quan Yanchi (权延赤), *Inside and Outside of the Red Wall* (红墙内外) (Beijing: Kunlun Press, 1989), 96.
(c) Mao spoke about it in his 'Anti-Revisionist Report' in September 1964. See Mao, *Mao Tse-tung Si Xiang Wan Sui*, 578.

4 Mao, *ibid*, 83, 578; Dong, Zhixin, *op. cit.*, 60; Quan, Yangchi, *op. cit.*, 95–6.

5 Chen, *Explaining Mao Zedong's Reading Notes*, 1217. My concept of *qi* has now been quite well known internationally since its appearance in 1995. Please refer to my works *The Role of Ch'i in Mao Tse-tung's Leadership Style* (1995) and *Mao Tse-tung's Ch'i and the Chinese Political Economy with Special Reference to the Post-Mao Modernization Revolution (2000)*. *Qi* (*ch'i*) is defined as a mental state which consists of the elements of an exaggerated inflation of capacity to an astronomical dimension and an exaggerated quantity of power of supernatural scale – which appear either singly or in unison.

6 Dong Zhixin, *op. cit.*, 215.

7 Dong Zhixin, *op. cit.*, 135, 141.

8 Lu Yude (陆儒德), *Jiang Hai Ge Mao Zedong* (江海客毛泽东) (Beijing: Ocean Press, 2009), 54.

9 Mao, *SW, Vol. V* (Beijing: Foreign Languages Press, 1977), 468. Mao argued that the masses were like the water in which the fish, i.e., the leaders of a nation to swim. Thus the leadership should not go against or divorce from them, because, first, the masses were the creators of history who possessed the power to change the world, and second, without the support of the masses the leadership was powerless. See also *Mao Tse-tung Si Xiang Wan Sui*, 106.

10 Li Ying (李颖) and Cheng Meidong (程美东), ed., *Experiencing History with Mao Zedong* (与毛泽东–起感受历史) (Wuhan: Hubei People's Press, 2005), 370.

11 Lu Rude (陆儒德), *Jiang Hai Ke Mao Zedong* (江海客毛泽东) (Beijing: Haiyang Press, 2009), 59–60.

Chapter Two

1 Mao, *Mao Tse-tung Si Xiang Wan Sui* (Beijing: 1969), 627, 694.

2 Snow, *Red Star Over China* (New York: Random House, 1961), 133.

3 Xu, *Mao Zedong's Comments on Five Classical Novels*, 132.

4 Chen, *op. cit.*, *Vol. II*, 1386.

5 Dong Zhixin, *op. cit.*, 230.
6 *Ibid.*, 232.
7 Dong, *op. cit.*, 361–2.
8 Li, Yinqiao, *Beside Mao Zedong for 15 Years* (在毛泽东身边15年) (Hong Kong: Cosmos Books Ltd Press, 1992), 111–12.
9 Li Yinqiao, *Beside Mao Zedong for 15 Years*, 111–12.
10 *Ibid.*
11 CCTV, Beijing: 19 March 2010, 7.15 p.m.–8.00 p.m.
12 Cao Cao, *The Cao Cao Anthology* (曹操集) (Beijing: Chung Hua Press, 1974), 11.
13 Cao Cao considers that he and Liu Bei are the only heroes of the time.
14 Chen, *Explaining Mao Zedong's Reading Notes*, 1217.
15 Xu, *Mao Zedong's Comments on Five Classical Novels*, 163.
16 Xu, *Mao Zedong's Comments on Five Classical Novels*, 156.
17 *Ibid.*, 156–8.
18 Li, Rui (李锐), *The Schooling Life of Mao Zedong at His Early Age* (毛泽东早年之读书生活) (Liaoning People's Press, 1992), 26.
19 Mao, *Mao Tse-tung Si Xiang Wan Sui*, 106, see also, Luo, G. Z., *Romance of the Three Kingdoms*, Chapter 38.
20 See Note 6, Chapter One.
21 If Cao Cao had won the battle, China would have been unified.
22 See Note 3, Chapter One.
23 Dong, Zhixin, *op. cit.*, 54. See also Sun Baoyi (孙宝义), Mao Zedong's Reading Life (毛泽东的读书生涯) (Beijing: Zhishi Press, 1993), 156–7.
24 Lu, *Jiang Haike Mao Zedong*, 56–60.
25 *Ibid.*, Chapter 98.
26 Lu, *Jiang Haike Mao Zedong*, 192–3; Luo, *Romance of the Three Kingdoms*, Chapter 42.
27 Luo, *ibid.*, Chapter 48.
28 Luo, *Romance of the Three Kingdoms*, Chapter 42.
29 *Ibid.*
30 Chen, *Explaining Mao Zedong's Reading Notes, Vol. I*, 481–2.
31 Xu, *Mao Zedong's Comments on Five Classical Novels*, 139, 140.
32 *Ibid.*, 141.
33 Containing 294 chapters, the work chronologically narrates Chinese history from the Warring States period in 403 B.C. to the beginning of the Song dynasty. Standard Chinese dynastic histories in terms of the Twenty-Four Histories including the *Records of the Three Kingdoms* primarily divided chapters between annals (纪) of rulers and biographies (传) of officials. In Chinese terms the *Guiding Mirror to aid in Government* changed the format of histories from biographical style (纪传体) to chronological manner (编年体), which is ideal for analysis and criticism.
34 Li Chuan Yin (李传印), *Zizhi Tongjian* (Beijing: Lan Tian Press, 2008), 44.

35 *Ibid.*
36 *Ibid.* See also Gong, Yuzhi (龚育之), etc., *Mao Zedong's Reading Life* (毛泽东的读书生活) (Beijing: San Lian Press, 1986), 208.
37 *Ibid.*
38 *Ibid.*
39 Si-ma Guang (司马光), edited Li Zongtong (李宗桐), etc, annotated, *Annotated Zizhi Tongjian* (资治通鉴今注) (Taiwan Commercial Press).
40 Mao, *Anthology of Mao Zedong's Comments on Chinese Classical Literature and History* (毛泽东读文史籍批语集) (hereafter *Anthology of Mao*), 106; see also Chen, Jin, *op. cit.*, *Vol. I*, 500.
41 *Ibid.*
42 *Ibid.*
43 *Ibid.*
44 *Yao Nai* (姚鼐), 'Comments on Distinguishing Different items' (论辩类), in *Classical Writing Types* (古文辞类纂); see also Chen, Jin, *op. cit.*, *Vol. I*, 500.
45 *Ibid.*
46 Mao, *Anthology of Mao*, 106.
47 Luo, *Romance of the Three Kingdoms*, Chapter 98.
48 *Ibid.*

Chapter Four

1 Strong, A. L., 'Reminiscences on Interview with Chairman Mao Tse-tung on the Paper Tiger', *Peking Review*, 29 November 1960, 13.
2 After a long negotiation, the soviets returned the Dalian and Lushun ports as well as the Changchun Railway in Manchuria to China in May 1955. See Lu Rude *Jiang Haike Mao Zedong*, 241.
3 Li and Cheng, *Experiencing History with Mao Zedong*, *Vol. I*, 370; see also Mao, *Mao Tse-tung Si Xiang Wan Sui*, 164.
4 I visited Professor Wang at the East Asian Institute, National University of Singapore on 5 May 2011, 5–6 p.m.
5 Li and Cheng, ibid., 388.
6 Lin Biao refused to serve as commander-in-chief under the pretext of recuperating in Russia. See Chu Yun (楚云), *The Korean War* (Beijing: Current Affairs Press, 2010), 87–8.
7 The interview took place on 23 July 1936. 'When the people's revolution has been victorious in China, the Outer Mongolian Republic will automatically become a part of the Chinese federation at its own will'. See Schram, Stuart, R., *The Political Thought of Mao Tse-tung* (New York: Frederick A. Praeger, 1963), 419. Also Lam,

L. S.' *Mao Tse-tung's Purposive Contention with the Superpowers* (Lewiston: Mellen University Press, 1994), 89. See also Lam, *The International Environment and China's Twin Models of Development* (Oxford: Peter Lang, 2007), 20–1.

8 Snow, *Red Star Over China*, 444–5.

9 *Ibid.*, 396.

10 Mongolian President Yumjaaglyn Tsedenbal related all this: see 'Mao's proposal on amalgamation of the MPR', *Far Eastern Economic Review* (Hong Kong: 7 February 1975), 37.

11 *Ibid.*

12 *Ibid.*

13 *Ibid.*

14 Mao, *Mao Zedong Wenji, Vol. 7* (Beijing: People's Press, 1999), 165.

15 This was stated by Mao's former security guard Chang Muqi (张木奇). Source: Phoenix Cable TV, Hong Kong, hosted by Lu Yu (鲁豫) (8.00–8.45 p.m., 5 January 2004).

16 Li, and Cheng, *Experiencing History with Mao Zedong, Vol. I*, 455–6.

17 Khrushchev, Nikita, *Khrushchev Remembers: The Last Testament* (trans. and ed.), Strobe Talbott (Boston: Little Brown & Co., 1974), 244.

18 Snow, *Red Star Over China*, 481.

19 Esposito, V. J., 'Korean War', *Encyclopedia Americana, Vol. 16*, International Edition, Grolier Incorporated, Danbury, Connecticut, 1982, 528k.

20 Li and Cheng, *Experiencing History with Mao Zedong, Vol. I*, 394.

21 'Strong, A. L., 'Reminiscences on Interview with Chairman Mao Tse-tung on the Paper Tiger', *Peking Review*, 29 November 1960, 17.

22 'President Eisenhower's Speech on the US Commitment in Vietnam', *New York Times*, 5 August 1953, 1, 10.

23 Lam, *Mao Tse-tung's Purposive Contention with the Superpowers*, 92.

24 Kaplan, L. S., International and Diplomacy' *Encyclopedia Americana, Vol. 27*, 759.

25 *Ibid.*

26. *The Times*, 13 January 1954, 2.

27 Li, and Cheng, *Experiencing History with Mao Zedong, Vol. II.*, 146.

28 *The Times*, 22 January 1954, 5.

29 *Ibid.*

30 *The Times*, 27 January 1954, 6.

31 Li, and Cheng, *Vol. II, op. cit.*, 146.

32 Snow, *The Other Side of the River*, 641.

33 *'Chairman Mao Assesses the Present International Situation'*, *People's Daily*, 19 November 1957, 1.

34 'Bandung Conference's Resolution Regarding Various Political Questions', *People's Daily*, 12 April 1955, 1.

35 'Long Live the Afro-Asian People's Great Consolidation', *People's Daily* (26 December 1957), 1; 'Afro-Asian Consolidation Conference on Disintegration of Imperialism' (28 December 1957), 5; 'All Afro-Asian Nations Condemned Colonialism' (30 December 1957), 5. Also see Lam, *Mao Tse-tung's Purposive Contention with the Superpowers*, 87.

36 *1967 Yearbook of Chinese Communism* (Taipei: Institute for the Study of Chinese Communist Problems, 1967), 403.

37 *Ibid.* This included the establishment of treaties of friendship and mutual non-aggression with 11 of these nations. China had already established (a) trade relationships with more than 50 nations, (b) cultural relationships with more than 50 nations and (c) aid commitments of US$970 million to 22 nations.

38 Yang, Min, 'Chairman Mao on the Twelve Year Plan for Agriculture', *Peking Review*, 18 March 1958, 12.

39 *Ibid.*

40 Li, and Cheng, *Experiencing History with Mao Zedong, Vol. II*, 58; see also Li, *Beside Mao Zedong for 15 Years*, 231.

41 Lam, *The Role of Ch'i in Mao Tse-tung's Leadership Style* (San Francisco: Mellen Research University Press, 1993), 186.

42 Part of this section depends on Lam's published work *Mao Tse-tung's Ch'i and the Chinese Political Economy With Special Reference to the Post-Mao Modernization Revolution* (Lewiston: Edwin Mellen Press, 2000), 138–47.

43 Li, and Cheng, *Experiencing History with Mao Zedong, Vol. I*, 405.

44 Private businessmen were the targets of the Five-Antis Movement, which was designed to aim against bribery, tax evasion, theft of state assets, cheating in labor and materials and stealing state economic intelligence.

45 Hughes, T. J., and Luard, Evan D. T., 'The Economic Development of Communist China', Oh, S. K., *Land Reform in Communist China and Postwar Japan* (Philadelphia: University of Philadelphia, 1966), 107.

46 Gurley, *China's Economy and the Maoist Strategy*, 213.

47 *Ibid.*

48 Zhou Enlai, 'Report on the Proposals for the Second Five Year Plan for Development of the National Economy to the Eighth Party Congress', 16 September 1956, Oh, *Land Reform in Communist China and Postwar Japan*, 107.

49 'To Strengthen the Cooperative Sector', *People's Daily*, 10 April 1952, 1.

Chapter Five

1 Dong, *Mao Zedong Du San Sanguo Yanyi*, 60.

2 Quan, *Inside and Outside of the Red Wall*, 95–6.

3 *Ibid.*
4 'Escalation Means Getting Closer and Closer to the Grave', *Peking Review*, 30 April 1965, 15.
5 *Ibid.*
6 'The Soviet New Maritime Strategy for Global Expansion', *People's Daily*, 30 April 1976, 25.
7 Lam, *Mao Tse-tung's Purposive Contention with the Superpowers*, 93–5.
8 Snow, *The Other Side of the River*, 640.
9 Snow, *The Other Side of the River*, 634.
10 This was contrary to the Chinese style of reception of 'friendly' heads of state, given that the Soviet Union was China's 'fraternal' ally.
11 Snow, *The Other Side of the River*, 641.
12 *Ibid.*
13 'China's Declaration of a Twelve-Mile Coastal Zone', *PD*, 4 September 1958, 1.
14 Snow, *The Other side of the Rive*, 634.
15 *Ibid.*, 635.
16 *Ibid.*, 634.
17 Li and Cheng, *Experiencing History with Mao Zedong*, 70–1.
18 Yahuda, M. B. writes: 'The signing of the partial Nuclear Test Ban Treaty in July 1963 was the turning point in Sino-Soviet relations'. See 'Chinese Foreign Policy After 1963: The Maoist Phases', in *China Quarterly*, no. 36 (October–December 1968), 93. However, I would argue that the turning point could even be dated further back to the outcome of the Taiwan Straits Crisis.
19 Mao, *Mao Zedong Wenji, Vol. 8* (Beijing: PP, 2001), 358.
20 'Soviet Military Aid to India against China', *Peking Review*, 8 November 1963, 25.
21 'Protagonists of New Colonialism', *People's Daily*, 22 October 1963, 1, 3.
22 This was because the Russians had denied them the resources to develop a nuclear bomb under the 'false claim that they would be prepared to defend Chinese interests'.
23 'Shameful Betrayal of Sino-Soviet Alliance', *People's Daily*, 30 August 1963, 2.
24 CCTV, Beijing, 19 September 2010, 8.00 p.m.
25 'Production and Militia Combined', Editorial, *People's Daily*, 4 September 1958.
26 'Get the Upsurge in Forming People's Communes', Editorial, *Hongqi*, tenth issue (1958), 1.
27 'The New Development of the Labor-Military Forces Combined', *Yenan Liberation Daily* (Yenan: 15 October 1944), 3; 'The Road of the Soldiers and People Behind the Enemy – Fighting and Production Combined', in *YLD* (Yenan: 2 March 1944), 1; 'The New Development of the Labor-Military Forces Combined in the Ch'in Sui (晋绥) Border Area Last Year', in *YLD* (Yenan: 1 February 1945), 3.
28 Editorial, 'Cooperative Contract Gives Efficient, Fast and Good Results', *People's Daily*, 3 September 1958, 1. See also Lethbridge, *The Peasant and the Communes* (Hong Kong: Dragonfly Books, 1963), 74.

29 Mao's commune system was meant to be the prototype for the whole of the oppressed and exploited third world with each nation as a basic unit. The dictum of 'uniting all that can be united' was meant to work for Mao's anti-capitalist and ultimately anti-imperialist schemes in which all self-sufficient and independent units represented by all third world oppressed and exploited nations were to be united with both anti-capitalist and anti-imperialist aims.
30 Stuart Schram, *The Political Thought of Mao Tse-tun* (New York: Praeger, 1969), 182.
31 Han Suyin, *China in the Year 2001* (London: C. A. Watts, 1967), 41.
32 'Resolution of the C.C. of the CCP on the establishment of People's Communes in the Rural Areas', *People's Communes in China* (Beijing: Foreign Languages Press, 1958), 2; see also *People's Daily*, 29 August 1958.
33 Han, *China in the Year 2001*, 46.
34 Geremie Barme, 'For Truly Great Men, Look to This Age Alone', Cheek, T. (ed.) *A Critical Introduction to Mao* (Cambridge: University Press, 2010), 257.
35 *Ibid.*, 140.
36 'Chairman Mao on Leftist Wind of Communism', *NCNA* (Beijing: 15 August 1967).
37 *Ibid.*
38 *Ibid.*
39 Teiwes, *Politics and Purges in China*, 401; *People's Daily*, 17 September 1959; also see Mao, *Wenji, Vol. 8*, 76.
40 'Chairman Mao Refuting Right Opportunists', *NCNA* (Beijing: 26 August 1959).
41 Li and Cheng, *Experiencing History with Mao Zedong, Vol. II*, 147.
42 Chiou, *Maoism in Action*, 56.
43 *Ibid.*
44 *Ibid.*
45 Teiwes, *Politics and Purges in China*, 311, 328.
46 *Ibid.*, 328.
47 Mao's letter the editor of *Shi Kan*, January 1959.
48 'Peng Teh-huai and His Behind-the-Scenes Boss Cannot Shirk Responsibility for Their Crimes', *PR*, 18 August 1967, 8; also see Note 33, Chapter One.
49 Li, 'Changes in China's Domestic Situation in the 1960s and Sino-US Relations', 298.
50 *Ibid.*
51 Mao's conversation with Wu Zhi-pu (吴芝圃) on 22 June 1959; see 'Documents of the Party' (党的文献), fourth edition (Beijing: 1959).
52 'Documents of the Party', fifth edition (Beijing: 1994).
53 Chen, *Explaining Mao Tse-tung's Reading Notes*, 1441.

Chapter Six

1 Even as far back as 1954, the entire length of the Trans-Siberian Railway was noted as 'military territory' and Khabarvosk on the Amur as a 'great military city'. See Salisbury, H. E., *The Coming War between Russia and China* (New York: W. W. Norton & Co., Inc., 1969), 105.
2 Lu, Rude, *Jiang Haike Mao Zedong*, 59–60.
3 *Ibid.*, 60.
4 'CPSU 20th Congress – Root of All Evils of Khrushchev Revisionists', *Peking Review*, 30 April 1965, 15.
5 'New Leaderships of the CPSU Preach Soviet-US Cooperation for World Domination', *PR*, 3 December 1965, 14.
6 'On Khrushchev's Phoney Communism and Its Historical Lessons for the World', *PR*, 17 July 1964, 7.
7 MacFarquhar, R., 'Perspective 2: Mao Zedong Lun', Cheek, T. (ed.), *A Critical Introduction to Mao*, 2010, 343–4, 352.
8 Myers, R., 'Agricultural Development', in Hinton, H., ed., *The PRC* (Boulder: Westview Press, Inc., 1979), 180.
9 Zhou, Bingde, *Wodebofu Zhou Enlai* (ManWeili Foundation, fourth edition), 2006, 249.
10 *Ibid.*, 239–62.
11 *Ibid.*
12 *Ibid.*, 254.
13 *Ibid.*, 251.
14 *Ibid.*, 259–62.
15 *Ibid.*
16 Zhou Bingde, *Wodebofu Zhou Enlai*, 259–62.
17 *Ibid.*, 449.
18 *Ibid.*
19 'Chairman Mao's Mechanization Strategy', *People's Daily*, 17 October 1955, 1.
20 Wong, *Land Reform in the PRC: Institutional Transformation in Agriculture*, 199.
21 'Chairman Mao on Liu's Mechanization Policy' *PD*, 17 October 1955, 2.
22 'On the Anti-Party Revisionists', *NCNA*, 1 June 1957.
23 Goldman, 'The Party and the Intellectuals', *Cambridge History of China, Vol. 14*, 257.
24 *Ibid.*
25 'A New Rectification Movement', *NCNA*, 10 September 1957.
26 MacFarquhar, R., *The Origins of the Cultural Revolution (2) The GLF, 1958–60* (London: Oxford University Press, 1974), 293–7.

27 'To Unite With All Possible', *NCNA* (Beijing: 18 June 1957); see also Harrison, J. P. *Long March to Power* (London: Macmillan, 1973, 474.
28 MacFarquhar, *op. cit.*, 295.
29 Skinner, W., 'Marketing and Social Structure in Rural China', *Journal of Asian Studies* (Ann Arbor: February 1965), 195–228. Richman, B., *Industrial Society in Communist China* (New York: Random House, 1969), 316–17. Hoffmann, C., *Work Incentive Practices and Policies in the People's Republic of China 1953–65* (New York: State University of New York Press, 1968), 108.
30 Liao, Yuen, 'Self-Management of Enterprises' in Yugoslav: The True Picture', *PR* (Beijing: 21 July 1961), 11.
31 The 'Capitalist Roader Liu Shaoqi', *PR*, 14 April 1967, 8.
32 'Fight for the Thorough Criticision and Repudiation of the Top Party Person in Authority Taking the Capitalist Road', *PR*, 14 April 1967, 8; 'The Revisionist-Capitalist Roader Liu Shaoqi', *PR*, 21 April 1967, 7.
33 'Anti-Party Activities of China's Khrushchev', *Peking Review*, 25 August 1967, 7.
34 Chen, Mingxian (陈明显), *The Old Aged Mao Zedong* (晚年毛泽东) (Nanchang: Jiangxi People's Press, 2008), 373.

Chapter Seven

1 Dong Zhixin, *Mao Zedong Du Sanguo Yanyi*, 54–66, Mao said, 'This statement in the *Romance of the Three Kingdoms* is dialectic'. See also Notes 3 & 4, Chapter One.
2 The editorial of the *People's Daily* on 1 October 1972 was much harsher towards Moscow than towards Washington. While 'US imperialism' came in for fewer lines and fewer attacks, the 'Soviet revisionist renegade clique', it elaborated, 'was reaching out it hands everywhere' … and was 'even more deceitful than the old-line imperialist nations and, therefore more dangerous'.
3 Lam, *Mao Tse-tung's Purposive Contention with the Superpowers*, 112.
4 *TASS News Agency*, see *The Guardian* (London: December 1971).
5 The essence of the Brezhnev doctrine was that when socialism itself was threatened in a socialist country, military intervention by other members of the socialist community might be necessary. Also see Lam, *ibid.*
6 Li Jie, 'Changes in China's Domestic Situation in the 1960s and Sino-US relations', Ross, S. R. and Jiang Changbin, ed., *Re-examining the Cold War: US-China Diplomacy, 1954–73* (Cambridge, MA, and London: Harvard University Press, 2001), 306.
7 *Ibid.*, 296.
8 Nixon, R., 'Inaugural Address', 20 January 1969, in *Public Papers of the Presidents of the United States: Richard Nixon, 1969* (Washington, DC: Government Printing

Office, 1971), 3; also see Gong Li, 'Chinese Decision Making and the Thawing of US-China Relations', in Ross, R. S & Jiang, C. B., *op. cit.*, 333.

9 'People from all over the world including the people from the US are our friends', *PD*, 25 December 1970, 1.

10 The Sino-Soviet talks began in September 1969 and ended in May 1971. It may be assumed that efforts had been made from both sides to relief the hostility. See *1971 Yearbook*, section 6, 4.

11 In February 1973, China invited Bulgaria's Vice Minister of Foreign Trade, K. Kozmov, to talk on trade, and agreements on exchange of commodities and payment were signed in February 1973. In mid-February 1974, Chen Chi led Chinese trade delegates to visit Bulgaria to sign agreements on commodity exchange and payment. China carried out similar trade relations with East Germany, Poland, Czechoslovakia, etc. See *1974 Yearbook*, section 6, 42–4.

12 *The Party's Documents*, 4th issue, 1973; also see Chen, *Explaining Mao Zedong's Reading Notes, Vol. I*, 617.

13 'Strive for the Four Modernizations', *PD*, Editorial (Beijing: 9 February 1979).

14 *Ibid.*

15 US Foreign Broadcast Information Service: *PRC Daily Report*, FBIS-CHI-75-13 (20 January 1975), *Vol. 1*, No. 13, D10–D11.

Chapter Eight

1 Deng, *SW of DXP 1982–1992* (Beijing: FLP, 1994), 72.

2 'Deng Xiaoping Theory is a Continuation and Development of Mao Zedong Thought', *Beijing Review* (Beijing: 6–12 October 1997), 14.

3 Lam, Lai. Sing, 'A Short Note on ASEAN-Great Power Interaction', in *Contemporary Southeast Asia* (Singapore: Institute of Southeast Asian Studies, March 1994), 454. Also see Lam, *Mao Tse-tung's Ch'i and the Chinese Political Economy*, 218.

4 Lam, *ibid.*

5 'The New Industrial Metropolis of Shenzhen', *SCMP* (Hong Kong: 22 June 2002), 14.

6 'China's Relations with Southeast Asia', *The Nation* (Sydney: 1 December 1982), 6.

7 In December 1989, the Soviet Union signed the arms-control treaty of reduction of the intermediate-range nuclear weapons with the US in Washington, in quest of the European security. In October 1990, they reached an agreement in New York in principle on the reduction of the conventional forces in Europe. In July 1991, they also reached an arms-control accord of slashing their arsenals of long-range nuclear weapons by about a third.

8 Estimates by the International Institute of Strategic Studies put total Soviet troop strength at 5.2 million of which about 2.2 million were deployed in Europe. See *Asian Wall Street Journal* (Hong Kong: 8 December 1988), 1.

9 Huang, T. W. and Li, Z. Y., 'The Changing Security Scene in East Asia – An Analysis of the US Perspective', in *ASEAN-China, Hong Kong Forum 1990* (Hong Kong: Royal Park Hotel, Shatin, 7–9 August 1990).

10 *Ibid.*

11 Rong, Zhi, 'A Retrospect of China's USSR and China-Russia Relations', *BR* (Beijing: 15 November 1999), 13.

Epilogue

1 'Minister Qian in bid to woo third world', *South China Morning Post* (*SCMP*) (Hong Kong), 8 January 1991, 11.

2 'Qian asserts role in new world order', *SCMP*, 15 December 1990, 11.

3 Xue, Chao, 'Foreign Minister Qian on world issues', *BR*, 7 January 1991, 9.

4 Cheung, Tai Ming, 'Gulf war mutes foreign concern', *Far Eastern Economic Review* (Hong Kong), 31 January 1991, 6.

5 Deng's perception of a new world order and the 'club of wealthy nations', *Ta Kung Pao* (*TKP*) (Hong Kong), 15 December 1990, 1.

6 'The wealthy nations' hegemonic contention over the third world', *International Problems Studies Magazine*, no. 4 (Beijing:, 1990), 5–6. See also *Inside China Mainland* (Taipei: Institute of Current China Studies, February 1990), 8.

7 'Qian Qichen on Our Changing World', in *TKP*, 15 December 1990, 1. Qian's thesis was based on Deng Xiaoping's new international political and economic order proposed in 1988 in accordance with the 'five principles of peaceful co-existence'.

8 US Defense Secretary Chenney's announcement was made in Tokyo in February 1990.

9 'Minister Qian in bid to woo third world', *SCMP*, 8 January 1991, 11.

10 'Premier Li's Guarantee', *Associated Press Report*, 15 December 1990.

11 'China's support of the East Asian Economic Caucus', *SCMP*, 13 January 1992, 8.

12 'Human rights will not destabilize China', *SCMP*, 12 January 1992, 5.

13 Huang and Li, 'The Changing Security Scene in East Asia', *op. cit., 1990*.

14 Baker assured firm American commitment to the region', *China Daily* (Hong Kong), 27 July 1992, 8.

15 *Ibid.*

16 Japanese new national defense program, *FEER*, 3 January 1991, 12.

17 *Ibid.*

18 Rizal Sukma, 'Jakarta-Beijing Relations and Security Challenges in Southeast Asia', *Indonesian Quarterly*, No. XVIII–4 (Jakarta: Centre for Strategic and International Studies), 284. See also *US & News Report*, 23 April 1990, 33.
19 The SDI consists of a ballistic-missile tracking system to be operated from space, energy-operated weapons systems to destroy ballistic missiles, a control system and research into support systems aimed at surviving an enemy attack.
20 Wang, Jisi, 'US China policy: containment or engagement?', *Beijing Review* (Beijing: 21–27 October 1996), 8.
21 'US containment strategists misled', *BR* (Beijing: 16 October 1995), 4. SEATO formed in 1954 was aimed at containing communism and China but disbanded in 1977.
22 Reportedly towards the end of 1996, the Chinese purchased two Sovremenny class destroyers equipped with SS-N-22 anti-ship cruise missiles, which the US feared most due to their deadly supersonic speed. See *SCMP*, 16 January 1997, 19.
23 'A new arms race warned', *SCMP* (Hong Kong: 18 April 1999), Sunday Focus Section, 3.
24 Zhen, Bingxi, 'Trade important for Sino-US ties', *BR* (Beijing: 28 February 2002), 8.
25 *Ibid.*
26 *Ibid.*, 7.
27 'Reality strikes US: China has arrived', *SCMP*, 25 June 2005, A5.
28 'Reality strikes US: China has arrived', *SCMP* (Hong Kong: 25 June 2005), A5.
29 'Sino-Russian cooperation', *BR* (Beijing: 15 November 1999), 13.
30 'Sino-Russian cooperation', *BR* (Beijing: 15 November 1999), 13.
31 'Yeltsin' on Sino-Russian economic cooperation', *NCNA* (Beijing: 23 April 1996).
32 Tang, Yuen Kai, 'China, Russia Good-Neighborly Treaty of Friendship and Cooperation', *BR* (Beijing: 2 August 2001), 8–11.

Bibliography

Chinese Sources

Texts

Cao, Cao (1974). The Cao Cao Anthology (曹操集) (Beijing: Chung Hua Press).
Jiang, Zemin (2006). *Selected Works of Jiang Zemin* (江泽民文选) (Beijing: People's Press).
Li Chuan Yin (李传印) (2008). *Zizhi Tongjian* (资治通鉴) (Beijing: Lan Tian Press).
Li, Yinqiao (李银桥) (1992). *Beside Mao Zedong for 15 Years* (在毛泽东身边15年) (Hong Kong: Cosmos Books Ltd).
Li, Ying (李颖) and Cheng, Meidong (程美东) (ed.) (2005). *Experiencing History With Mao Zedong* (与毛泽东一起感受历史), two volumes (Wuhan: Hupei People's Press).
Lu Bi (卢弼), 'Lu Sun Biography' (陆逊传), Wu Volume 58 (吴书), in *Anthology of the Records of the Three Kingdoms* (三国志集解).
Luo, Guanzhong (罗贯中) *Romance of the Three Kingdoms* (三国演义) (Hong Kong: Kwong Chi Press).
Mao, Tse-tung (1950). *Fight For the Basic Improvement of the National Financial and Economic Situation* (为争取国家财政经济状况的基本好转而斗争) (Beijing: People's Press).
—— (1966). *Vol. II* (Beijing: People's Press).
—— (1967). *Poems of Chairman Mao* (毛主席诗词) (Beijing: People's Literature Press).
—— (1969). *Mao Tse-tung Si Xiang Wan Su*i (Beijing: no publisher given).
—— (1969a). *Selected Works of Mao Tse-tung, Vol. I* (Beijing: People's Press).
—— (1969b). *Vol. II* (Beijing: People's Press).
—— (1969c). *Vol. III* (Beijing: People's Press).
—— (1969d). *Vol. IV* (Beijing: People's Press).
—— (1969e). *Vol. V* (Beijing: People's Press).
—— (1976). *Mao Tse-tung's Works* (毛泽东集), The Research Section of Chinese Communism (ed.) (Hong Kong: I Shan Press).

——(1977). *Vol. V* (Beijing: People's Press).
——(1999). *Mao Zedong Wenji* (毛泽东文集), *Vol. 6* (Beijing: People's Press).
——(1999a), *Vol. 7* (Beijing: People's Press).
——(1999b), *Vol. 8* (Beijing: People's Press).
Si-ma Guang (司马光) (ed.) Li Zongtong (李宗桐), etc, annotated, *Annotated Zizhi Tongjian* (资治通鉴今注) (Taiwan Commercial Press).
Yao Nai (姚鼐), 'Comments on Distinguishing Different items' (论辩类), in *Classical Writing Types* (古文辞类纂).

General reference

Chang Muqi (张木奇) (2004). Source: Phoenix Cable TV, Hong Kong, hosted by Lu Yu (鲁豫) (8.00–8.45 p.m., 5 January).
Chen, Jin (陈晋) (ed.) (1996). *Explaining Mao Tse-tung's Reading Notes* (毛泽东读书笔记解析), two volumes (Shenzhen: Guangdong People's Press).
Chen, Mingxian (陈明显) (2008). *The Old Aged Mao Zedong* (晚年毛泽东) (Nanchang: Jiangxi People's Press).
Chu, Yun (楚云), *The Korean War* (Beijing: Current Affairs Press, 2010).
Dong, Zhixin (董志新) (2009). *Mao Zedong Du Sanguo Yanyi* (毛泽东读三国演义) (Shenyang: Wan Juan Press).
Gong, Yuzhi (龚育之), etc (1986). *Mao Zedong's Reading Life* (毛泽东的读书生活) (Beijing: San Lian Press).
Li, Rui (李锐) (1977). *Comrade Mao Tse-tung's Early Revolutionary Activities* (Beijing: The Chinese Youth Press, 1957); *see also* Sariti, A. W., tran (New York: M. E. Sharpe).
Li, Rui (李锐) (1992). *The Schooling Life of Mao Zedong at His Early Age* (毛泽东早年之读书生活) (Liaoning People's Press).
——(1994). *Report on the Lushan Conference* (庐山会议实录) (Zhengzhou: Henan People's Press).
Liu Suinian and Wu Qungan (1986). (ed.) *China's Socialist Economy* (Beijing: Beijing Review Press).
Lu Rude (陆儒德) (2009). *Jiang Haike Mao Zedong* (江海客毛泽东) (Beijing: Haiyang Press).
Mao (n.d.). *Anthology of Mao Zedong's Comments on Chinese Classical Literature and History* (毛泽东读文史籍批语集).
——(1990). *Selected works of Mao Zedong's Foreign Diplomacy* (毛泽东外交文选) (Beijing: People's Press).

——(1959). Mao's Letter to *Shi Kan* (诗刊) (Beijing: January).

Quan Yanchi (权延赤), *Inside and Outside of the Red Wall* (红墙内外) (Beijing: Kunlun Press, 1989).

Wang, Shuzeng (王树增) (2009). Lecture Room (百家讲坛), 'Zunyi Conference', 4.15 p.m.–5.00 p.m., 24 April, CCTV, Beijing.

Wu Jiqing (吴吉清) (1983). *On those Days Beside Chairman Mao* (在毛主席身边的日子里) (Nanchang: Jiangxi People's Press).

Wu, X. J. (2005). 'Mao Zedong and the Normalization of the SinoUS Relations', in Li Ying and Cheng Meidong, *op. cit.*, 34–653.

Xu, Zhongyuan (许中远) (1997). *Mao Zedong's Comments on Five Classical Novels* (毛泽东读评五部古典小说) (Beijing: Chinese Language Press).

Zhou Bingde (周秉德) (2006). *Wodebofu Zhou Enlai* (我的伯父周恩来) (Hong Kong: Manweili Foundation, 4th edition).

Articles in periodicals and newspapers (by year)

Editorial (1944). 'The New Development of the Labor-Military Forces Combined', *Yenan Liberation Daily* (Yenan: 15 October), 3.

Editorial (1944). 'The Road of the Soldiers and People Behind the Enemy – Fighting and Production Combined', *Yenan Liberation Daily* (Yenan: 2 March), 1.

Editorial (1945). 'The New Development of the Labor-Military Forces Combined in the Ch'in Sui (晋绥) Border Area Last Year', in *Yenan Liberation Daily* (Yenan: 1 February), 3.

Mao (1950). 'Chairman Mao on the Sino-Soviet Treaty and Agreements', *People's Daily* (Beijing: 13 April).

Editorial (1952). 'To Strengthen the Cooperative Sector', *People's Daily* (Beijing: 10 April), 1.

Correspondent (1954). China's New Constitution, *People's Daily* (Beijing: 21 September), 2.

Correspondent (1955). 'Bandung Conference's Resolution Regarding Various Political Questions': *People's Daily* (Beijing: 12 April), 1.

Correspondent (1955). 'Chairman Mao's Mechanization Strategy', *People's Daily* (Beijing: 17 October), 1.

Mao (1955). 'Chairman Mao on Liu's Mechanization Policy' *People's Daily* (Beijing: 17 October), 2.

Correspondent (1957). 'Afro-Asian Consolidation Conference on the Disintegration of Imperialism', *People's Daily* (28 December), 5.

Correspondent (1957). 'All Afro-Asian Nations Condemned Colonialism', *People's Daily* (30 December), 5.

Correspondent (1957). 'Long Live the Afro-Asian People's Great Consolidation', *People's Daily* (Beijing: 26 December), 1.

Correspondent (1957). 'A New Rectification Movement', *NCNA* (Beijing: 10 September).

Correspondent (1957). 'On the Anti-Party Revisionists', *New China News Agency* (*NCNA*) (Beijing: 1 June).

Correspondent (1957). 'To Unite with All Possible', *NCNA* (Beijing: 18 June).

Mao (1957). *'Chairman Assesses the Present International Situation', People's Daily* (Beijing: 19 November), 1.

Correspondent (1958). 'China's Declaration of a Twelve-Mile Coastal Zone', *People's Daily* (Beijing: 4 September), 1.

Editorial (1958). 'Cooperative Contract Gives Efficient, Fast and Good Results', *People's Daily* (Beijing: 3 September), 1.

Editorial (1958). 'Get the Upsurge in Forming People's Communes', *Hongqi*, tenth issue (Beijing: October), 1.

Editorial (1958). 'Production and Militia Combined', *People's Daily* (Beijing: 4 September).

Mao (1959). 'Chairman Mao Refuting Right Opportunists', *NCNA* (Beijing: 26 August).

Mao (1959). 'Letter to the editor of *Shi Kan* (*Poetry*) (诗刊)' (Beijing: People's Press, January).

Mao (1959). *'On Right Opportunism', People's Daily* (Beijing: 17 September), 1.

Editorial (1963). 'Protagonists of New Colonialism', *People's Daily* (Beijing: 22 October), 1, 3.

Editorial (1963). 'Shameful Betrayal of Sino-Soviet Alliance', *People's Daily* (Beijing: 30 August), 2.

Mao (1967). 'Chairman Mao on Leftist Wind of Communism', *NCNA* (Beijing: 15 August).

Yearbook of Chinese Communism Editorial Committee (1967, 1971, 1974). 'Organizational structure and management of the Shen-Kan-Ning Border Government's cooperative system', *The Yearbook of Chinese Communism* (中共年报) (Taipei: Institute for the Study of Chinese Communist Problems), refer to the following yearbooks:
(a) *1967 Yearbook*, section 6, 403.
(b) *1971 Yearbook*, section 6, 4.
(c) *1974 Yearbook*, section 6, 42–4.

Editorial (1970). 'People from all over the world including the people from the US are our friends', *People's Daily* (Beijing: 25 December), 1.
Editorial (1976). 'The Soviet New Maritime Strategy for Global Expansion', *People's Daily* (Beijing: 30 April), 25.
Editorial (1979), 'Strive for the Four Modernizations', *People's Daily* (Beijing: 9 February 1979).
Editorial (1990). 'Deng's perception of a new world order and the "club of wealthy nations"', *Ta Kung Pao* (Hong Kong: 15 December), 1.
Correspondent (1990). 'Qian Qichen on Our Changing World', *Ta Kung Pao* (Hong Kong: 15 December), 1.
Correspondent (1990). 'The wealthy nations' hegemonic contention over the third world', *International Problems Studies Magazine* (Beijing: no. 4), 5–6.
Correspondent (1996). 'Yeltsin on Sino-Russian economic cooperation', *NCNA* (Beijing: 23 April), 12.
Editor (1998). 'Song Jiang was a capitulationist-revisionist', *The Chinese Youth* (中国青年报), 24 September), 3.

English Sources

General literature

Adie, W. A. C. (1974). 'World Or Power? China as an Alternative Model of the International System' (Canberra: The Australian National University Seminar Paper).
Akira, Iriye (1992). *Across the Pacific: The Sino-American Crisis* (Chicago: Imprint Publications Inc.).
Burns, A. (1969). 'Military-Technological Models and World Order', in *International Journal*, autumn.
Barme, G. 'For Truly Great Men, Look to This Age Alone', in Cheek, T. (ed.) (2010). *A Critical Introduction to Mao* (Cambridge: Cambridge University Press), 243–71.
Bernstein, T. P. (1993). 'A Giant Economy', in Morley, James, W. (ed.), *Driven by Growth: Political Change in the Asia-Pacific Region* (New York: M. E. Sharpe, Inc.).

Camilleri, J. (1980). *Chinese Foreign Policy: The Maoist Era and Its Aftermath* (Oxford: Martin Robertson Press).

Chang, Kang (1985). 'Politics and Performance in Industry', Eckstein, A., Galenson, W., and Liu, T. C., *Economic Trends in Communist China* (Edinburgh: Edinburgh University Press).

Chang, Kingyuh (ed.) (1985). *Perspectives on Development in Mainland China* (Boulder: Westview Press).

Chang, P. H. (1987). 'Peking's Perceptions of the Two Super Powers and of American-Soviet Relations', in Ilpyong Kim, ed., *The Strategic Triangle; China, the United States and the Soviet Union* (New York: Paragon House Publishers (A PWPA Book), 90–108).

Cheek, T. (2010). (ed.) *A Critical Introduction to Mao* (Cambridge: Cambridge University Press).

Chen, Yuen (1985). 'The Responsibility System in Mainland China: An Analysis', in Chang, King-yuh, ed., *Perspectives on Development in Mainland China* (Boulder: Westview Press, 1985).

Chi Chao-ting (1966) 'Capitalists Cross Over in China in Transition', in Oh, S. K., *Land Reform in Communist China and Post-war Japan*, PhD dissertation in International Relations (Philadelphia: University of Pennsylvania).

Chiou, C. L. (1974). *Maoism in Action* (Brisbane: University of Queensland Press).

Clegg, J. (2009). *China's Global Strategy: Towards A Multipolar World* (New York: Pluto Press).

Deng, Xiaoping (1957). Report on the Rectification Campaigns delivered at the Third Plenum (Enlarged) of the Eighth Central Committee of the CCP (Beijing: Foreign Languages Press, 23 September).

—— (1983). *Selected Works of Deng Xiaoping* 1975–82 (Beijing: Foreign Languages Press).

—— (1994). *Selected Works of Deng Xiaoping, 1982–92* (Beijing: Foreign Languages Press).

Dikötter, F. (2010). *Mao's Great famine: The History of China's Most Devastating Catastrophe 1958–62* (New York: Walker Publishing Co., Inc.).

Dittmer, L. (1987). 'The Strategic Triangle', in Ilpyong Kim (ed.) *The Strategic Triangle: China, the United States and the Soviet Union*, 29–46.

Eckstein, A. (1975). *China's Economic Development* (Ann Arbor: The University of Michigan Press).

Eckstein, A. Galenson, W., and Liu, Ta-Chung (1985). *Economic Trends in Communist China* (Edinburgh: Edinburgh University Press).

Esposito, V. J. (1982). 'Korean War', *Encyclopedia Americana, Vol. 16* (Danbury, Connecticut: Grolier Incorporated), 528.

Foot, R. (2001). 'Reflections: The Domestic Context of America's China Policy in the 1960s', in Ross, R. S. & Jiang, Changbin. *Re-examining the Cold War: US–China Diplomacy, 1954–73* (Cambridge, MA, and London: Harvard University Press).

Garver, J. W. (2003). 'The Opportunity Costs of Mao's Foreign Policy Choices', in *The China Journal*, no. 49 (Canberra: Contemporary China Centre, Research School of Pacific and Asian Studies, The Australian National University).

Gong, L. (2001). 'Chinese Decision Making and the Thawing of US–China Relations', in Ross, R. S. & Jiang, Changbin. *Reexamining the Cold War: US–China Diplomacy, 1954–73* (Cambridge, Mass. & London: Harvard University Press).

Goodman, D. S. G. (1994). *Deng Xiaoping and the Chinese Revolution: A Political Biography* (London: Routledge).

Goldman, M. (1987). 'The Party and the Intellectuals', in *Cambridge History of China, Vol. 14* (Cambridge: Cambridge University Press).

Gurley, J. G. (1976a). *China's Economy and the Maoist Strategy* (New York: Monthly Review Press).

Han, Suyin (1967). *China in the Year 2001* (London: C. A. Watts, Ltd).

Harrison, J. P. (1973). *Long March to Power* (London: Macmillan Press).

Hinton, H. C. (ed.) (1979). *The People's Republic of China* (Boulder: Westview Press).

Hoffmann, C. (1968). *Work Incentive Practices and Policies in the People's Republic of China 1953–65* (New York: State University of New York Press), 108.

Hsiung, J. C. (1987). 'Internal Dynamics in the Sino-Soviet-US Triad', in Ilpyong Kim, *The Strategic Triangle: China, the United States and the Soviet Union*, 230–52.

Hsu, C. Y. I. (1995). *Rise of the Chinese People's Republic*, 5th edition (New York: Oxford University Press).

Huang, T. W., and Li, Z. Y. (1990). 'The Changing Security Scene in East Asia – An Analysis of the US Perspective', in *ASEAN-China, Hong Kong Forum 1990* (Hong Kong: Royal Park Hotel, August 7–9).

Kaplan, L. S., 'International and Diplomacy' *Encyclopedia Americana, Vol. 27*, 759.

Kau, M. Y-M and Marsh, S. H. (1993). *China in the Era of Deng Xiaoping: A Decade of Reform* (New York: M. E. Sharpe, Inc.).

Khrushchev, Nikita (1974). *Khrushchev Remembers: The Last Testament* (trans. and ed.) by Strobe Talbott (Boston: Little Brown & Co.).

Khrushchev, Sergei Nikitich (2000). *Nikita Khrushchev and the Creation of a Superpower* (tran) Benson, Shirley (University Park, PA: The Pennsylvania State University).

Kim, Ilpyong (ed.) (1987). *The Strategic Triangle: China the United States and the Soviet Union* (New York: Paragon House Publishers, A PWPA Book).

Kissinger, H. (1979). *White House Years* (Boston: Little Brown).
—— (1994). *Diplomacy* (New York: Simon & Schuster).
Lam, L. S. (1993). 'From Mikhail Gorbachev's Policy to China's Regional Role', in *The Journal of East Asian Affairs* (Seoul: The Research Institute of International Affairs, August).
___ (1993). *The Role of Ch'i in Mao Tse-tung's Leadership Style* (San Francisco: Mellen University Press).
—— (1994). 'A Short Note on ASEAN-Great Power Interaction', in *Contemporary Southeast Asia* (Singapore: Institute of Southeast Asian Studies, March).
—— (1995). *Mao Tse-tung's Purposive Contention with the Superpowers: The Theory of Ch'i* (Lewiston: Edwin Mellen Press).
—— (2000). *Mao Tse-tung's Ch'i and the Chinese Political Economy With Special Reference to the Post-Mao Modernization Revolution* (Lewiston/Queenston/Lampeter: Edwin Mellen Press).
—— (2007). *The International Environment and China's Twin Models of Development* (Bern: Peter Lang AG,).
Lardy, N. R. (1987). 'The Chinese Economy Under Stress, 1958–65', in Twitchett, D. C., and Fairbank, J. K., *The Cambridge History of China, Vol. 14* (Cambridge: Cambridge University Press).
Lethbridge, H. J. (1963). *The Peasant and the Communes* (Hong Kong: Dragonfly Books).
Levine, S. I. (1987). 'Soviet Perspectives of Chinese-US Relations', in Ilpyong Kim, *The Strategic Triangle: China, the United States and the Soviet Union*, 72–89.
Li Jie (2001). 'Changes in China's Domestic Situation in the 1960s and Sino-US Relations', in *Re-examining the Cold War: US-China Diplomacy* (ed.) in Ross, R. S., and Jiang Changbin (Cambridge, MA and London: Harvard University Press).
Lieberthal, K. (1987). 'The GLF and the Split in the Yenan Leadership', in *Cambridge History of China, Vol. 14*.
Liu, Suinian and Wu, Qungan (ed.) (1986). *China's Socialist Economy* (Beijing: Beijing Review Press).
McDonald, W. A. (2002). 'Nixon, Kissinger, and the Détente Experiment', in *Britannica Macropaedia. Vol. 21.*
MacFarquhar, R. (1974). *The Origins of the Cultural Revolution: Contradictions among the People* (London: Oxford University Press).
—— (1983). *The Origins of the Cultural Revolution: The GLF 1958–60* (Oxford: Oxford University Press).
—— (1997). *The Origins of the Cultural Revolution: The Coming of Cataclysm 1961–66* (Oxford: Oxford University Press).

—— (2010). 'Two Perspectives on Mao Zedong', in Timothy Cheek, *A Critical Introduction to Mao* (Cambridge: Cambridge University Press) 343–52.
Mao (1954c). *Selected Works of Mao Tse-tung: Vol. III* (Beijing: Foreign Languages Press).
—— (1960c). *Vol. IV* (Beijing: Foreign Languages Press).
—— (1967c). *Vol. I* (Beijing: Foreign Languages Press).
—— (1967d). *Vol. II* (Beijing: Foreign Languages Press).
—— (1967e). *Vol. III* (Beijing: Foreign Languages Press).
—— (1967f). *Vol. IV* (Beijing: Foreign languages Press).
—— (1977c). *Vol. V* (Beijing: Foreign Languages Press).
—— (1976). *Mao Tse-tung Poems* (Beijing: Foreign Languages Press).
Meisner, M. J. (1977). *Mao's China: A History of the People's Republic* (New York: The Free Press).
Morley, J. W. (ed.) (1993). *Driven by Growth: Political Change in the Asia-Pacific Region* (New York: M. E. Sharpe, Inc.).
Nixon, R. (1969). *Public Papers of the Presidents of the United States: Richard Nixon.*
—— (1978). *The Memoirs of Richard Nixon* (New York: Grosset & Dunlop).
Oh, S. K. (1966). *Land Reform in Communist China and Postwar Japan* (Philadelphia: University of Pennsylvania).
The Party's Documents (黨的文献) (1994). (Fourth issue, 1959 and 5th issue).
People's Communes in China (1958). (Peking: Foreign Languages Press).
Polomka, P. (1990). 'Strategic Stability and the South China Sea: Beyond Geopolitics', in *International Academic Conference on Territorial Claims in the South China Sea.* (Hong Kong: University of Hong Kong, 4–6 December).
Richman, B. (1969). *Industrial Society in Communist China* (New York: Random House), 316–17.
Rizal, S. (1990). 'Jakarta-Beijing Relations and Security Challenges in Southeast Asia', in *Indonesian Quarterly*, No. XVIII–4 (Jakarta: Centre for Strategic and International Studies).
Robinson, T. W. (1987). 'On the Further Evolution of the Strategic Triangle', in Ilpyong Kim (ed.), *The Strategic Triangle: China, the United States and the Soviet Union*, 4–26.
—— (1994). 'Chinese Foreign Policy: 1940s–1990s', in Robinson, W., and Shambaugh, D. (ed.), *Chinese Foreign Policy: Theory and Practice*, 557–72.
——, and Shambaugh, D. (ed.) (1994). *Chinese Foreign Policy: Theory and Practice* (Oxford: Clarendon Press Paperbacks).

Ross, R. S. & Jiang, Changbin (2001). *Re-examining the Cold War: US–China Diplomacy, 1954–73* [Cambridge, Mass. & London: Harvard University Press].

Rummel, R. J. (1987). 'Triadic Struggle and Accommodation in Perspective', in Ilpyong Kim, *The Strategic Triangle: China, the United States and the Soviet Union*, 253–78.

Salisbury, H. E. (1969f). *The Coming War Between Russia and China* (New York: W. W. Norton & Co. Inc.).

—— (1992). *The New Emperors, Mao & Deng: A Dual Biography* (London: HarperCollins Publishers).

Schram, S. R. (1963). *The Political Thought of Mao Tse-tung* (New York: Frederick A. Praeger).

Shambaugh, D. (1994). 'Patterns of Interaction in Sino-American Relations', in Robinson, T. W. and Shambaugh, D. (ed.), *Chinese Foreign Policy: Theory and Practice*, 197–223.

Skinner, W. (1965). 'Marketing and Social Structure in Rural China', in *Journal of Asian Studies* (Ann Arbor: February), 195–228.

Snow, E. (1961). *Red Star Over China* (New York: Random House).

——(1966). *The Other Side of the River* (London: Victor Gollanez Ltd).

——(1973) (Grove Press).

Teiwes, F. C. (1979). *Politics and Purges in China* (New York: M. E. Sharpe, Inc.).

——(1993). *Politics and Purges in China*, second edition (New York: M. E. Sharpe, Inc.).

——(1987) 'Establishment and Consolidation of the New Regime', in *Cambridge History of Chinese History, Vol. 14*, Twitchett, D. C., and Fairbank, J. K. (ed.) (Cambridge: Cambridge University Press).

Teng, Hsiao-ping (Deng, Xiaoping) (1957). *Report on the Rectification Campaigns* (Peking: Foreign Languages Press).

Tow, W. (1994). 'The International Strategic System', in Robinson, W. T. and Shambaugh, D. (ed.), *Chinese Foreign Policy: Theory and Practice*, 118–52.

Twitchett, D. C., and Fairbank, J. K. (1987). *The Cambridge History of China, Vol. 14* (Cambridge: Cambridge University Press).

Union Research Institute (ed.) (1968). *CCP Documents of the GPCR*, 1966–67 (Hong Kong, Union Press).

Van Ness, P. (1970). *Revolution and Chinese Foreign Policy: Peking Support for Wars of National Liberation* (Berkeley: University of California Press).

Welfield, J. B. (1974, April). *Australia and Japan in the Sino-US Cold War, 1949–72, Some Notes and Observations* (Canberra: Australian National University Seminar).

Womack, B. (2006). *China and Vietnam: The Politics of Asymmetry* (New York: Cambridge University Press).

Wong, J. (1973). *Land Reform in the PRC: Institutional Transformation in Agriculture* (New York: Praeger).

Yu, A. C. (1977). (trans. & ed.), Journey to the West (Chicago & London: The University of Chicago).

Articles in periodicals and newspapers (by year)

Eisenhower (1953). 'Speech on the US Commitment in Vietnam', *New York Times* (New York: 5 August), 1, 10.

Correspondent (1954). 'President Eisenhower's scheme of peaceful transformations', *The Times* (London: 13 January), 2.

Correspondent (1954). 'Secretary Pospelov of Soviet Communist Party promised to ease international tension by peaceful means', *The Times* (London: 22 January), 5.

Correspondent (1954). 'US-USSR to bar PRC to join Berlin Conference', *The Times* (London: 27 January), 6.

Yang, Min (1958), 'Chairman Mao on the Twelve Year Plan for Agriculture', *Peking Review* (18 March), 12.

Strong, A. L. (1960). 'Reminiscences on Interview with Chairman Mao Tse-tung on the Paper Tiger', *Peking Review* (29 November), 13.

Ho, Chi-Fang (1961). 'Preface to 'Stories About Not Being Afraid of Ghosts', *Peking Review* (Beijing: 10 March), 6.

Liao Yuan (1961). 'Self-Management of Enterprises' in Yugoslav: The True Picture', *Peking Review* (Beijing: 21 July), 11.

Editorial (1963). 'CPSU 20th Congress – Root of All Evils of Khrushchev Revisionists', *Peking Review* (Beijing: 30 April), 15.

Special correspondent (1963). 'Soviet Military Aid to India against China', *Peking Review* (Beijing: November 8), 25.

Editorial (1964). 'On Khrushchev's Phoney Communism and Its Historical Lessons for the World', *Peking Review* (Beijing: 17 July), 7.

Editorial (1965). 'Escalation Means Getting Closer and Closer to the Grave', *Peking Review* (Beijing: 30 April), 15.

Editorial (1965). 'New Leaderships of the CPSU Preach Soviet-US Cooperation for World Domination', *Peking Review* (Beijing: 3 December), 14.

Editorial (1967). 'Anti-Party Activities of China's Khrushchev', *Peking Review* (Beijing: 25 August), 7.
Editorial (1967). 'Fight for the Thorough Criticision and Repudiation of the Top Party Person in Authority Taking the Capitalist Road', *Peking Review* (Beijing: 14 April), 8.
Editorial (1967). 'Peng and His Behind-the-Scenes Boss', *Peking Review* (Beijing: 25 August), 6.
Editorial (1967). 'Peng Teh-huai and His Behind-the-Scenes Boss Cannot Shirk Responsibility for Their Crimes', *Peking Review* (Beijing: 18 August), 8.
Editorial (1967). 'Resolution of 8th Plenary Session of 8th C.C. of CPC on the Anti-Party Clique Headed by Peng Teh-huai', *Peking Review* (Beijing: August 18), 8.
Editorial (1967). 'The Revisionist-Capitalist Roader Liu Shaoqi', *Peking Review* (Beijing: 21 April), 7.
Li, Hsin-Kung (1967). 'Peng's Heinous Crimes of Usurping Army Leadership and Opposing the Party', *Peking Review* (1 September), 12.
Correspondent (1975). 'Mao's proposal on amalgamation of the Mongolian People's Republic', *Far Eastern Economic Review (FEER)*, (Hong Kong: 7 February), 37.
US Foreign Broadcast Information Service (1975). *PRC Daily Report*, FBIS-CHI-75-13 (20 January), *Vol. 1*, No. 13, D10–D11.
Correspondent (1976). 'Moscow Test Ban Treaty', *China Reconstructs* (Beijing: April), 5.
Editorial (1976). 'Song Jiang's Capitulationist Line', *Peking Review* 27 February) 11.
Editorial (1976). 'Chao Kai Killed by a Poisonous Arrow', *Peking Review* (27 February), 11.
Correspondent (1982). 'China's Relations with Southeast Asia', *The Nation* (Sydney: 1 December), 6.
An IISS scholar (1988). 'On Soviet Troop Strength', *Asian Wall Street Journal* (Hong Kong: 8 December), 1.
Lam, Wo-Lap, Willy (1990). 'Qian asserts role in new world order', *South China Morning Post* (*SCMP*) (Hong Kong: 15 December), 11.
Rizal Sukma (1990). 'Jakarta-Beijing Relations and Security Challenges in Southeast Asia', *Indonesian Quarterly*, No. XVIII–4 (Jakarta: Centre for Strategic and International Studies), 284.
Cheung, Tai Ming (1991). 'Gulf war mutes foreign concern', *FEER* (Hong Kong), 31 January), 6.
Correspondent (1991). Japanese new national defense program, *FEER* (Hong Kong: 3 January), 12.

Correspondent (1991), 'Minister Qian in bid to woo third world', *SCMP* (Hong Kong: 8 January), 11.

Xue, Chao (1991). 'Foreign Minister Qian on world issues', *Beijing Review* (Beijing: 7 January), 9.

Correspondent (1992). 'China's support of the East Asian Economic Caucus', *SCMP* (Hong Kong: 13 January), 8.

Correspondent (1992). 'Human rights will not destabilize China', *SCMP* (Hong Kong: 12 January), 5.

Foreign correspondent (1992). 'Baker assured firm American commitment to the region', *China Daily* (Hong Kong: 27 July), 8.

Editorial (1995). 'US containment strategists misled', *Beijing Review* (Beijing: 16 October), 4. SEATO formed in 1954 was aimed at containing communism and China but disbanded in 1977.

Wang, Jisi (1996). 'US China Policy: Containment or Engagement?', *Beijing Review* (Beijing: 21–27 October), 8.

Editorial (1997). 'Deng Xiaoping Theory is a Continuation and Development of Mao Zedong Thought', *Beijing Review* (Beijing: 6–12 October), 14.

Correspondent (1999). 'A new arms race warned', *SCMP*, Sunday Focus Section (Hong Kong: 18 April), 3.

Rong, Zhi (1999). 'A Retrospect of China-USSR and China-Russia Relations', *Beijing Review* (Beijing: 15 November), 13.

Tang, Yuen Kai (2001). 'China, Russia Good-Neighborly Treaty of Friendship and Cooperation', *Beijing Review* (Beijing: 2 August), 8–11.

Correspondent (2002). 'The New Industrial Metropolis of Shenzhen', *SCMP* (Hong Kong: 22 June), 14.

Zhen, Bingxi (2002). 'Trade Important for Sino-US Ties', *Beijing Review* (Beijing: 28 February), 8.

Correspondent (2005). 'Reality strikes US: China has arrived', *SCMP* (Hong Kong: 25 June), A5.

Index